Data Bases, Computers, and the Social Sciences

Information Sciences Series

Editors

ROBERT M. HAYES
Director of the Institute of Library Research
University of California at Los Angeles

JOSEPH BECKER
President
Becker and Hayes, Inc.

Consultants

CHARLES P. BOURNE
Director, Advanced Information Systems Division
Programming Services, Inc.

HAROLD BORKO
System Development Corporation

Joseph Becker and Robert M. Hayes:
INFORMATION STORAGE AND RETRIEVAL

Charles P. Bourne:
METHODS OF INFORMATION HANDLING

Harold Borko:
AUTOMATED LANGUAGE PROCESSING

Russell D. Archibald and Richard L. Villoria:
NETWORK-BASED MANAGEMENT SYSTEMS (PERT/CPM)

Charles T. Meadow:
THE ANALYSIS OF INFORMATION SYSTEMS, A PROGRAMMER'S INTRODUCTION TO INFORMATION RETRIEVAL

Launor F. Carter:
NATIONAL DOCUMENT-HANDLING SYSTEMS FOR SCIENCE AND TECHNOLOGY

George W. Brown, James G. Miller and Thomas A. Keenan:
EDUNET: REPORT OF THE SUMMER STUDY ON INFORMATION NETWORKS CONDUCTED BY THE INTERUNIVERSITY COMMUNICATIONS COUNCIL (EDUCOM)

Perry E. Rosove:
DEVELOPING COMPUTER-BASED INFORMATION SYSTEMS

F. W. Lancaster:
INFORMATION RETRIEVAL SYSTEMS

Ralph L. Bisco:
DATA BASES, COMPUTERS, AND THE SOCIAL SCIENCES

Data Bases, Computers, and the Social Sciences

EDITED BY

Ralph L. Bisco

University of Pittsburgh
Pittsburgh, Pennsylvania

WILEY-INTERSCIENCE

A DIVISION OF JOHN WILEY & SONS
NEW YORK · LONDON · SYDNEY · TORONTO

Copyright © 1970, by John Wiley & Sons, Inc.

All rights reserved. No part of this book may be reproduced by any means, nor transmitted, nor translated into a machine language without the written permission of the publisher.

10 9 8 7 6 5 4 3 2 1

Library of Congress Catalogue Card Number: 75-94917

SBN 471 07550 7

Printed in the United States of America

To Magdalena

Preface

This book was written with several diverse audiences in mind: (1) social and behavioral scientists and their students, (2) librarians and library-science students who are favorable about employing computers and computer-usable information in their work and classes, and (3) archivists and their employees who desire to have more than a current overview of the problems and their tentative solutions. Because of the diversity of material, it is not expected that all readers will use the book in the same way. Rather, it is assumed that readers will supplement a subset of the book with bibliographical materials from the reference sections.

The book is a product of the Fourth Annual Conference of the Council of Social-Science Data Archives. The conference and preparation of this book were supported by National Science Foundation Grant GS–1258, awarded to Columbia University. It is a product, but not a proceedings. After the conference, held at the University of California in Los Angeles, some of the papers that had been presented were selected for inclusion in this book. Then they were rewritten, edited, and otherwise revised to make a reasonably coherent manuscript concerning the interrelations between data banks, computer technology, and the needs of the social sciences. Needless to say, these tasks have taken considerable time and largely explain the delay between the conference itself and the publication of this book.

I am especially appreciative of the work the chapter authors did after the conference to make their manuscripts more suitable to the purpose of this book. A special note of appreciation must go to Dwaine Marvick of the University of California in Los Angeles and to William Glaser of Columbia University, who were very helpful to me when I was Program Chairman for the conference and who were seemingly always willing to help me, as editor, to evaluate ideas about organization, orientation, priorities, and content. They constituted an "invisible hand" that guided the development of the manuscript in numerous ways leading to many improvements. The gaps and inadequacies are the responsibility of the editor.

Finally, the manuscript would never have seen the form of a hardcover, formal publication without the help of Judy Hansen and Maryon Wells, who undertook numerous and diverse technical tasks indispensable to bringing a set of papers into a form suitable for publication.

RALPH L. BISCO

University of Pittsburgh
August 1969

Information Sciences Series

Information is the essential ingredient in decision making. The need for improved information systems in recent years has been made critical by the steady growth in size and complexity of organizations and data.

This series is designed to include books that are concerned with various aspects of communicating, utilizing, and storing digital and graphic information. It will embrace a broad spectrum of topics, such as information system theory and design, man-machine relationships, language data processing, artificial intelligence, mechanization of library processes, non-numerical applications of digital computers, storage and retrieval, automatic publishing, command and control, information display, and so on.

Information science may someday be a profession in its own right. The aim of this series is to bring together the interdisciplinary core of knowledge that is apt to form its foundation. Through this consolidation, it is expected that the series will grow to become the focal point for professional education in this field.

Contents

Introduction, Ralph L. Bisco   1

PART I

Problems and Prospects   17

    1   THE IMPACT OF COMPLEX DATA BASES ON THE SOCIAL SCIENCES, *Karl W. Deutsch*   19

    2   SOME QUESTIONS ABOUT THE NEW JERUSALEM, *Angus Campbell*   42

    3   THE JOYS AND SORROWS OF SECONDARY DATA USE, *Charles G. Bell*   52

PART II

Government as the Major Producer, User, and Archivist of Social Science Data Bases   61

    4   THE IDEA OF A FEDERAL STATISTICAL DATA CENTER— ITS PURPOSES AND STRUCTURE, *Raymond T. Bowman*   63

    5   FEDERAL INFORMATION SYSTEMS—SOME CURRENT DEVELOPMENTS, *Roye L. Lowry*   70

PART III

Case Studies in the Development and Use of Complex Data Bases   81

xii   *Contents*

    6   Working with Complex Data Files: I. Development and Analysis of Complex Data Files in a Regional Transportation Study, *Robert J. Miller and Noreen J. Roberts*   83

    7   Working with Complex Data Files: II. The Wisconsin Assets and Incomes Studies Archive, *Richard A. Bauman, Martin H. David, and Roger F. Miller*   112

PART IV

Computer Systems for Managing Complex Data Structures   137

    8   Data Management Techniques for the Social Sciences, *Paul A. Castleman*   139

    9   The Informatics MARK IV File-Management System, *Fred Braddock*   158

PART V

Handling Missing-Data Problems   173

   10   Some Ways of Handling Missing Data— A Case Study, *Roger F. Miller*   177

   11   Regression Analysis with Missing Data, *R. M. Elashoff and Janet D. Elashoff*   198

PART VI

Data-Linkage Problems and Solutions   209

   12   Problems of Area Identification, *William T. Fay*   211

   13   Grid Coordinate Geographical Identification Systems, *Edgar M. Horwood*   220

   14   Some Aspects of Statistical Data Linkage for Individuals, *Joseph Steinberg*   238

PART VII

The Protection of Privacy 253

15 PROTECTING PRIVACY: PROS AND CONS, *Stanley Rothman* 255
16 PROTECTION OF PRIVACY THROUGH MICROAGGREGATION,
Edgar L. Feige and Harold W. Watts 261

PART VIII

Summing-Up, *Ralph L. Bisco* 273

Index 287

Data Bases, Computers, and the Social Sciences

Introduction

Ralph L. Bisco

A beautiful theory, killed by a nasty, ugly, little fact.

> Thomas Huxley

Social science data banks or data archives are a new facility for social science teaching and research. They developed out of the need by many social scientists to exploit better the masses of governmental, academic, and commercial data produced and accumulated over the past three decades. Their creation was made possible by the capabilities of modern computing technology. Although usage of these new facilities has rarely equaled or exceeded the expectations of their creators, they have in their brief existence been found beneficial by thousands of graduate students and by hundreds of social scientists.

Generally the purpose of these data-bank organizations is to make data already collected and useful for social science research available for computer analyses on a large-scale basis. Presently the majority of data stored in archives is copies of computer-usable collections prepared by various social research organizations around the world. However, an increasingly significant proportion of the holdings is coming to be various kinds of data—historical and administrative records, texts of publications, important speeches, and news reports. Also, statistical data, heretofore available only in printed form, are being converted to a computer-processable form by the archive organizations themselves.

2 Introduction

In the future social science data archives can be expected to play an especially important role instoring, maintaining, and distributing the many computer-usable materials that are increasingly a by-product of the printing process. For the same reasons that libraries were invented to preserve books, it will be more and more necessary to have libraries of the future—organizations that can service the ournalistic, academic, commercial, and statistical products of society for computer use as well as "hand use" by human beings. Social-science data archives of today are developing experience and procedures for acquisitions, data maintenance, control, documentation, and services to users. Some of the knowledge obtained will be important for the development of libraries of the future.

Although originally developed for social-research purposes, archives are currently used most for teaching research methodology and data analysis. Their use for social science rresearch is demonstrated in numerous doctoral dissertations and by the publications of Lipset, Alford, and Pool, Abelson, and Popkin.

In addition to meeting the teaching and research needs of social scientists, data banks are a necessary development in the provision of facilities because social science data collections are very expensive, and therefore taxpayers benefit if these data collections can be made accessible to researchers who can use copies for the same or other analytic purposes. The cost of acquiring a copy of a data set can be as little as one fifteen-thousandth the cost of conducting a new data-collection operation. A new data collection may cost $75,000 or more; a copy of an appropriate computer-processable data collection may cost as little as $5.

More important perhaps, data archives are necessary if researchers and policy makers are to be able to compare current research findings with previous findings. Increasingly social research requires an ability to compare current with past information; this need can be most efficiently met if previously collected data can be adopted to the task. For one thing much bias is introduced when respondents in a current survey are asked to report their behavior of 10 or 15 years ago. Another problem is that there are many situations in which respondents are unable to recall changes in their reactions, reasons, opinions, behavior, or attitudes over the past 5 or 10 years. A greater problem is that in the past very few data-gathering activities involved panel or time-series methods. Currently researchers needing trend data *must* rely on archives to provide a set of comparable but different data collections because there are few panel studies or other data collections highly integrated over time. The capability to locate and obtain copies of previous studies containing information that is or can be made comparable to currently collected data requires organizational and technical facilities that are beyond the requirements of any single data-collecting organization. It is a task that necessitates cooperation among organizations—data archives —designed to fulfill needs for previously collected data. This need for cooperation among organizations with similar purposes was one reason for establishing the Council of Social Science Data Archives.

However, it will be increasingly unsatisfactory simply to acquire and preserve data that have been collected. In many cases it is necessary, but also reasonably sufficient, if the archives provide one of several alternative strategies for making data collected for the use of a small research group or individual social scientist more understandable and usable. The next step will be to improve data-collection methods, documentation standards, and other aspects of the data-collection process known to be critical if large investments in data collection are to benefit more than the original data collector.

Now the social science information system tends to be a hodgepodge of almost randomly articulated components. What worked reasonably well in the past may become inefficient and uneconomical in the future. But it might be that it is sufficient to change established values so that *almost* as much attention and reward is given to making data collections more publicly useful (i.e., more "archivable") as to reporting research findings: however, we know that changing "system values" is not easy. Whatever the necessary solutions, it is known that many data collections can be used for research and teaching purposes not even conceived of by the original data-collection organization. Perhaps only for the sake of economy it is necessary that we give more attention to determining the conditions that make some data collections useful for more purposes and for a longer time period.

SOME PROBLEMS IN DEVELOPMENT

Development of archival facilities has necessarily been slow. First, support has to be found to establish or to continue them: fees charged users for services cannot yet, and perhaps never will, make these organizations completely self-supporting. Data archives can be likened to libraries, cyclotrons, and medical research facilities whose benefit to society as a whole often requires more, or something other, than a strictly commercial justification for continuance. Needless to say, finding the necessary support is neither easy nor fast.

4   Introduction

Second, because these facilities are new and their requirements for staff are also new, they cannot usually recruit people with the necessary training and experience through established academic or other channels. The kinds of people needed are not ordinarily described in personnel-classification systems or manuals, and in some cases such description could not yet be made because we do not yet have enough experience to routinize the various duties and responsibilities. Today people who work in the archive organizations must usually have unique combinations of social research and computer skills, and have reasonably great tolerance for uncertainty and ambiguity regarding personal status, career lines, intra- and inter-organizational relationships, and the future of both themselves and their organizations. Thus the organizations must often recruit their staffs in ways that will displease personnel officers and typically must rely on on-the-job training and other ways to make the new person an effective archivist. Inability to rely on established ways of selecting and recruiting personnel and in many cases the requirement to establish in-house training programs are not the kinds of conditions that permit a rapid development of capabilities responding effectively and efficiently to the needs of users of these new facilities.

Third, the rapid growth and change that have characterized the computer industry have had detrimental effects on the ability of archive organizations to develop with speed and efficiency. Late deliveries of equipment, the additional training that archival computer specialists must have in order to use the new computers, and the discrepancies between promised and actual computer capabilities have all caused significant differences between the plans of archival organizations and any current ability to meet those plans. Almost all who read this book have experienced the problem described, and further discussion would only belabor the point. However, the reader should not conclude that we blame the computer manufacturers for the problem of slow perfection of archival services. Archive organizations suffer from the same effects of rapid growth and change that cause problems for the computer manufacturers. Blaming is useless and irrelevant: it is necessary that we learn better ways of coping with rapid growth and change, because these seem to be major and general challenges of the twentieth century in almost every area.

Finally, the development of archival organizations has been slowed by healthy debate among the organizations about the relative priorities of various ways of implementing the several goals and purposes. For example, a critical problem is to increase the use of archival facilities already available: on the one hand, we know that there is a large number of potential users; on the other hand, we also know that these potential users confront many problems in trying to take advantage of the services offered. In order to increase usage of the services should we concentrate on better ways of matching the specific needs of the user with the service capabilities of the archives, or should we concentrate on training programs that will help users make local computing and other facilities more responsive to their data-storage, manipulation, and analysis needs, and otherwise to take better advantage of already offered archival services? As another example, we know that the present set of archives does not store certain kinds of data that some potential users need. However, there is another serious problem, because there presently is no searching facility for matching data needs with the specific, current holdings of the various data-bank organizations. Should we emphasize the development of more thorough coverage in data acquisitions, or should we give higher priority to information systems that will improve the ability of users to determine whether any current holdings of archives match their immediate needs? Stressing the former alternative would improve the coverage of the network of archive organizations but would not necessarily improve the access of users to the network assets. Stressing the latter alternative might improve the ability of users to locate specific data collections in the network but might cause considerable frustration if the network is unable to service the majority of requests.

ACTIVITIES OF ARCHIVES

Let us now turn to a more specific description of the activities of archives. An account, written by the editor for *Social Science Information,* is relevant and follows:

"The computer-based archive of social science data is such a new organizational phenomenon in the academic world that some general comments about the problems archives attempt to solve are warranted. First, it is important to recognize that at the present time, each data collection added to an archive typically was designed in the first place for the specific use of a particular analyst or research group. A study involving the collection of data is hardly ever carried out so that the data and ancillary documentation are left in a form useful for subsequent widespread dissemination to other scholars who would put the data to other uses. . . .

"Second, for the above reasons, data and documentation come to an archive in varying degrees of "cleanness." Archive staffs ordinarily

6 Introduction

check information they acquire to determine whether data, codebooks, and ancillary information agree. One basic reason is simple self-protection: to prepare in advance, and one time only, answers to questions that users inevitably raise about discrepancies. When an archive staff has access to original source records, it may examine data for codes not described in codebooks, and inconsistencies and illogical relationships among variables. Errors in the data and codebooks are then corrected before the information is released to users. Also, the "cleaning" operations benefit both the user and original data supplier in very direct ways. Cleaning is usually complex, and often involves extended communication by mail and telephone with the data collection organizations. Clearly, the data supplier does not desire to provide the same kinds of information to hundreds or thousands of individual users of a given data set. Similarly, it is wasteful for hundreds of individual users of a data set to duplicate operations that a central organization, such as a data archive, can perform. Finally, the objectives of social research are better met if the individual social scientist undertaking a "secondary" analysis can move directly to his research purposes, rather than suffer the long delays that data "cleaning" typically involve.

"Third, once a number of data collections or data sets are brought together in an archive, an increasing number of users desire to combine individual data sets for concerted use.... The archive may also include environmental data, election statistics, and economic and demographic characteristics for political units, such as congressional districts and counties. The data required (for a particular analysis) may originally have come from five or more different sources.

"The integration, for analysis purposes, of such a data base, consisting of many individual data sets, has important implications for the processing of data and documentation for inclusion in an archive. For instance, coding schemes must be developed for identifying information so that various data sets can be linked or merged, and standard codes are also needed for similar variables in order that combinations of data sets or comparisons between information files can be easily made.

"Fourth, the users of an archive may differ widely in the computer and data-processing resources available to them, in their training in the use of quantitative data and data-processing facilities, and in their analysis requirements. Some users have the use of only unit record equipment. Some have access to appropriate data-processing equipment and computers, but these installations are not properly staffed or are insensitive to the needs of social scientists. Many users will need only a specified subset of variables from a single data set, while others will require that selected variables from several data sets be combined in a special format for a single analysis. Some researchers can take advantage of the data base provided by an archive only if the archive itself can provide analysis output, such as frequency tables, correlation matrices, regression equations, and factor scores. In each case there are implications for the staff specialization an archive may need to maintain. Specialists in mathematics may be required to handle the diverse demands for services.

"Fifth, archives may have unique capabilities to collect and convert to a machine-readable form certain kinds of data, particularly published aggregative information such as election statistics and census data, not easily assembled by the individual scholar. This is most likely to be the case if an archive has a large clientele of potential users so that capitalization costs can be justified. In addition, the extent of the other parts of the data base may have already required the kinds of staff and computer facilities necessary to manage and service such collections. If so, only a relatively small, incremental addition to the staff and equipment facilities may be needed to support the acquisition of large amounts of other kinds of data.

"Sixth, there are the mundane, but large, problems of data maintenance: insuring that data and documentation are kept in a complete and current form. Data in machine-readable form are highly perishable —cards can get lost or destroyed; tapes can be damaged by high temperatures, improper humidity conditions, exposure to certain electromagnetic phenomena, and frequent use; cards can warp; and tapes can be stretched or broken during those infrequent times when machines malfunction; disks have unique vulnerabilities. Consequently, specialists are required simply to maintain data in an accurate and usable form: time and resources must be devoted to providing "backup" reserves of data, and otherwise insuring against irretrievable losses of information.

"Over time, a data base is also subject to dynamic change as errors are discovered or more accurate sources of basic information are located or defined. For example, a particular frequency table may generate questions about a data set: a search of original sources, such as interview protocols, may reveal previously undetected errors in coding or keypunching. Another example: a more accurate and valid set of election statistics for a particular state and time may turn up in some obscure place in a state's archives. In such cases, a data archive will ordinarily want to update its files to include the best source of information.

"The size of modern archives creates still more problems. Until recently, archives were small enough that traditional methods of information retrieval appeared adequate. Currently, a number of archives are approaching dimensions such that traditional methods are no longer adequate. The information retrieval problem is accentuated by the increasing complexity of data sets themselves, and by the increasing complexity of research needs. Before a scholar can exploit a given archive, he must know in great detail what data are available. The servicing facilities of the archive can be brought into play only if the researcher can match his needs against the store of data.

"These problems lead to the use of computers to automate the documentation of data bases, and to provide for complex retrieval of information from large and complex data bases. Some experimental retrieval systems are under development, but there is no computerized system in operation today which meets the varied needs of the new social science archives. The result is that these archives must train and employ specialists who can keep up with developments in the field of information retrieval, who can undertake the design and development of information retrieval systems, experiment with promising systems, and eventually maintain operational systems and keep the systems, current as the data base expands.

"The above commentary can be reorganized as a functional description of data archives.

"The initial function of a social science data archive is *information acquisition*. This includes locating relevant data and ancillary information, and arranging for their acquisition, duplication, and subsequent diffusion.

"A second function is *processing information* in preparation for distribution and analysis—the creation of the data base. The information-processing phase includes eliminating multiple punches and performing other transformations that facilitate computer analyses, conversion of data to standard coding schemes that permit easy comparisons and concerted analyses, and locating and correcting errors in both data and documentation.

"A third important activity is *information maintenance,* insuring that data are current and accurate, and providing "backup" copies of machine-readable data and documentation in order to prevent irreparable losses of information.

"An archive must remain sensitive to the wide range of *services* required by its users. Services include preparing duplicates of and subsets from data sets on demand, supplying analysis output from com-

Introduction 9

puters, and providing consultation in mathematics, statistics, methodology, programming, and social research.

"The above functions imply *development activities for computers.* Computer programs are needed to process data into an archive, to provide services requested by users, and to maintain data and documentation. Development activities include the design and programming of systems to handle a complex of related data-processing and analysis functions in an integrated way, and to provide information-retrieval capabilities.

"As archives become larger and more complex, they must provide *training programs and research seminars* so that potential users can develop and expand needed skills and so that the data bases can be fully exploited.

"In summary, archives are complex social organizations with specialists in statistics and mathematics, computer technology and programming, data processing, systems analysis, information retrieval, social science research and methodology, language translation, teaching, and administration. The required complex of specialists must be adequately housed and provided with access to modern and appropriate data-processing and computer facilities. Each archive must provide efficient and effective capabilities and procedures for communication with individual users and with other archives. The staff of each must keep reasonably current with developments in a number of specialized areas."

Figure 1 illustrates the interrelationships of these archival functions.

PROBLEMS OF USERS

It is useful now to review the major problems that the users of these new archive facilities confront. The foremost difficulty, already mentioned, is that users have no efficient means of determining the sources of specifically needed machine-processable information. Users are now confronted with a time-consuming, inefficient, and costly means for determining what specific data holdings match their immediate research needs. They must first identify which of the several score archival organizations are likely to maintain the *kinds* of data they might need, and then they must call, visit, or write each of the likely sources to determine whether these specific organizations have individual collections that meet their present requirements. The Council of Social Science Data Archives has plans that our studies indicate will attenuate this problem and these plans will be duly reported.

10   Introduction

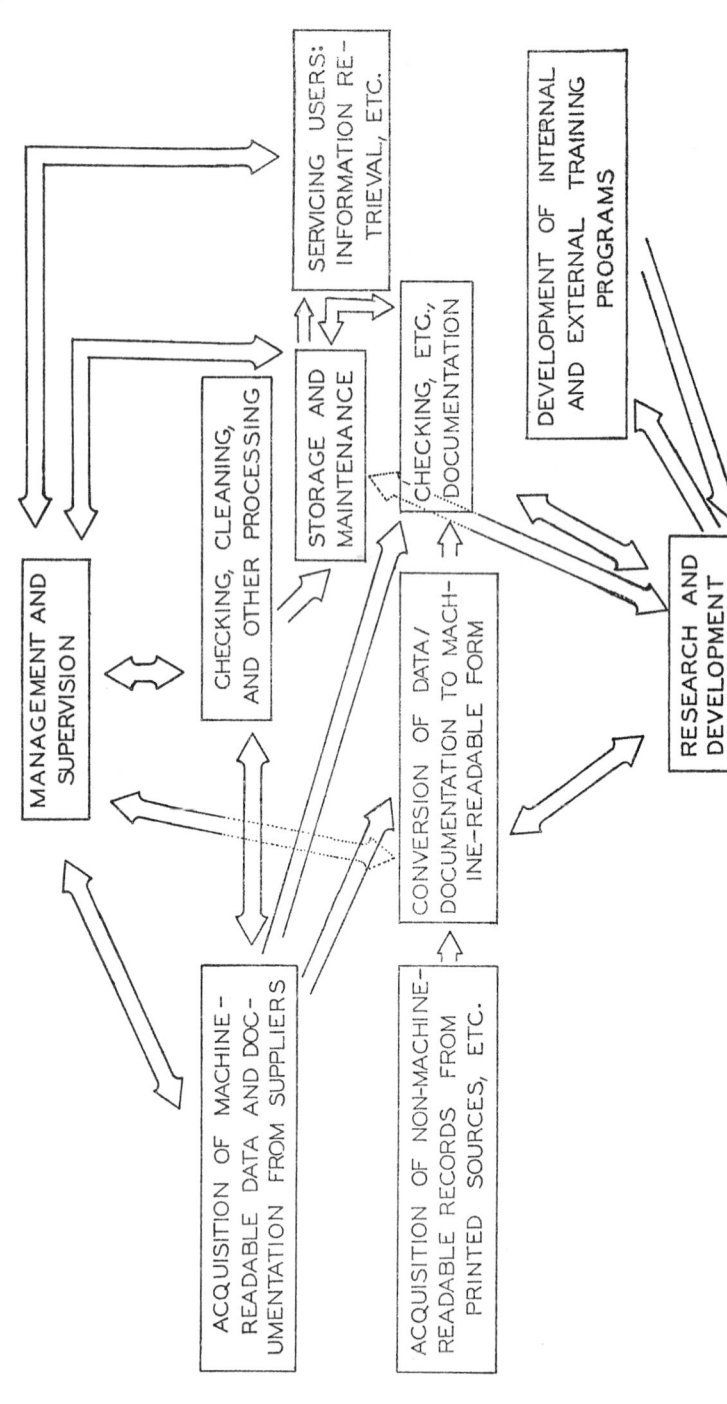

Figure 1.1. Internal functions of archives.

The next problem for the user is that he has no guarantee from the archive and often has insufficient information and inadequate skills to determine whether the data he obtains from an archive can be processed and analyzed by using his locally available hardware and software. Can the data tape be mounted on the local facility? Will the data format be compatible with the requirements of locally available software? Often the number of questions that can be asked are so many that the user does not effectively confront them until he actually has data from archives in hand. The problems involved have lead to the development of new kinds of specialization within university social science departments and research units and have motivated the Council's concerns about standards for archive services and for software capabilities and documentation, and about improved ways of sharing software.

There are still other issues that determine the useability of data from an archival organization. Often fairly rich data collections are reduced to more limited data sets in the coding process. For example, the information gathered by an open-ended question in a survey can be reduced in the coding process to a highly conceptual and project-limited representation. Also, variables such as age and income may be coded as gross ranges or brackets, which are inappropriate for the analytic requirements of a given secondary user. It is a fact that most data available to archives were collected, coded, and otherwise processed according to the immediate and short-term needs of a specific research group. Thus for currently held data holdings we must develop methods for imputation that permit a kind of simulation of needed data from available data.

To improve the data that will eventually constitute the majority of archival holdings it is necessary that we begin now, in cooperation with the data-collecting institutions that supply archives, to establish standards and guidelines that encourage richer, more empirical coding and that ensure capturing information about demographic and other basic variables. We must now commence work on still other ways to improve the utility of data that archives will need to store, maintain, and diffuse in the future. This means better guidelines for documentation and cleaning, and other standards that will improve the utility of future data collections for widespread use by present researchers and teachers as well as by historians in the future. The ability to predict how a data collection will be used or useful in the future becomes more and more difficult as the definition of "future" involves longer time periods.

Some important breakthroughs in the ability to make data collections more widely available to researchers and more useful for historical

Introduction

research will come when the data-collection organizations themselves give greater attention to the problems and values involved. In any case it is necessary that organizations that support research be interested in helping to resolve this general set of problems and be willing to fund or find support for some of the additional costs that may be required.

ALTERNATIVE ARCHIVE ORGANIZATIONS

There are at least three alternative sets of experiences that can guide our approach to these problems of data usability. One is the solution offered by the Inter-University Consortium for Political Research at the University of Michigan; the second is that developed by the data bank of the Center for International Studies at the Massachusetts Institute of Technology; the third has been implemented, independently by the Data and Program Library Service of the Social Systems Research Institute at the University of Wisconsin and by the Social Science Information Center at the University of Pittsburgh.

The first alternative, that of the Consortium, involves a highly specialized archive staff that operates between the data supplier and the data user, and requires the investment of considerable resources in editing and revising both data and documentation, as well as otherwise "cleaning" and preparing data and documentation for multiple use. This approach tends to give priority to data that are known to be of reasonably high quality and that have a large probability of high usage rates. Other major advantages of this approach are that the user can be confident that there will be few discrepancies between data and documentation and that the documentation will be reasonably understandable. Disadvantages are that the user must accept the philosophy and values the archive follows in preparing the data and documentation, that the data-preparation process is very expensive, and that the process of cleaning and editing often means delay in the availability of data from the archive.

The MIT alternative makes the following assumptions:

1. Research requires access to a wide range of data, and there are valid ways of overcoming deficiencies in the quality of data.

2. It is often impossible to ascertain in advance the usage of some data collections, and therfore the expense of pre-use-cleaning and other data-preparation operations cannot be justified for many data collections available to archives.

Introduction 13

3. Some analyses require that any data and documentation transformations must be under the control of the analyst.

Consequently, the MIT group has developed a user-oriented computer system, called ADMINS, which provides automated aids to the user for determining discrepancies between data and documentation or for locating inconsistencies within the data, thus permitting the user to move directly from cleaning to analysis tasks. Advantages of this system are that the user can change from a given level of cleaning to a given level of analysis at will, he is not constrained by the philosophy about cleaning and data preparation of any given archive organization, and he does not have to rely solely on the data and services available from archival organizations. The main disadvantages are that the ADMINS system is not now transferable from project M.A.C. at MIT without a reprogramming effort of at least six months, possibly that using the system requires something more than elementary knowledge of computer technology, and that the data-cleaning task may be duplicated by many users unless there are organized ways of sharing the products of the ADMINS system among many users.

The third alternative is based on a combination of the assumptions made for the other two alternatives. Like the Consortium, this assumes that there must be some kind of human interface between the data source and the user, and, like the MIT group, it assumes that the user must have considerable control over the processing and analysis of archivally available data. It differs from the Consortium alternative in that the interface organization limits itself to finding and supplying to the user information required for cleaning data or for handling internal discrepancies and then systematically organizing such information for the benefit of other potential users. It differs from the approach of the MIT group in that it does not limit the user to a specific software system for cleaning and editing the data and documentation, or for analyzing the information, but rather provides or adapts from other sources any specific items of software that users feel they need to use the available data resources. The major disadvantages of this organizational alternative seem to be that the user is dependent on the human skills of the people that the local data-bank organization can recruit and train, and that a given user may have to become familiar with several computer programs that perhaps involve very different procedures and assumptions —in short, the programs do not necessarily constitute a "system."

These three alternative strategies for archival services also indicate the general kinds of archive organizations that are currently operational.

14   Introduction

Basically the existing archives can be characterized according to the scope of their data collections and the geographical range of their services. There are four types of archives:

1. General-purpose, general-service archives—such as the National Archives and Records Service or the Social Science Research Council Data Bank at the University of Essex, England.

2. Special-purpose, general-service archives—such as the International Data Service and Reference Library at the University of California, Berkeley; the Roper Public Opinion Research Library at Williams College, Williamstown, Massachusetts; the Zentralarchiv at the University of Cologne; and Datum in Bad-Godesberg, West Germany.

3. General-purpose, local-service archives—such as the Data and Program Library Service at the University of Wisconsin and the Social Science Information Center at the University of Pittsburgh.

4. Special-purpose, local-service archives—such as the Political Behavior Archives at the University of California at Los Angeles and the Political Science Research Library at Yale University.

A description of the archive organizations that are members of the Council of Social Science Data Archives is contained in *Social Science Data Archives in the United States,* a publication of the Council.[2]

The Inter-University Consortium for Political Research (special purpose, general service) is successful because it involves its users in the determination of data-acquisition policies and offers training programs for its actual and potential users. The Data and Program Library Service at the University of Wisconsin and the Social Science Information Center at the University of Pittsburgh show high usage rates because the local staffs have workable means for determining the data needs of local users and because the organization has good communication channels with other data archives and with many data-supplying organizations. Each of these general-purpose, local-service archives has a staff whose main purpose is to help researchers, students, and teachers use archived and other available data, and to locate and use needed file handling, analysis, and other needed computer programs. Present information indicates that archives with high usage rates give first priority to the various needs of their users and in the process of providing services "buffer" and otherwise protect their users from the inadequacies of the social science information system as it exists today. At the time of this writing it is a reasonable hypothesis that the general-purpose, local-service archives will become the major sources of data and services to users. Reasons for this apparent trend are that local users are so diverse in their needs that national organizations can respond only in gross ways to their problems, and that the computer and other facilities available to these local users require special kinds of attention to almost unique local problems.

At present the usage rates for most archives probably do not justify their existence, at least on a commercial basis. I have tried to stress that archive organizations can provide special benefits to policy makers, researchers, teachers, and students. Archived data *will* be better used if better data-delivery systems can be developed, if the data-producing organizations can better prepare their data collections for more widespread use, and if users can have improved access to the software required for analysis tasks. However, data archives are now in a stage of development similar to the Wright brothers' airplane: they have demonstrated that some problems, previously considered insoluble, can be solved, but they have not evolved to the point where they can be economically used. In the case of the airplane laissez-faire mechanisms eventually permitted the establishment of the required development mechanisms. If the ultimate potential of data-archive organizations is to be realized, then universities, private and governmental funding agencies, and relevant commercial organizations must continue for a reasonable period to support the efforts of the archives to perfect their instruments and procedures. The organization required to make data available for uses beyond the purposes of the original collection must be complex: archives cannot be simple warehouses and copying mechanisms. However, there also must come a time when archives "sink or swim" strictly on merits and no longer on promises.

This book is the product of many persons who are intensively involved in improving ways to make data available to those who are committed to accelerating progress by continually confronting data with theory and theory with data. Understandably, but unfortunately, some archive managers are so concerned with their own internal problems that they give no attention to the complex problems of necessary interrelations between data bases, computers, and users. However important internal needs are in the short run, the ultimate success of archives and other data-base organizations depends on considerable attention to necessarily complex dependencies among the various components of the social science information system.

REFERENCES

1. Bisco, Ralph L. "Social Science Data Archives: Progress and Prospects," *Social Science Information,* Volume VI, No. 1, Paris: February, 1967.
2. *Social Science Data Archives in the United States, 1967,* New York: Council of Social Science Data Archives, 1967.

Part I Problems and Prospects

In this part, Deutsch gives a historical account of how the data needs of scientists have been served by at least four different kinds of social organizations (or social revolutions). Campbell warns us of some modern problems in developing truly effective social science data archives. Bell reports empirical findings (the looseness which he describes) about some problems users meet in taking advantage of the services offered by the new data-bank organizations.

Chapter One

The Impact of Complex Data Bases on the Social Sciences

Karl W. Deutsch*

In order to appraise the probable impact of today's new complex data bases on the social sciences we begin best by looking back at the data bases that the social sciences have had since their inception. The first ways of looking at human society and at the way people behave toward each other (even before people began to divide their behavior neatly into politics, economics, sociology, psychology, and all the other ways of dividing up the behavior of human beings in society) were usually in terms of remembering *qualities* and types, comparing society with society, and comparing particular traits at different times and places. This goes back to Herodotus and Aristotle, who put his research assistants to work comparing the constitutions of 120 city states; it went

---

* Harvard University, Cambridge, Massachusetts.

to Montesquieu; and we can find it in Raymond Aron today.[1] It is still a great and important tradition.

Almost equally old is the effort to develop highly abstract *models* that leave out most of the social reality in order to deal more powerfully with a few drastically simplified aspects. Plato's *Republic* is in many ways a conceptual model showing both the limitations and the power of this approach. Machiavelli's *Prince* is another one. The Theory of Games would be a modern example as it is applied to conflict behavior.[2] In each case we try first to simplify reality quite radically and then to pursue a very few selected aspects of human behavior in considerable depth. Social science thus has begun with broad descriptions and comparisons, and also with abstract models and powerful, though narrow-beamed, methods of analysis from the very outset, but the systematic development of data that went beyond qualitative description is recent. I should like to think of four data revolutions that have occurred in the history of the social sciences.

THE FOUR DATA REVOLUTIONS

Perhaps the first data revolution is the one of the late seventeenth century. A milestone for it was Sir William Petty's book *Political Arithbetick,* which appeared in 1683–1689. Incidentally, the first data revolution gave the word "statistics" to various languages because statistics meant information important to the state. The statistics of the seventeenth and eighteenth centuries consisted largely of disjointed facts and figures collected chiefly for administrative, tax, and military purposes. Efforts were then made, of course, to interpret these statistics. These efforts furnished part of the intellectual background for Adam Smith's notion of the wealth of nations; then and thereafter statistics were used for inquiries as to what would make a country richer or less rich, more powerful or less powerful.

The tradition of using statistics was continued by Werner Sombart and others in the late nineteenth century.[3] As large bodies of mostly aggregative data (such as tax records, price histories, or trade statistics) were collected, efforts were made to apply them to the practical needs of statesmen and administrators, and also to use them as aids or challenges for the development of relatively grand theory. After all, Adam Smith had already been thinking of a nation as a whole, trying to describe what would make it more wealthy.

The second data revolution came about nearly two centuries later.

I would put its beginnings into the 1840s, although there were forerunners in the 1820s. It was inspired by a long series of the evolutionary models that were usually phrased in qualitative terms. Hegel and Kant were among its typical philosophical forerunners. The efforts of social scientists, such as Herbert Spencer, to develop a more detailed theory of "increasing complexity" in modern countries was a later step. Karl Marx, of course, and his contemporaries tried to develop, again, ideas as to where society might go. The data involved here were primarily historical data, dealing with the succession of types of societies and stages of society. Johann Heinrich von Thünen and the people who began with economic geography and location theory would be another example of these early efforts to produce longitudinal and cross-sectional models and series of data.[4]

The third data revolution is quite recent. Some of us experienced it as students. Typically those of us who are old enough to remember having been at universities when it happened will remember that universities knew next to nothing about it when it was happening. This third revolution began around 1935, and it began with a really large wave of new methods for gathering partial and sectoral data, and of new quantitative methods for organizing and interpreting them.

One such sector was the development of national income accounting, pioneered by Colin Clark and Simon Kuznets.[5] It was characteristic of this revolution that many previously disjointed data were now being put in relationship to each other. National income is a concept that involves the interrelations of very many different series of economic data. We may still call it sectoral because national income accounting of course takes no note of attitudes, political behavior, and many other things outside economics; but also within the field of economics national income accounting was supplemented by another one of the methods developed in the 1930s. Wassily Leontiev's input-output analysis consists in putting together many more time series and many more data than had previously been put in relation to each other.[6] The main characteristics of the data revolution of the 1930s was this double discovery: (1) methods for getting new data and (2) techniques for putting existing data into a more rigorous relation to each other.

Specialists in survey research know more about a similar revolution in the sector they are most familiar with, the work of George Gallup, Elmo Roper, Hadley Cantril, and others who brought sampling theory into surveys and polls; and on the technical side, again, the work of the psychologists, such as L. L. Thurstone and others who developed factor analysis.[7] The Michigan group of course probably goes back to the

1940s rather than the 1930s, but it is a very significant part of the same general development. Rensis Likert, Angus Campbell, and the people who have worked with them have continued this work from that time.[8]

The work of Bernard Berelson, Harold D. Lasswell, and others played a similar role in lifting and liberating content analysis from the scholars of literary history who invented it and used it back in the 1920s and before, and bringing it into the social sciences in the late 1930s and 1940s. Harold Lasswell deserves an extra note in the history of social science for the skill with which he extracted, during World War II, Department of Justice funds from the U.S. Government for developing methods of content analysis. Both the national interest and social science benefitted, and there were results that even now ought to be published. And, of course, clinical interviews, begun by the psychiatrists and the Freudians, were then developed into an instrument for social and political research. In recent years Robert Lane has used this depth-interviewing technique in political science, and motivation-research workers have applied it in psychology and in industrial organization research.[9]

At the same time that the wave of new data-gathering and data-interpretation methods developed there came a whole series of new middle-range theories. Max Weber probably can be classed either as a general theorist or a middle-range theorist, depending on how you want to look at him. Karl Mannheim was trying to develop his notions of what he called the "fundamental democratization" of society.[10] The Theory of Games of Neumann and Morgenstern is in many ways a middle-range theory, and its development for experimental applications by Anatol Rapoport and his collaborators has shown what can be done with such a theory. The notions of Leon Festinger about cognitive dissonance, the work of Kenneth Boulding on images, the tremendous work by Paul Lazarsfeld, Seymour Martin Lipset, and Alexander Inkeles, which brings together a wealth of data and middle-level theories, the work of Norbert Wiener and Claude E. Shannon on communication theories and information theory, or cybernetics, the work of Herbert Simon,[11] the development of a mathematical psychology, of a mathematical sociology, the development of simulation and modeling—all these are other aspects of the same revolution that started in the mid-1930s and stretched over the next two decades. Currently this revolution is represented by the works of Bauer, Pool, and Dexter on *American Business and Public Policy*,[12] and by Pool, Abelson, and Popkin on *Candidates, Issues, and Strategies*.[13]

All these have produced building blocks on the one hand and challenges on the other to the work of the grand theorists, and again we see men such as Talcott Parsons and Harold Lasswell working at grand theories. From time to time Robert Dahl works on grand theory: his *Preface to Democratic Theory* is an example. At other times he has moved to more limited theories in such works as *Who Governs?* and *Government and Opposition,* but in his essential style Dahl is a grand theorist.[14] I think that all these events and products can still be described as the outcomes or continuations of the data revolution that began in the late 1920s and early 1930s.

The fourth data revolution is the one that is beginning now. It is represented by many of the participants in the work of the Council of Social Science Data Archives. It is marked by the rise of multiple methods and of complex data bases, and its eventual aim, the implication of its development, is probably the development of *all-to-all comparisons.* That is to say, eventually we will want to reach a stage in social science at which a set of data found by one particular method or applied to one particular sector of social development will be at least not flagrantly incompatible, at least not flagrantly inconsistent, with all the other data and with all the other theories and methods that we have. I am formulating this in the most extreme and radical form. I am under no illusion that we will reach this stage very soon, and indeed I suspect that we will not do any better than the physicists. We will find quite often that we will have to live with major inconsistencies, much as the physicists had to live with the wave theory of light and the corpuscle theory of light for 200 years until it turned out that both of these were inadequate or badly posed formulations.

THE SEARCH FOR REPLICABILITY AND ALL-TO-ALL COMPATIBILITY OF FINDINGS

We must not forget that this is the way that the natural sciences developed. Eventually every formula any alchemist had found had to be shown either to be erroneous or—if it was not shown to be nonsense, if it turned out to be a correct description of a chemical compound—it had to be compatible with everything chemists knew about other compounds. To a very large degree this cumulative growth of knowledge and this multiple consistency of *all-to-all* comparisons characterized the change from alchemy to chemistry.[15]

Something similar happened in astronomy. All the information all the astronomers had recorded anywhere and everywhere about the positions of heavenly bodies had to be shown either to be based on mistaken observations—or else they had to be shown to be consistent or at least as not mutually incompatible. It turned out that the result was not the dreary mechanism of the eighteenth century astronomers. It turned out that there was room in all this for astrophysics and for novae—that is, for the rise of new stars, for comets, for quasars, and for any number of quite unexpected phenomena. The tests for mutual consistency do not preclude new discoveries. On the contrary, they make new discoveries eventually more likely.

In the social sciences, too, we may have to consider the task to be awareness of all that has been observed and found of relevance to our fields, just as the chemists, the physicists, the astronomers, the biologists, and the medical researchers are aware of all the more important things that have been found in theirs. In the end we cannot dodge the task of determining whether our findings and observations are really true and whether they are replicable. Insofar as we are dealing with events that are not exactly replicable, we must ask whether the aspects in regard to which they resemble each other are replicable and whether, to the extent that they are not replicable, they are not, at least flagrantly, inconsistent.

The data movement of the 1960s—and presumably the 1970s—is the beginning of this fourth revolution because it means that we are taking our findings seriously. We find now that surveys are important enough for the results not to be thrown away after the survey is over. We find that our experiments are important enough to be recorded in sufficiently specific detail so that tests can be made for implications and mutual consistency of results. The data revolution of today is going on at a time when we are seeing for the first time a cumulative improvement in the social sciences. Such a cumulative improvement in the performance of the social sciences has taken place and can be demonstrated. The most obvious examples of improvement in the performance of a social science can be found of course in economics. We should remember first the old qualitative ideas of a "just price" and the medieval regulations that led to the chaos of little-city economies in Europe. Then we should review the first attempt to build a consistent theory—the "invisible hand," or laissez-faire, theory of Adam Smith and his successors —then we must remember the improvement in Smith's ideas through the theories of Malthus, Ricardo, and Marx, which predicted increasing troubles, mounting depressions, population problems, wars, and therefore essentially increasing instability in what Adam Smith had imagined was going to be a perpetually harmonious system. Now we can see how much better, how much more sophisticated and effective, after another century of work, the economics of John Maynard Keynes and his successors have become.[16]

At present economists in both Western Europe and the United States can advise governments on courses of action in private-enterprise systems that will keep unemployment very roughly below 5 percent of the work force and peacetime secular inflation perhaps at below a 3 percent price increase per year. This is not yet a very good performance. An unemployment rate of 5 percent in a national average can easily mean 10 percent unemployment for disadvantaged minorities, and as much once again for disadvantaged age groups thus we still have 20 or 25 percent unemployment among young Negroes in American cities. Similarly a 3 percent rise in general prices can conceal of course considerably higher price increases—in some particularly important goods and services. We may hope that the economists' performance will further improve, so that it might become possible to run a more or less free, consumer-choice-oriented economy with no more than, say, 2 percent unemployment of the work force and with no more than a 1 percent price increase per year. However, at the moment my colleagues in economics assure me that this time is not yet, although regarding a 3 percent increase and a 5 percent unemployment rate they feel pretty confident.[17]

Over on the Marxist side of the world's borders the economists now can run planned economies, and it seems that they can guarantee something like an average peacetime growth rate of 5 or 6 percent over the fairly long run. They cannot guarantee, however, any high and uniform quality of consumers' goods and services or any high degree of consumer satisfaction, and they have at least as many troubles and needs for improvement in their brand of economics as we do in ours.[18] But there is no comparison between the quality of economics in the 1960s, both east and west of the Iron Curtain, and what passed for economics in the 1920s and early 1930s at the time of the Great Depression, on the one hand, and the great Stalin campaign for the collectivization of the Soviet Union on the other. Another example of progress in economics is the change from the false prediction of Adam Smith that competition would always lower prices to the improved predictions by Thorstein Veblen, Edward Chamberlin, and Joan Robinson that, under more realistic conditions of imperfect competition, the arrival of more businessmen in a small country town might well increase prices because a limited trade would now have to be split among more firms and hence more separate overhead costs. This is the theory of monopolistic competition.[19]

In other fields we may think of what has been done in psychology. There is little doubt that after Freud and after some of the modern empirical psychologists we know a great deal more than before. We have learned to consider the "Festinger effect" according to which, when prophecy fails, the man whose predictions have not come true will redouble his efforts to go on reasserting his old theories.[20] This does not only apply to the cases considered in Leon Festinger's studies; it might even apply to certain high echelons in the State Department. The work by S. E. Asch on the effects of group suggestion and the work of W. P. Livant and others on cumulative distortion are other examples of performances of social sciences that are significantly better than what existed 30 or 50 years ago.[21] In political science we once had the good old naive theories about the supposedly almost automatic progress of bigger and better integration—from the village to the province, from the province to the duchy, from the duchy to the kingdom, from the kingdom to the empire, and from the empire to the world government. Today we know a good deal more about the countervailing trend toward the self-closure of large systems. We know something about communication overload and about the tendency toward a decline of central government attention to the outlying districts and to marginal political units or groups; and we know now therefore that political integration is likely to be self-terminating or a self-limiting process unless certain conditions are fulfilled.[22] In short, political science as well as psychology, economics, and the other social sciences have become cumulative in a demonstrable way.[23] We know what the forerunners in social science knew as well or as badly as they knew it, but now we know a little more —not too much more but significantly and demonstrably more.

With this modest but real growth of cumulative knowledge has come also a significant increase in our ability to apply it. Sometimes we focus our attention on what social science cannot do and what governments cannot do, and we forget that present-day governments keep doing things that earlier were considered impossible. To insure practically all working people in this country against old age was considered impossible and unthinkable 100 years ago, and in some countries even 60 years ago, but it is by now fairly current practice in almost all civilized countries. To insure people through the government against illness was considered years ago a bold and impractical thing, but Medicare is here in the United States; and in many countries even broader schemes became law much sooner. Race relations were supposed to be beyond serious control by law or by social science. But Thurgood Marshall, the lawyer who pleaded the case of Commonwealth vs. Brown in 1954, joined the Supreme Court of the United States in 1967. With all the troubles we have in race relations, we have been trying the last 13 years to do things that were considered to be impossible in the preceding 100 years.

In short, the background of the growth of social science on one hand and of the secular change in social climate on the other is incomparably more favorable for the new data revolution than anything any previous generation of social scientists encountered in their lifetime. However, if the capabilities of social science have increased, its burdens have increased still more: perhaps this is why our feeling that social science is inadequate is now more oppressive and intense. What we are concerned with is not what social science can do but the margin between what it can do and what it ought to do and *has* to do, and that margin has become reassuringly smaller.

It is under these conditions that a fourth data revolution is now taking place—the attempt to get systematic collections of all theory-relevant social science data; that is, of all data that could be relevant to social science.[24] Secondly, the fourth data revolution is concerned to get on permanent computer-usable records many more of the ratios that various social scientists have found important and interesting. Thirdly, we must have two kinds of implication analysis. We need an implication analysis of propositions for most of the more live or more relevant social science theories. Such an implication analysis would say, "If this theory is correct, what observable facts ought to be the case?" And we need an implication analysis of data—namely, an analysis that will say, "If these data have been correctly observed, what other observable facts or data would they imply?"

Such an implication analysis of data could involve, for instance, an analysis of the latent meaning of survey questions. In the 1950s various samples of German respondents were asked, "With what countries do we need to collaborate closely?" About 80 percent named the United States, about 20 percent named the Soviet Union, and about 14 percent named Israel. There also was asked the question, "With what countries should be *not* collaborate particularly closely?" About 61 percent named the Soviet Union, 60 percent named Poland, and 37 percent named Israel. Now we can compare the latent meaning of this result with the ballot question, "What is generally your attitude toward the Jews?" About 34 percent of the respondents gave antisemitic responses. It must be noted that the 37 percent who felt no need for good relations with Israel and the 34 percent who did not like Jews may be the same population. Since these were different samples, we cannot get at the actual overlap between the two, but an analysis of the common latent meaning of these two differently worded questions is revealing. Incidentally, at the time of the 1956 Suez war of Britain, France, and Israel against Egypt 56 percent of German poll respondents sympathized with Egypt and the Arabs, but 11 years later, at the time of the brief Arab-Israeli war of 1967, 50 percent of the German public sympathized with Israel and only about 12 percent sympathized with the Arabs [25] according to press summaries of the latest opinion poll. Apparently there as in other areas public opinion has been shifting. These examples suggest that we need more cross-examination of different poll data and of the latent meaning of different kinds of survey responses. If the data are right, what would they mean, what do they mean for other data, and what do they mean for other theories?

This brings us back to the question of complex data bases. What are they? They embody a very basic philosophy—the principle of the multiplicity of sources and the multiplicity of operations. This is an intellectual principle that runs exactly against one of the most cherished principles of modernization in all countries. Since the Untied States is like all other countries, only more so, it runs particularly against a basic tenet in the United States—namely, the principle of technical specialization.

According to the principle of technical specialization a survey expert should not worry about content analysis, and he should not bother about economic data; he should not waste his time on historical time series nor should he bother too much with depth interviews or with Jungian symbols or Freudian complexes. But if our main job as social scientists is not merely or primarily to be technical auxiliary experts, then we shall need and cherish technical experts on everything from Egyptian papyrus inscriptions to our specialists on mid-twentieth-century survey data. If our main task is to develop social science data archives, then our main specialty will be to develop through our work the collective working memory of social science in this country and in the world.

And here we come back to an old philosophic principle. About 2500 years ago the Greek philosopher Thales of Miletus said that it was not true that the gods were behind things. In reality, said Thales, the gods were within them. This was one of the beginnings of the philosophy of science.

Today we can go perhaps a step further and say that truth is not in the facts, truth is in the relationships among them. Truth is among the facts, not in them. No single indicator, no single operation, no single source of information, no single class of facts is going to help us very much in understanding social reality or indeed any other kind of reality. Our judgment of reality is a judgment about the relationships among different kinds of streams of evidence.

"Reality" and "truth" are labels for predicted relationships among present and future streams of different information from diverse verifying operations. As Dr. Johnson said to his interlocutor, "If you doubt whether this brick exists, sir, try kicking it." He was saying that the evidence of a man's eyes looking at the brick would be confirmed by the evidence of his toe when he tried to kick it. The difference between a pair of real white mice and a pair of white mice that appear to a man in certain stages of delirium tremens is not a difference in the vividness of the impression—the mice in the delirium may seem to be more vivid. But the mice in the delirium leave no droppings; they leave no footprints in flour; they do not excite a dog or a cat; and they can not be caught in traps with cheese. Real mice can, even though they do not look as vivid nor as plausible. The difference between the imagined mouse and the real mouse is in the multiplicity of verifying operations, of convergent evidence, of consistent operations. Whenever we are after real rather than imagined mice, or after any other piece of reality, we need evidence for many different streams of information.

I have tried sometimes to give an inventory and a list, and even some numerical estimates of what eventually not any one data archive but rather the collectivity of data archives would need as a data basis for research just on politics (Table 1.1).

Speaking in the parochial and narrow ways of a political scientist, the first set of such data would begin with the people of power and influence, and thus consist of elite data. Such elite data would involve biographies, some survey data, some social background data, and tabulations of who are the incumbents of the different elite levels in different countries of the world: the top elites, the different functional elites, the middle-level elites, and the broader politically relevant strata. As of 1965 our stock of elite data was on the order of 100,000 card equivalents or more. The annual accession rates may probably by now be on the order of 200,000 cards. By 1970 we might have about a million card equivalents of elite data in the world.

Survey data can be collected on the mass level, on the top elite level, and on something I would like to call the mid-elite level. Samples of this mid-elite level could be obtained by pulling out of the various surveys the top 5 percent level of respondents in terms of income, education, and socioeconomic status. We could then distinguish even

Table 1.1
Expectable Information Requirements of Political Science *
(In Million Cards or Equivalents) †

Type of Information	Data Stock 1965	Data Stock 1970	Data Stock 1975	Annual Additions 1965	Annual Additions 1975
Elite data	0.1	1.0	3.0	0.2	0.4
Mass opinion	10.0	12.5	15.0	0.5	1.0
Voting statistics	5.0	7.5	10.0	0.5	0.5
Legislative voting data	0.05	0.2	0.8	0.05	0.05
Content analysis	0.1	0.6	1.6	0.05	0.2
Aggregative data	0.1	2.5	7.5	0.5	1.0
Other social sciences	0.15	0.4	0.9	0.05	0.1
Mathematical routines and secondary data	—	2.5	7.5	0.5	1.0
Historical data	0.7	2.1	4.1	0.4	0.8
Total	16.20	29.3	50.4	2.65	5.05

* Source: Karl W. Deutsch, "Recent Trends in Research Methods in Political Science," in *A Design for Political Science*, Monograph No. 6 of the American Academy of Political and Social Science, Philadelphia (December 1966).

† All these figures merely illustrate orders of magnitude. Some of them may well be subject to an error margin of up to 50 percent.

the core mid-elites, which are those for whom these three indicators all agree, and the marginal elites, consisting of those who are in the top 5 percent on one or two of those grounds but not on the others.

Talcott Parsons had a theory that the men who were in the top 5 percent or better on money but not on education and not on status were particularly susceptible to a peculiarly militant type of populist conservatism;[26] whereas on the other hand, the people who have champagne tastes and beer pocketbooks—that is, the people with the high education and the middle to lower income—are frequently on the liberal or radical side of opinion: this category of course includes many members of university faculties. But the serious collection of data on all three levels—top elite (which are cabinet members, undersecretaries and assistant secretaries of state, and so on) mid-elite, and mass—would begin to give us considerably more. We already have a data stock of about 10 million card equivalents on mass opinion data, and we may now have an annual accession rate of at least half a million cards or card equivalents. We may have, therefore, by 1970 about 15 million card equivalents in the world on mass survey data, and more may be coming.

Through the systematic secondary analysis of this wealth of survey data we could carry out more serious comparisons than ever before. We can compare much more seriously across space. Inkeles and others have begun to compare cross-nationally, and we can of course compare across groups and classes. We can use much larger samples and begin therefore to break down our groups much more finely, or we can use the Simulmatics method on a larger scale and more consistently all over the world to put answers to identical questions in successive years together as if they had been given in a single survey—thus, for the moment, deliberately throwing away the impact of time on the group but getting many other cases in each of the finer categories.[27] For instance, if this is done for American poll data on the recognition of Red China over 10 years, it turns out that the American Negroes have a quite different image of Red China from that held by American whites. In no single survey can this result be seen because there are always too few Negroes. If we take 6 or 10 surveys together, we get enough Negro respondents for statistical analysis, and then it turns out that *they* would recognize Red China without any trouble and always would have. It also turns out that we know now who are the most adamant opponents of recognizing Red China. Our real backbone, or our most hard-line group in the United States, are white, Republican farmers over 50 years of age with no more than a grade-school education.[28]

We can do much more in the cross-examination of both overt and latent meanings of questions. We can begin to develop quantitative data on the effects of question wordings and of interviewers. We all know that they exist, but it would be good to know under what conditions an interviewer is likely to have a distorting effect of 5 or 10 percent on the outcome, and in what cases he will have a 20 percent effect or a still larger one. Similarly in what cases is the wording of a survey question in itself likely to produce more than a 10 or 15 percent shift in the kind of answers that are obtained? We also might want to get more data on what I would call the Guttman dimensions of attitudes—that is, intensity, salience involvement, and closure.[29] This would involve on the one hand changing the instruments of questionnaires to get more explicit answers *that* can be used but then keeping these and beginning to find out what the correlations are between these secondary dimensions of attitudes and the attitudes themselves.

We might have to do much more comparing across time. We already have panel methods that Lazarsfeld and others have developed, and we have some historical data. However, in Japan, for instance, Chikio Hayashi in his studies of the Japanese national character combined the two methods. He used large samples—2500 people. The first 2500 were polled in 1953. Half of them were reinterviewed as panel members five years later, in 1958. The other half was a new sample, freshly drawn according to standard sampling methods; and all this was repeated once more in 1963. We could use this technique much more often and find out much better what are panel effects and what are new-sample effects.[30]

We ought to know much better what is the generation effect on an age group that has had a formative experience and what is the sheer effect of biological aging. We all know the old tag that young men at twenty ought to be socialists and at fifty ought to be conservatives. It touches at best only a small part of the truth, but it is observable that many people do become somewhat more conservative as they become either older, or richer, or both. But we do not know their numbers. Ronald Ingelhardt of the University of Michigan shows that the 15-year olds in Europe are now distinctly more pro-European than their elders. We do not know whether or not this is a secular shift indicating a wave of the future; that is, whether 20 years from now the 15-year olds, who will then be 35 years old, will be just as pro-European as they were at 15 years of age. We do not know by how much they may shift back into conformity with their elders with every year that they get older. On the other hand, their views might have been formed by the simple fact that they were born in 1950 and that they grew up in an atmosphere in which at least a fair amount of present or future European unification was taken for granted.[31] We do know that the generation that was 20 years old at the time of the Great Depression is not going to take laissez-faire economics quite as seriously again as the people who were born earlier. In some ways we find that the depression generations—or war generations—behave at least somewhat differently in politics from those who came before or after them. However, we do not have precise data about them, and we could.

Serious data archives that make data available for such comparisons and that *even carry out* some of these comparisons themselves or encourage scholars to do this and store the results could then eventually produce data similar to the ones we all get when we bring our baby home from the clinic. There we get a weight chart, and if we find that a baby's weight is within a channel marked on it, we know that the baby is gaining weight just about satisfactorily. Should we not have something like a weight chart saying that the memory of a historical enmity or other past event will decay at a certain speed and, so long as it is within its channel, this is what is to be expected? If it is forgotten faster or if it is remembered more tenaciously, we ought to learn more about the particular reasons.

I would like to know from our social scientists what is the half-life of a prejudice; that is to say, how long does it take until a particular prejudice is held only by one-half of the percentage of the population who held it originally? And we have actually two half-lives; namely, the half-life of the prejudice among the people who originally held it, and (a somewhat shorter half-life) the half-life of the prejudice among the general population, which in the meantime has received members of a younger age group who may never have had it. But these two data ought to be known, and we ought to know roughly what it is for deeply held prejudices by strong interest groups. I would put the half-life at about 25 years—which would accord well with the resistance to the St. Lawrence Seaway in the 1930s and its acceptance in the 1950s. The resistance toward school integration and its acceptance would give us ample test cases. The fluoridation test cases might give us other data on this. We ought to know much more about the rates and speeds of habit change, straight from survey data together with age cohort analysis, generation data, and other relevant information. Something similar of course can be extracted from voting statistics, and voting statistics again give us about, I should say, five million card equivalents and an accession rate of about half a million by the end of the decade. We need more legislative voting data, and, again, many more are becoming available from roll calls and various research data on legislative behavior.[32] At the moment we have probably no more than 50,000 card equivalents of this type of data, but we are getting at least as much as that in each year, and we might therefore have about 200,000 card equivalents on legislative voting by 1970.

Content analysis can now move forward much faster because of the work of Philip Stone and others on the *General Inquirer*.[33] But what is now needed is a real comparison of content-analysis data with survey and attitude data. At Yale this spring two studies were made. One was on Soviet May Day slogans, which is the continuation of the old work of Lasswell and Jacobsen, and the series now runs from 1917 to 1967. It turns out the Russians are currently about as internationalistic and world-minded as they were in the 1920s; that is, the international symbols and the national symbols are now close to a ratio of 1.1 to 1. In the peak of the Stalin period, between 1938 and 1948, they were 10 to 1, national. So we can see the tremendous difference that has occurred there. But we also find that on the whole militant langauge, symbols of violence, and military imagery have steadily declined in the imagery of the May Day slogans. On the whole supportive and friendlier phrases have increased.[34]

Another Yale doctoral candidate, a Jesuit priest has run three papal encyclicals through the *General Inquirer* using the *Lasswellian Value Dictionary*. He finds, comparing *Rerum Novarum* of 1890, *Quadragesimo Anno* of 1930, and *Mater et Magistra* of the 1950s, a steady decline of the symbols of power and authority; a steady decline of the negative affect symbols; a decline of exclusion; and an increase of friendly, supportive, and inclusive statements.[35] It seems that both the Vatican and the Kremlin have been getting somewhat more dovelike in the long run. Again, these are small bits of findings. What we need is to compare them much better with data on the level of the top elite of the organizations concerned, with data of the mid-elite, and with data about their rank-and-file constituents. But in more nearly closed societies, where we cannot very well go around with questionnaires, content analysis is one of the most effective ways of listening in on how the leadership of these groups is talking to their own constituencies and in particular how they are talking to their own middle-level management.

Content-analysis data currently stored in archives are on the order of 100,000 card images, and we are getting probably another 50,000 card equivalents each year. We may have 600,000 or more card equivalents by the end of the 1970s. We also should have by then survey data and relevant content-analysis data in archives, stored next to each other. We also should store in the data archives the standard texts of important documents for new runs with computerized content-analysis methods. Then, when a new social scientist has a different question to ask, he will not have to spend again $50,000 or $100,000 to get the original texts punched, edited, and cleaned all over again. If we had standard, cleaned, and edited texts for content analysis, we could run from time to time new questions against old texts; and we could again and again run an old or new question against contrasting texts. We could say then, "Let us run a program searching for symbols of authority, or of questioning, or of integrative attitudes against four standard texts." For instance, the texts of the social encyclicals since 1890 should now be punched cards in the data archives. The May Day slogans of the Communists since 1919 ought to be there, as should be U.S. political party platforms and presidential messages to Congress from their beginnings. Preliminary efforts at hand content analysis suggest that at times certain symbols have almost disappeared from American electoral discourse. Thus property symbols were frequently used in party platforms in the nineteenth century but declined in the twentieth, particularly after 1930, and have not come back successfully so far. California might be a recent exception, but for quite a while in national elections the platforms have been playing down such symbols.

We need other social science data. First of all we need aggregative data of actual behavior. The German opinion-survey organizations asked people, "Do you have friends or relatives in East Germany?" "Are you writing them letters?" "Are you sending them packages?" About half the population said *yes*. These numbers obtained from survey data accord very well with the data on actual letters sent and actual packages sent, as recorded by the German Federal Post Office. In ways like these we often can check, as the market-research people very frequently do, the relationship between an expressed attitude and actual behavior. We can now get vast amounts of such aggregative data from the United Nations and from other organizations, and our data archives should not neglect such information about social phenomena.

From aggregative data we can compute interesting ratios. For instance, we have the Human Relations Area Files, which tell us a great deal about the food habits of various tribes. From some of these data we could compute innovation rates regarding various products, methods, and societies, and discover some median, mean, and modal values for some types of them. What is the half-life of a prejudice in food? How long did it take until half the villages in a country planted potatoes or half the African Negro tribes planted tapioca or manioc? We have some data on this by now. Just as we can get learning rates by using survey research and changes in political attitude from voting data, we can get the speed of change in food habits from the anthropologists. And we can get some ratios of change, incidentally, for economics and innovation from the historians of economics and the historians of technology. Together all this will give us for societies something that is similar to a turning radius for vehicles. We know that a Chevrolet takes 41 feet to turn around, a Volkswagen can be turned in a little bit less, and the Queen Mary takes $1\frac{1}{2}$ miles to stop, even when her engines are reversed when she is at full speed—because of her momentum. What is the turning radius of a society? How long does it take to change the behavior of a society in some important respect? What is the fastest that it can be done under optimal conditions? What is the slowest?

We are oversupplied with statements to the effect that mankind must change many of its old habits or it will perish in a modern atomic age. But we do not know which habits can be changed, how quickly, and under what conditions. Our data archives could help our social scientists find this out. We can get many more experimental data. Think of the 100,000 experimental game plays that Anatol Rapoport and his associates alone collected.[36] Think of the Festinger or Asch data and many others. We can begin to work with historians on historical data. What was the military participation ratio in the crusades or in ancient Rome? From historical research we have a great deal of data in cases for which we know one thing—the outcome of an event. If we can get more data as to what were the proportions of the forces involved and if we know the outcome in the historical cases, our historical wisdom could be made a very great deal more effective in looking at the possible effects of shifts in proportions or shifts in size and quantity that we find in our societies today. Finally, we could try to get ratios and indices on a much larger scale. I suspect that eventually we shall find that the total volume of derived data—such as per capita incomes, growth rates, and military participation ratios—will be as large or larger than our primary data. We can choose of course to throw away all secondary ratios and to store only primary data, but then we should have to generate over and over again all ratios whenever they are needed. However, even if computers become much cheaper than they are now, the cost in time and programming might be prohibitive. I think we ought to work toward a consensus among social scientists and data-archive leaders about which derived data and ratios—rates of change, indices, or indicators—are so likely to be generally useful that they should be kept permanently available to new users. For instance, Robert Angell computed an indicator of integration for cities by developing a ratio of Community Chest contributions to the crime rate. His argument was that what people were voluntarily doing for a town is an indicator of integration—and crimes, particularly violent crimes, are an indicator of disintegration. Perhaps this could be improved, but he computed it for over 100 cities.[37] The archives keep available these 1941 data from Angell, and corresponding indicators could be easily enough computed for 1951 and 1961. Updated sequels to a limited number of series of such social indicators should be computed routinely, and we could then see what is happening to these indicators over time and across different regions and countries.

We also need to store many more of our computer programs in the social sciences, and our data archives can begin to struggle against dialect formation. Just as the peasants in Tyrolean villages speak mostly with each other but rarely to strangers—and so develop a peculiar local speech in each village—so computer programmers in some great universities talk mostly to each other and less often to people out of town. After a while they have their own shortcuts, notations, and abbreviations, and many of the computer programs developed at one university somehow do not work very well at any other. Tyrolean peasants find that this is an excellent way of keeping strangers out of their village. Similarly computer programmers find that this works like a protective tariff. However, Tyrolean peasants do not belong to the richest, happiest, or most progressive people, and I think that the computer programmer in the long run can do better than the Tyrolean peasantry. That is to say, what we need to develop, and I think our sociologists can give us some pointers here, there will be a profession, a nationwide and eventually a worldwide profession, with interchangeable talents, with its own professional standards, and, incidentally, with its own career lines in the pecking order of the academic chicken yard. What we need is a career line for data-archive directors and computer programmers who will be the equivalent of everything a university has to offer in the way of professorships together with the security, the tenure, and all the other tangible and intangible attractions of academic administration and research.

Similar problems have been solved by the physicists and the astronomers. The man who runs a large observatory or a large electron accelerator has to be as skilled and competent, in his own way, as the professor of astronomy or physics with whom he is working. If he is, then he is likely to prove as valuable; he has to be as well paid, and as secure economically and professionally. We need just this kind of career for the social science directors and the leaders of the social science observatories that we are getting now. We may even have to invent a word for their emerging contribution, but we are beginning to get it in effect. What we now need is the social and professional recognition for this emerging group of specialists whom we are now getting and of whom we need more.

In the end, if we put all these things together, we shall find that we can even store and test some of our information about theories. As propositional inventories are developed, they will tell us only a small fraction of what theories have to say. The most interesting things about a theory often are not its detailed propositions but the overall patterns that it embodies. For some time to come these patterns will not go well on punched cards, although eventually we may find ways for pattern recognition in the computer age. But long before we get methods for the comparison of theoretical patterns or for comparative surveys of entire models, we shall already be able to get propositions down and to say which proposition is common to 10 or 20 theories.

38 Problems and Prospects

We can, in short, develop in the data archives a three-way synthesis. First, synthesis between the archive and the laboratory—and thus a synthesis between the storage of information, which is typical of archives and libraries, and the development of new inquiries, observations, and experiments, which is typical of laboratories. Second, a synthesis of each of these with the function of an analysis center, devoted to theory development through the disassociative and combinatorial function that is characteristic of the human memory at its best and its most creative.

In a very serious sense social science today, if it is to cope with its tasks, has to improve its capacity to think. But it has to improve this capacity, including among other things its capacity to remember relevantly and effectively, by a whole order of magnitude. To improve our intellectual capabilities in the social science field by an order of magnitude may be in the course of the next half century a matter of life and death for all of us. In the task of improving the intellectual capabilities of social science by an order of magnitude social science data archives will prove to be an essential link and will make an indispensible and vital contribution.

REFERENCES

1. W. W. Jaeger, *Aristotle*. Oxford: Clarendon Press, 1934; Montesquieu, *The Spirit of the Laws*. New York: Hafner, 1949; Raymond Aron, *Peace and War: A Theory of International Relation*. Garden City, N.Y.: Doubleday, 1966.
2. John von Neumann and Oskar Morgenstern, *Theory of Games and Economic Behavior*, 3rd ed. Princeton, N.J.: Princeton University Press, 1953; Anatol Rapoport, *Fights, Games and Debates*. Ann Arbor, Mich.: University of Michigan Press, 1960; R. D. Luce and H. Raiffa, *Games and Decisions, Introduction and Critical Survey*. New York: Wiley, 1957; Martin Shubik, *Game Theory and Related Approaches to Social Behavior*. New York: Wiley, 1964.
3. Werner Sombart, *Die deutsche Volkswirtschaft im neunzehnten Jahrhundert*. Berlin: G. Bondi, 1903; *Der moderne Kapitalismus*. Leipzig: Duncker & Humblot, 1902.
4. J. H. von Thünen, *Der isolierte Staat in Beziehung auf Landwirtschaft und Nationalekonomie*. 3rd ed. Jena: Fischer, 1930.
Eric Roll, *A History of Economic Thought*. New York: Prentice-Hall, Inc., 1942.
5. Colin Clark, *The Conditions of Economic Progress*, 3rd ed. New York: St. Martin's Press, 1960 (the three editions differ in part in the empirical data used); Simon Kuznets, *Modern Economic Growth*. New Haven, Conn.: Yale University Press, 1966.
6. Wassily Leontiev and others, *Studies in the Structure of the American Economy*. New York: Oxford University Press, 1953.

7. L. L. Thurstone, *Multiple-Factor Analysis*. Chicago: University of Chicago Press, 1947; for a recent survey see H. H. Harmon, *Modern Factor Analysis*. Chicago: University of Chicago Press, 1960; R. J. Rummel, *Applied Factor Analysis*. Evanston, Ill.: Northwestern University Press, 1967.
8. Angus Campbell and others, *The American Voter*. New York: Wiley, 1960; *Elections and the Political Order*. New York: Wiley, 1966.
9. R. E. Lane, *Political Ideology*. New York: Free Press of Glencoe, 1962.
10. Karl Mannheim, *Men and Society in an Age of Reconstruction*. New York: Harcourt, Brace and World, 1967; M. S. Lipset, *The First New Nation*. New York: Basic Books, 1963; and *Political Man*. Garden City, N.Y.: Doubleday, 1960; P. F. Lazarsfeld, *Mathematical Thinking in the Social Sciences*. Glencoe, Ill.: Free Press, 1954; P. F. Lazarsfeld and Morris Rosenberg, *The Language of Social Research*. New York: Free Press, 1955; D. H. Smith and Alex Inkeles, "The OM Scale: A Comparative Socio-Psychological Measure of Individual Modernity," *Sociometry*, 29, No. 4, (December 1966), pp. 353–377; Alexander Inkeles, *What is Sociology?* Englewood Cliffs, N.J.: Prentice-Hall, 1964.
11. Herbert Simon, *Models of Man: Social and Rational*. New York: Wiley, 1957.
12. R. A. Bauer, I. S. Pool, and L. A. Dexter, *American Business and Public Policy*. New York: Atherton, 1963.
13. Ithiel de Sola Pool, R. P. Abelson, and S. L. Popkin, *Candidates, Issues, and Strategies*. Cambridge, Mass.: MIT Press, 1964.
14. R. A. Dahl, *A Preface to Democratic Theory*. Chicago: University of Chicago Press, 1956; *Who Governs?* New Haven, Conn.: Yale University Press, 1961; cf. also R. A. Dahl, *Political Oppositions in Western Democracies*. New Haven, Conn.: Yale University Press, 1966.
15. For a discussion of some aspects of this change see J. B. Conant, *Science and Common Sense*. New Haven, Conn.: Yale University Press, 1951.
16. For the earlier stages of this development see again Eric Roll, op. cit., passim. For more recent development see ref. 29.
17. For recent discussions see Wassily Leontif, *The New Outlook in Economics*. University of York, 1967; James Tobin, *National Economic Policy*. New Haven, Conn.: Yale University Press, 1966; W. W. Heller, *New Dimensions of Political Economy*. Cambridge, Mass.: Harvard University Press, 1966; Simon Kuznets, ref. 5; B. H. Higgins, *What Do Economists Know?*. Melbourne: Melbourne University Press, 1951.
18. For views of economists in Soviet bloc countries see, for example, Joseph Goldmann, "Fluctuations and Trend in the Rate of Economic Growth in some Socialist Countries," *Economics of Planning*, 4, No. 2, 1964; for views of Western observers of East bloc economic problems see Abram Bergson, *The Real National Income of Soviet Russia since 1928*. Cambridge, Mass.: Harvard University Press, 1961; J. M. Montias, *Central Planning in Poland*. New Haven, Conn.: Yale University Press, 1962; W. F. Stolper, *The Structure of the East German Economy*. Cambridge, Mass.: Harvard University Press, 1960; Alexander Eckstein, *The National Income of Communist China*. New York: Free Press of Glencoe, 1961.
19. Thorstein Veblen, *The Theory of Business Enterprise*. New York, 1904; Edward Chamberlin, *The Theory of Monopolistic Competition*. Cambridge, Mass.: Harvard University Press, 1938; Joan Robinson, *The Economics of Imperfect Competition*. London: Macmillan, 1936; W. J. Fellner, *Competition among the Few*. New York: Kelley, 1960.

Problems and Prospects

20. Leon Festinger, Henry W. Riecken, and Stanley Schacter, *When Prophecy Fails*. Minneapolis: University of Minnesota Press, 1956; Leon Festinger, *A Theory of Cognitive Dissonance*. Stanford, Calif.: Stanford University Press, 1962; *Conflict, Decision and Dissonance*. Stanford, Calif.: Stanford University Press, 1964, for example, pp. 30–31, 97–100, 152–158.
21. S. E. Asch, *Social Psychology*. Englewood Cliffs, N.J.: Prentice-Hall, 1952; "Effects of Group Pressure upon the Modification and Distortion of Judgments," in *Readings in Social Psychology*, 3rd ed. Eleanor E. Maccoby, T. M. Newcomb and E. L. Hartley (eds.). New York: Holt, Rinehart, and Winston, 1958, pp. 174–183; W. P. Livant, "Cumulative Distortion of Judgment," *Perceptual and Motor Skills*, 16 (1963), pp. 741–745; R. C. Jacobs and D. T. Campbell, "The Perpetuation of an Arbitrary Tradition through Several Generations of a Laboratory Microculture," *Journal of Abnormal and Social Psychology*, 62 (1961), pp. 649–658. (The last two articles are reprinted in *Human Behavior and International Politics*, J. D. Singer (ed.). Chicago: Rand McNally, 1965, pp. 274–278, and 278–287, respectively.)
22. For a modern and sophisticated analysis of the integration problem see Amitai Etzioni, *Political Unification*. New York: Holt, Rinehart, and Winston, 1965; cf. also P. E. Jacob and J. V. Toscano, *The Integration of Political Communities*. Philadelphia: Lippincott, 1964.
23. For example of cumulative developments in political science see the series of yearbooks of behavioral political research, edited by Heinz Eulau, such as most recently, J. D. Singer, (ed.), *Quantitative International Politics*. New York: Free Press, 1968; for a general discussion see H. D. Lasswell, *The Future of Political Science*. New York: Atherton, 1963.
24. C. J. Friedrich, "Some General Theoretical Reflections on the Problems of Political Data," in *Comparing Nations*, R. L. Merritt and Stein Rokkan (eds.). New Haven, Conn.: Yale University Press, 1966, pp. 57–79; and K. W. Deutsch, "The Theoretical Basis of Data Programs," *ibid.*, pp. 27–55.
25. Elisabeth Nölle and E. P. Neumann, *Jahrbuch der öffentlichen Meinung 1947–1955*, 2nd ed. Allensbach: Verlag für Demoskopie, 1956, pp. 128, 331; E. P. Neumann, "Nützt Ungarn der CDU?", *Der Spiegel*, 11, No. 2 (January 2, 1957), p. 13; K. W. Deutsch and L. J. Edinger, *Germany Rejoins the Powers*. Stanford, Calif.: Stanford University Press, 1959, pp. 41–42, 226; K. W. Deutsch "The German Federal Republic," in *Modern Political Systems: Europe*, R. C. Macridis and R. E. Ward (eds.). Englewood Cliffs, N.J.: Prentice-Hall, 1963, pp. 315–317.
26. Talcott Parsons, "Social Strains in America," in his *Structure and Process in Modern Societies*. New York and Glencoe, Ill.: Free Press, 1960, pp. 226–247.
27. See Ithiel de Sola Pool, R. P. Abelson, and S. L. Popkin, ref. 13.
28. J. R. Sacks, unpublished research, Yale University, 1963–1965.
29. Louis Guttmann, "The Principal Components of Scalable Attitudes," in *Mathematical Thinking in the Social Sciences*, P. F. Lazarsfeld (ed.). Glencoe, Ill.: Free Press, 1954, pp. 216–257.
30. Chikio Hayashi, *A Study of Japanese National Character*. Tokyo: Shiseido, No. 1–11, 1961.
31. Ronald Inglehardt, "An End to European Integration?", *The American Political Science Review*, LXI, No. 1 (March 1967) p. 91.
32. D. B. Truman, *The Congressional Party*. New York: Wiley, 1959.

33. P. J. Stone and others, *The General Inquirer: A Computer Approach to Content Analysis.* Cambridge, Mass.: MIT Press, 1966.
34. Ruth Greenstein, *Soviet May Day Slogans 1918–1966,* unpublished research, Yale University, 1967.
35. Gerald Costigan, S. J., unpublished research, Yale University, 1966–1967.
36. Anatol Rapoport and A. M. Chammah, *Prisoner's Dilemma.* Ann Arbor, Mich.: University of Michigan Press, 1965.
37. R. C. Angell, *The Integration of American Society.* New York: McGraw-Hill, 1941; cf. W. S. Landecker, "Types of Integration and their Measurement" in *The Language of Social Research,* P. F. Lazarsfeld and Morris Rosenberg (eds.). New York: Free Press, 1955, pp. 19–27.

Chapter Two

Some Questions about the New Jerusalem

Angus Campbell[*]

There exists in some sections of the world of social science a hopeful expectation that social science researchers are all about to achieve salvation; that social research is about to be lifted out of the ignominious condition in which it has labored these many years and conducted into the divine presence. The instrument of this elevation is to be the data archives and computers that are now springing up around the land.

I want to make it clear at once that I am as anxious to be saved as many readers of this chapter. I regard myself as rather enthusiastic about the development of data archives in the social sciences; I have even played a kind of avuncular role in the creation of a rather sizable one at the University of Michigan. I am supportive and optimistic about everything the Council of Social Science Data Archives stands for, and in raising the questions I shall shortly come to I do so not in any curmudgenoly spirit of skepticism but as a true believer who is ready to join you all on the Glory Road.

---

[*] University of Michigan, Ann Arbor.

Some Questions About the New Jerusalem

The first question concerning the New Jerusalem is, "What is going into the new archives that we hope to see develop?" The answer will probably be, "Both too much and too little." Too much because it seems likely that in our enthusiasm to exploit the new capacities that computer developments are making available there will be a great temptation to sweep up every imaginable kind of data in a vast **omnium gatherum**. The Reuss Committee on the use of social research by the federal government [1] has already criticized what it refers to as "the current fashion of indiscriminate accumulation of large bodies of facts" and suggests that this "often leads away from rather than toward greater social understanding." The Reuss Committee report does not offer any evidence to support this latter statement, and one may doubt if it can be convincingly supported. However, there is no question that accumulating large bodies of facts and rendering them machine readable, whether indiscriminate or not, is very expensive and that some order of priorities will have to be set as to what is accumulated and what is not.

It would be very difficult to develop a set of criteria for the selection of materials to be archived that would please everyone in the social sciences. There are, perhaps, certain bodies of data that are so obviously important that everyone would agree they should be high on a priority list; for example, in the field of political science it was certainly outrageous that the basic data on voting in the United States were permitted to lie in a disreputable state of scatteration for as long as they were. With the support of the National Science Foundation those data are now being assembled at the University of Michigan's Survey Research Center. It is relevant to the previous remark about costs to note that the accumulation and treatment of these data, along with certain related census materials, will cost over a million dollars.

Assuming that there is a limited number of other acts of rescue that are obviously desirable, there will remain more difficult decisions as to where the limited funds available for archiving should be invested, and it may well be asked, "Who is going to make such decisions? And on what basis will they be made?" Since most of the funds that will support large-scale archiving will almost certainly come either from federal agencies or from private foundations, it can be assumed that the ultimate "yes" or "no" to specific proposals will be said by the officers of these granting agencies based on the suggestions and recommendations of their advisory panels. However, these advisory panels also need advice, and it is time for the various social science disciplines that are interested in these matters to give organized consideration to the kinds of advice they want to give.

44   Problems and Prospects

To some extent this is already happening. The Social Science Research Council's Committee on the Preservation and Use of Economic Data, the so-called Ruggles Committee, was for some time concerned with drawing up a statement regarding bodies of data needed for economic analysis.[2] The Committee for the Collection of Basic Quantitative Data of American Political History, recently created by the American Historical Association, is pursuing similar interests. Other disciplines will eventually have to follow suit, because it is quite clear that no matter how wide ranging our acquisitive instincts may be, no matter how strong our tendency to turn the archives of the future into a vast dustbin of data, we are going to be severely restricted by financial limitations. There will have to be an order of priority, and some bodies of data will inevitably stand in line longer than others.

Consider now the question of what is *not* going into the archives. Although we may feel that in some respects too much information will be collected, it is quite clear that in other respects there will be far too little. This is because many of the important data that we need for meaningful social analysis are simply not available: they have never been gathered. If we look beyond the data collected by the various federal agencies—the Bureau of the Census, the Department of Commerce, the Department of Labor, the Public Health Service, and so on—if we look beyond the data made available by the federal establishment itself, we see a rather dismal picture.

It is not exaggeration to say that the typical data gathered by social scientists in the universities have the following characteristics:

1. They are based on a population universe that is not the universe of choice. They are based on a single town, community, a school, a factory, even a classroom, although the results of the study have meaning only if they can be thought to apply to a far larger population.

2. They employ sampling procedures that vary from second best to deplorable. The techniques of probability sampling have been known for nearly 20 years, but they are seldom applied. In the discipline of psychology there seems to be a tacit agreement never to mention the word "sample" because of the destructive effect it would have on the credibility of the research reports that fill the psychological journals.

3. They very seldom have any significant time depth. The number of research programs that have gathered comparable data through time on some significant population is very small indeed.

These lugubrious remarks are not offered in criticism of the social scientists themselves. Most of them presumably would prefer not to live in sin. The problem is that they cannot afford to live honestly. Social research has had very meager financial support over the years, and even with the substantial increases of the last few years we are still very inadequately supported. It is sometimes said that poverty brings out the homely natural virtues in man. It is doubtful if that is true of people, and, insofar as research is concerned, it is clear that what poverty brings out is substandard methods, inadequate scope, and restricted and unconvincing results.

Of course some prominent members of the social science establishment believe that social research currently has all the support it can use effectively and that every social scientist who is competent to do research is well taken care of. Disregarding the strong air of intellectual arrogance that is implied in this attitude, I must say I disagree profoundly with the statement itself. For example, in the University of Michigan's Survey Research Center virtually every study undertaken would profit greatly if its sample were double the actual size used. Sample sizes are constantly trimmed in order to bring the budget within what the granting agency will tolerate. There is also great difficulty in finding financing for longitudinal studies that require repeated interviews through time and the expensive pursuit of a mobile population. Social science researchers are all acquainted with the difficulties of long-term financing by federal agencies and the skittishness of the private foundations in involving themselves in anything more than short-term obligations. The result is that a great deal of what is known about change in our society—especially in the perceptions, attitudes, behavior of our population—is based on highly fragile, recollective information and scattered cross-sectional surveys rather than the integrated programs of measurement through time that would be desirable.

There are many important areas of social life in this country concerning which social scientists have learned almost nothing. We are very careful about counting births and deaths, and pretty fussy about marriages and divorces; we count the amount of money people earn and the number of crimes they commit, neither of them perfectly but well enough to be useful. Recently we have received a marvelous new array of data on morbidity and mortality from the National Health Survey. Many other indices and social indicators have become part of the social record.

But consider for a moment the important facts that are not known. What do social scientists know, for example, about the revolution of rising aspirations that has sent the Negro population into the streets during the last five years? With the notable exception of the heroic efforts of the National Opinion Research Center to gather trend data in the area of race relations—with very limited financial support—it can be said that the entire convulsion in the relationships between white and black people in this country during the last few years has gone almost entirely undocumented and hence largely not understood.

What do we know about the sense of alienation that is presumably spreading through our society? We hear that our modern affluent urban life is producing declining levels of social commitment, disrespect for authority, and a general privatization of life. But in fact no one *knows* whether this is true because there has been no research of any consequence to demonstrate whether it is true or not. We know that the structure of the work force and the nature of employment are changing profoundly, but we know very little about the human consequences of these changes. As Secretary of Labor Willard Wirtz stated in his testimony before the Harris Committee hearings on the National Foundation for Social Sciences, "Advancing technology is now moving thousands of people a day from hand tools to machine tools and from work benches to buttons and panels. We know virtually nothing of what this is doing to the meaning of work in the human life."

As a final example consider the statement made by the Report of the Behavioral Sciences Subpanel of the President's Scientific Advisory Committee that we do not even know how people spend their time, much less how they would prefer to spend it if they had their choice.

The fact of the matter is that we are being carried along by an unprecedented wave of social and physchological change that for the most part social scientists failed to anticipate and now understand but poorly. The population is growing, the birthrate is falling, people are moving from farm to city and from city to suburb, the labor force is shifting toward service occupations; these changes in the structure of our society we monitor with regularity and care, and these data have become a major resource for social analysis. Many additional measurements of this kind would be desirable. The need for a wider range of so-called social indicators has become a matter of growing concern.

However, the greatest lack results from our failure to develop anything like an adequate program of measurement of the human meaning that these great social changes have for our population. We have not organized any systematic effort to evaluate the quality of life as it is perceived by the members of our society. Consequently these data are not going to be in the archives now being built, and they are not going to be available for computer analysis. Our understanding of the nature of social life will be the poorer until they are.

Some Questions About the New Jerusalem

A further question to be considered is the relationship between the archive and the individual social researcher. This relationship has two aspects: (1) when the archive gets data from the individual and (2) when the individual gets data from the archive. Considering the first question first, what obligation does an individual researcher or research organization have to make its data available to a social science archive or to turn them over to some other interested individual for secondary analysis? There are no accepted standards at the present that would govern such questions of access. As is well known, some people are very possessive about what they regard as *their* data, and it seems unlikely that any sanction could be imposed to make such material available to others. I have never seen a clause in any foundation or federal-agency grant that requires, or even suggests, that the data generated under the grant should eventually become generally available. Historically it has been the privilege of the individual researcher to disseminate his data as narrowly or as widely as it suited him, and this is generally still the case.

It is not difficult to foresee that with the increasing availability of computing facilities and increasing sophistication about their use there will develop a growing interest in secondary analysis and a growing feeling that all substantial bodies of data ought to become part of the public domain. Perhaps social science researchers should be thinking about drawing up a code of ethics to govern the conduct of people who come in possession of important files of data.

This may not prove as easy as it looks. It might be proposed, for example, that every researcher have a period of grace during which he had exclusive access to his material, but after this time had expired he should make it generally available. How long should that grace period be? Two years perhaps? Surely not more than five years. However, there are two or three projects at the University of Michigan's Survey Research Center in which analysis is still going on six or eight years after the data were gathered, and the people involved would not be very happy to see their material worked on and published by somebody else.

Carrying the matter a step or two further it might be asked if there are not certain conventions that ought to be followed in the planning of every major study so that when the data are eventually turned over to a data bank they will be more widely useful. For example, nearly every social survey takes some kind of a recording of the age of the respondent. This may be done in individual years, decades, or rough categories of young, middle aged, and old. Since having age in individual year categories is the most flexible form for anyone who may subsequently want to use these data, perhaps everyone should be expected to ask and code age by the individual year.

Furthermore, there may be some kinds of data that are so generally useful that they should never be omitted from important population surveys. For the past 20 years the Survey Research Center's Economic Behavior Program has been conducting an annual sample survey called the Survey of Consumer Finances. Although the Center gathers a wide array of economic data in this study and numerous other data that are useful in analysis, we typically do not ask respondents their religion. Perhaps, in view of the fact that the Bureau of the Census is enjoined from asking this sensitive information, research centers should undertake, as an obligation to the scholarly community, to add a question on religion to all questionnaires, even though the information is not especially useful for a particular study.

Whatever the answers to these questions may be, it is unfortunate that the questions themselves have not been much discussed in social science circles, and it will probably be some time before social scientists come to any general agreement about them. There is, however, one aspect of the issue of access that everyone who gathers data from individual respondents thinks about and takes seriously; that is the question of the protection of privacy. This is certainly not a new issue, but it has taken on new significance lately as the Gallagher and Long Committees, and other agencies of the Federal Government have become concerned about what they regard as invasions of the right of privacy.

It seems to me that we social scientists can take a certain amount of satisfaction in our record over the last 20 years in the protection of confidential information that we have gathered in interviews. Even though we have conducted hundreds of studies and interviewed probably hundreds of thousands of people, there has not, to my knowledge, been a single serious case of revelation of confidential information either by intent or by accident. Although social science researchers are not specifically restricted by the kinds of legal restraints that govern the Bureau of the Census and the Internal Revenue Service, they have guarded their files very effectively.

It must be obvious, however, that the development of centralized data archives is going to create new kinds of problems. When an individual researcher turns over his data to an archive for transmission to second, third, and fourth parties his control over this information is at an end. This makes it imperative that when these data leave his hands the possibility of identification of any individual respondent must be reduced to a minimum. If the honesty and good judgment of the person to whom the data will eventually go could be assumed, the problem would not be serious; but, since it is not known who these people are going to be, data contributors cannot afford to take chances.

The necessity of protecting privacy undoubtedly means that some important bodies of data will never become available for archival use. The Survey Research Center has in its files a collection of several hundred interviews with candidates for the House of Representatives. Many of these men are well known, and, even if all of the so-called identifying information were removed from the interviews, many of them could still be easily recognized. It might be possible to extract certain limited specific data from each of these interviews that could be made publicly available, but this would have to be done with great care. At the moment the interviews are locked up in a vault, and they will probably stay there for quite some time.

Turning back to access we encounter the problem of how the individual scholar can gain access to the data held by an archive and what the archive's obligations are to him. It is obvious that an archive that is not accessible is not very useful or valuable, and the first obligation of any archive, certainly, is to make sure that its accumulated data are actually available to the people who want to use them. The communication problem between the archive and the user may turn out to be serious, because archives consist of computer tapes that can be reached only through the use of computer programs. Generally speaking the people who seek access to these archives are going to be less sophisticated about computer technology than the people who manage the data banks.

If the experience of the Survey Research Center is any basis for judgment, there is going to be a considerable investment in person-to-person education, a good many false starts, and a certain amount of frustration. Difficult as it may be, this communications problem can be bridged. The record of the Inter-University Consortium for Political Research over the last five years demonstrates very well what a computerized archive can accomplish when it is well supplied with intelligence, perseverance, patience, and—last, but not least—money.

Certainly the second indispensable responsibility that a computerized archive has to its clients is accuracy. The gap that now exists between the analyst and the computer is bridged by the computer expert, and in a very real sense the analyst is at his mercy. He turns in his computer requests and he accepts what he gets back. Although an experienced analyst learns to develop a sense of error in data, he is really in a rather precarious situation. There has been at least one publication that had to be repudiated by its author because of undetected computing errors, and there certainly will be other such events. Of course many social researchers will become competent in computer technology—but many will not, and for them the problem of quality control is serious.

As a final question, are the new data banks and their related computing facilities going to carry social scientists triumphantly into the Promised Land or not? It should be noted that some people are convinced that they are rapidly carrying social science research in the opposite direction. There is more than a little apprehension in some quarters that the innocent archiving of personal records in centralized data banks will eventually lend itself to a real-life facsimile of *1984*. Maybe these people are just Nervous Nellies; maybe they are not. The prospect of some unscrupulous public official laying his hands on some master data bank of the future is not very reassuring.

However, my own opinion is that social research is not going to enter either of these nonterrestrial alternatives in the near future; I think we are going to remain earthbound for some little time yet. Not that these new developments will have no substantial effect on the social sciences. On the contrary, it seems certain that, as more substantial bodies of data are assembled in the data banks and as the problems of access are simplified and routinized, the impact will be tremendous. The extraordinary developments in the last few years in the field of political science, due in part at least to the archiving and training activities of the Inter-University Consortium for Political Research, give a convincing demonstration of what we may expect.

With all their capacity and all their promise the data banks and the computers lack one crucial quality that will be needed for the ultimate breakthrough to the state of grace to which we all aspire. That quality is imagination. Unless social scientists are able to take off on an occasional flight of inspired creativity, they are fated to remain earthbound indefinitely. All the tapes and computers that can be assembled will not by themselves get social science research off the ground. They will hopefully help bring about circumstances in which creativity will flower. Ultimately, however, the inspiration necessary to exploit the growing possibilities the archives and the computers will provide will have to come from common mortals and not from the machines. That may seem a rather discouraging prospect to some, but others will find it reassuring that man still contributes something essential to the research process that the computers cannot. The computers may take social science research to the gates of Paradise, but social scientists will have to provide the key themselves.

REFERENCES

1. U. S. House of Representatives Committee on Government Operations, *The Use of Social Research in Federal Domestic Programs.* 90th Congress, 1st Session, 1967. (A staff study for the Research and Technical Programs Subcommittee.)
2. Richard Ruggles et al., *Report of the Committee on the Preservation and Use of Economic Data to the Social Science Research Council.* Washington: Social Science Research Council, April 1965.

Chapter Three

The Joys and Sorrows of Secondary Data Use

Charles G. Bell[*]

In recent years many colleges and universities have begun the acquisition of various kinds of data for purposes of secondary use. The data, originally collected by researchers at other institutions, are brought together to facilitate research and education. However, since these data are secondary, they do not always meet the needs of the user. Quite often this collecting of secondary data is on a haphazard basis as part of an overall growth pattern. A good example of this may be seen in Fullerton State College, one of the newer California state colleges.

Fullerton came into being about 10 years ago in one of the Orange County high schools and was then moved to a few small temporary wooden buildings. Four years ago the college moved into the first of several multistory buildings that have been, and will continue to be, built. The student and faculty population is growing at an equally rapid rate— about 20 percent last year and 15 percent this year. Many problems accompany rapid growth of this kind: staffing problems, library prob-

---
[*] Fullerton State College, Fullerton, California.

The Joys and Sorrows of Secondary Data Use 53

lems, curriculum problems, and of course the problems of trying to establish all of the accoutrements of a large department. Since these so-called fringe items seldom receive much financial support—particularly in a rapidly growing institution—they must be established and funded on the proverbial shoestring.

The Political Science Department at Fullerton wanted to establish a center for governmental studies and an adequate data bank. It is this latter goal that will be discussed at greater length. In the past two years Fullerton has gathered together an assortment of data covering a wide range of topics from many different sources by purchase, trade, contract by-product, and for services rendered, as well as through its own research. Most of these data are of course secondary data.

What are the joys and sorrows of secondary data use? First there is the problem of the search for usable data. This might appear to be much like the traditional bibliographic library research. The inefficient trial-and-error method often used in library research is unfortunately carried over into searches for data. According to L. Uytterschaut the pattern of bibliographic research for both experienced and inexperienced researchers is initially to consult leading authors and standard works.[1] Such an approach provides an instant bibliography, which is obviously advantageous, but there may also be severe conceptual limits to such a list in addition to the fact that it is inescapably out of date.

Another advantage of such bibliographies is that the researcher can reasonably hope to find most of the citations in a nearby university or college library. Here the parallel to archival research ends. When the researcher finds reference to one or possibly two or three data decks, it is highly unlikely that he can turn to a nearby data archive and scan the relevant questionnaires and code books. As a result valuable data go unused for want of a system that would make it as easy to scan such archived data as it is to scan the more traditional library data.

Thus, as Philip H. Ennis found in a survey of 15 major American sociological journals published in 1962, secondary data analysis is still a fairly rare occurence.[2] Out of 612 data sources used 69 percent were freshly gathered, 21 percent had supported previous publications, whereas 10 percent had been previously gathered but had never been published in some form. This is obviously a tremendous waste of resources. It appears that only a relative handful of social scientists engage in secondary analysis of the rich supply of available data. There are of course some outstanding examples of the use of secondary data. The Simulmatics Project is a case in point;[3] Robert Alford's *Party and Society* is another.[4] But on the whole the list is smaller than we would expect.

54   Problems and Prospects

Examination of the list of International Data Library and Reference Service (IDLRS) users and Inter-University Consortium members substantiates this conclusion. There is no secondary use of data by the vast majority of social scientists in the United States. All IDLRS users come from less than 40 colleges and universities in the United States. Of those institutions only three could be called small. One will look in vain for users from most of the California state colleges—there are only three: one at San Francisco, one at Chico, and one at Fullerton. San Diego belongs to the Consortium. Examination of the Inter-University Consortium lists leads one to the same conclusion. It is the social scientists at the major universities and a few leading colleges who use this vast supply of ready-made data. Yet, ironically, data archives offer an unparalleled opportunity to the majority of social scientists whose institutions cannot afford directly to support the research they wish to undertake.

It has been suggested that the cost factor is a major restriction on the use of secondary data. However, data are not that expensive. The expenditure of one or two hundred dollars will provide a great deal of data. With the exception of Consortium and Roper Center membership, acquisition costs should not be a basic factor limiting secondary data use. There are some other problems, however.

First there may be a communications problem. It is quite possible that many potential secondary data users are under the impression that such data are expensive. Probably the greatest limiting factor, however, is a basic inability to use secondary data (or any data). The IBM card is still a strange and wonderful beast to many social scientists, and statistics remains a dirty word to many. For too many social scientists the intellectual cost of tooling up to use secondary data appears too great. Although most new Ph.Ds now come equipped to make use of the available data, there are still many social scientists who do not know how to use this new data form or even how to find it. Finally, in many situations there is a problem of computer hardware and software. All of this of course is not to say that there are no substantial problems in the use of secondary data.

The following information is the result of a modest effort to find out why more use has not been made of the data available in the many data banks and archives now in existence. To that end a one-page questionnaire (Figure 3.1) was mailed to 48 IDLRS users. Fifteen usable questionnaires were returned (31 percent). Although tests of statistical significance are not applicable, the patterns of response were consistent enough to encourage some use of the data. In light of the comments above,

The Joys and Sorrows of Secondary Data Use

it should be remembered that the questionnaire data can be applied to only a relatively small proportion of social scientists—the users of secondary data.

QUESTIONNAIRE

Please answer these questions in regard to the last survey data which you received from any data archive

1. Generally, when you ordered the survey data, how adequate was the information that you had about them? Please indicate on the Adequate-Inadequate Semantic Differential Scale.

    a. Publications that may have resulted from the survey?..... A : : : I
    b. General focus of the survey?......................... A : : : I
    c. Conceptual framework of the survey?.................. A : : : I
    d. Operational definitions of the survey?.................. A : : : I
    e. Specific questions used in the questionnaire?............ A : : : I
    f. Sample size? .... A : : : I
    g. Sample techniques? .... A : : : I
    h. Coding techniques? .... A : : : I
    i. Limits on statistical analysis imposed by coding?.......... A : : : I

2. How did you first learn about the existence of the data?_____

3. Were you able to make as much use of the survey data as you had hoped when ordering them? Yes_____ No_____

    If "No," why not?_____

4. Did you use other survey data in conjunction with these last data? Yes_____ No_____

    If "Yes," where did you get them?_____

    Were those data compatible with these last data? Yes_____ No_____

Comments on back side.

Figure 3.1 Questionnaire mailed to IDLRS users.

56   Problems and Prospects

Apropos of the Uytterschaut and Ennis findings, users of archival data did not appear to rely on published results as a guide to available data. Only one respondent out of 15 stated that he had first learned of the data he subsequently ordered from a publication. On the other hand, eight discovered the data in lists published by archives. The remaining six found out about the data through casual conversations or correspondence with colleagues. It appears that the analogy between bibliographic and data-search patterns is superficial. At best potential secondary data users employed a sort of "card catalog" level of citation search. However, the rapid expansion of archival holdings will soon make these sophomoric search patterns impossible.

One result of this poor search technique seems to be an all too frequent disappointment with the data after they have been acquired from the archives. When asked "Were you able to make as much use of the survey data as you had hoped when ordering them?" 10 respondents answered "no" compared to 5 who answered "yes."

Analysis of the differential-scale item responses suggests that when ordering data potential users were not well informed about them. This lack of information was greatest in the area of research techniques—for example, sample and coding techniques, and operational definitions. This may be related in part to the fact that users' information about publications based on earlier use of the data was also poor (Table 3.1)

Table 3.1
Adequacy of Information about Data when Ordered*

Factor	Adequacy Score†	Range
Publications that may have resulted from the survey	5.29	2–9
General focus of the survey	4.60	2–9
Conceptual framework of the survey	4.60	1–8
Operational definitions of the survey	5.13	2–8
Specific questions used in the questionnaire	4.07	2–9
Sample size	4.46	2–8
Sample techniques	5.93	2–8
Coding techniques	5.27	1–8
Limits on statistical analysis imposed by coding	4.92	2–8

* Based on responses to the question, "Generally, when you ordered the survey data, how adequate was the information that you had about them?"
† Adequate = 1; inadequate = 9.

The respondents who felt that they had had adequate information about earlier publications more often felt that the other information that they had was also more adequate. For example, the Pearsonian correlation between information about prior publications and adequate knowledge about sample techniques was 0.48; that between prior publications and statistical limits imposed by coding was 0.59. This suggests that those who were aware of other uses of the data had a better chance of doing what they wanted with the data when they got them. However, calculation of the biserial correlation between adequacy of information about earlier publications and ability to make use of the survey data (question 3) was only 0.29. According to the results of this survey, having information about publications based on the data had little relationship to the success of secondary use.

Other factors do relate to the success of secondary data use. Examination of Table 3.2 suggests that problems with codes, questions used, operational definitions, and sample techniques did relate to the ability of secondary users to make use of data. Use of the biserial correlation revealed that the greatest problem associated with unsuccessful use of the data was coding ($r_{\text{bis}} = 0.49$). Other factors were not as significant. Additional comments written on the back of the questionnaires support

Table 3.2

Factors Relating to the Ability To Use Secondary Data

	Adequacy Score		*Difference*
Factor (Knowledge about)	*Able To Use Data*	*Unable To Use Data*	
Publications that may have resulted from the survey	4.60	5.67	−1.07
General focus of the survey	4.40	4.70	−0.30
Conceptual framework of the survey	4.80	4.60	0.20
Operational definitions of the survey	4.40	5.50	−1.10
Specific questions used in the questionnaire	3.20	4.50	−1.30
Sample size	4.00	4.70	−0.70
Sample techniques	5.20	6.30	−1.10
Coding techniques	4.00	5.90	−1.90
Limits on statistical analysis imposed by coding	3.40	5.22	−1.82

the conclusion that coding is the greatest single problem in secondary data use. Respondents made comments such as the following:

1. Extremely bad coding.
2. Discrepancies in coding, keypunching errors.
3. Poor coding (i.e., multiple punches).

Coding was also quite clearly a major problem faced by those who tried to use more than one set of data.

Another comment, comparing one archive to another, was directed to the problem of knowing what it is one has after he has read the codes, thus:

"The direction the Berkeley archive is headed—i.e., to concentrate on one geographic region, screen studies for quality before accepting them, and carefully document and clean data—should be strongly encouraged... The motto of data archives should be quality over quantity."

In light of the fact that so many users first locate their data through lists published by archives, it was surprising that these lists were not a very satisfactory source of information. Of those who first learned of the data through an archival list 78 percent were disappointed with the data. Of those who first learned of them through other ways, only 56 percent were disappointed. This suggests that those who learned of the data through other ways knew more about them before they attempted to use them than did those who learned of them through an archival list. Perhaps archives ought to provide more information about their data. This of course has nothing to do with the quality of the data.

There has been, and correctly so, much concern with the quality of secondary data. Although the quality of data is obviously important, there is only so much any archivist can and ought to do in this area. However, there is much more that can be done to inform potential data users about the codes and questionnaires. Secondary data users need more of this kind of information. It is true of course that some efforts have also been made to standardize question format and codes. This may not be much of an answer.

Few researchers can be expected to modify their research goals to suit some possible secondary data user of the future. And, although the archivist may be applauded for cleaning up poor data, he can hardly be criticized for the original sins of those who collected the data. The solution, it seems, is more information about the data.

The Joys and Sorrows of Secondary Data Use

Returning for a moment to IDLRS users, examination of requests for codes, questionnaires, cards, and tape or combinations thereof revealed some interesting use patterns. First, the more experienced researchers appeared to order only codes and questionnaires more often than did less experienced researchers, who ordered everything at once—codes, questionnaires, and data (either on card or tape). Second, IDLRS users who were not on the Berkeley campus ordered only questionnaires and codes more often (35 percent of orders) than did those who were on campus (23 percent of orders). This suggests that researchers on campus had better knowledge about available data than did those off campus.

In order to be constructive about these comments it should be suggested that some archives prepare and distribute on a subscription basis microfilm editions of code books for data collections. These subscriptions should be largely sold to libraries. They would include an index or codex to the materials. Surely the research establishment can support such a guide to archival holdings. The cost would be minimal. One-thousand-page volumes of microfilm would cost about $6.50. The codex would cost more, but paying $30 or even $50 for an annual codex would not be unreasonable. If so much time is devoted to traditional library retrieval, why not an equal devotion to the retrieval of data on which so much of library material is based?

In summary, given the growing number of data archives, their different interests or areas of concern, the differences in equipment and procedures, and the psychological investments involved, it seems safe to predict that secondary users of data will find that shopping around from outlet to outlet will become increasingly expensive, time consuming, and futile. Better information about the data already available would increase the secondary use of data and thus reduce the costs of research. Considering the substantial frustrations inherent in research one should at least try to eliminate or reduce the procedural frustrations. Thus I applaud current efforts of the Council of Social Science Data Archives to develop "inventories" of archivable holdings and to develop manual and computer-assisted methods for matching user needs with specific data holdings.

REFERENCES

1. L. Uytterschaut, "Literature Searching Methods in Social Science Research: A Pilot Inquiry," *American Behavioral Scientist*, **IX**, No. 9 (May 1966) p. 23.
2. P. H. Ennis, "Data Galaxies in the Social Sciences," *American Behavioral Scientist*, VII, No. 10, (June 1964). p. 19.

3. Ithiel de Sola Pool, R. P. Abelson, and S. L. Popkin, *Candidates, Issues, and Strategies.* Cambridge, Mass.: MIT Press, 1964.
4. Robert Alford, *Party and Society.* Chicago: Rand McNally, 1963.

BIBLIOGRAPHY

American Behavioral Scientist, June 1964. A special issue devoted to information retrieval in the social sciences.

Bisco, R. L., *Policies and Standards for Coding Data,* Inter-University Consortium for Political Research Memorandum, 1964.

Bisco, R. L., *Information Services for Political Science: Progress and Prospects,* American Political Science Association Convention, Chicago, 1964.

Bisco, R. L., "Information Retrieval from Data Archives: The ICPR System," *American Behavioral Scientist,* June 1964, pp. 45–48.

Rokkan, S., and Viet, J., *Comparative Survey Analysis: An Annotated Bibliography.* Paris: International Committee for Social Sciences Documentation, 1962.

Rokkan, S., "Archives for Secondary Analysis of Sample Survey Data: An Early Inquiry into the Prospects for Western Europe," *International Social Science Journal,* **XVI**, No. 1 (1964), pp. 49–62.

Rokkan, S., *"The Case for Comparative Secondary Analysis of Survey Data: An Example from Political Sociology.* Oslo: Institute for Social Research, September 1965, p. 5.

Scheuch, E. K., and Bruning, Iris, "The Zentralarchiv at the University of Cologne," *International Social Science Journal,* **XVI**, No. 1 (1964), pp. 77–85.

Wilcox, A. R., Bobrow, D. B., and Bwy, D. P., "System SESAR," *American Behavioral Scientist,* January 1967.

Part II Government as the Major Producer, User, and Archivist of Social Science Data Bases

It is probable that the U.S. Government both produces more data useful for the study of social problems and is also the largest user of such data. This is not to say, however, that the federal government always collects the most useful information, is the most efficient user of these data, or has the best organized set of agencies and institutions involved in the storage and maintenance of data for future uses.

However, it should also be pointed out the agencies of government are under more constraints than most of those in the private sector regarding the collection, use, and preservation of data. Limitations include laws that certain data shall not be collected, administrative regulations about how data shall be obtained and used, laws and administrative rulings about access to these data, and informed political boundaries that administrators wisely take into consideration when deciding how they shall fulfill their missions. It might be easy for a nongovernment researcher to demonstrate how he could better use the financial, computer, and other resources government officials have available, but it is not so easy to make such demonstrations when the legal, moral, administrative, judicial, and political constraints are not assumed to be absent.

In the United States at least, there are probably more problems regarding the development and use of complex data bases, and each problem in turn is more difficult to resolve in the government context than in the private sector. In this part Lowry describes the efforts of various agencies to resolve the problems, and Bowman suggests that useful solutions of at least some of the problems may require a new kind of governmental institution—a federal statistical data center.

Chapter Four

The Idea of a Federal Statistical Data Center—Its Purposes and Structure

Raymond T. Bowman[*]

The proliferation of statistical materials, the rapid development of computer technology, and the increasingly widespread and more scientific use of quantitative information by business, government, and the academic community have created certain very important needs for the further improvement and accessibility of compatible statistics for interrelated uses in comprehensive analyses. The emphasis here is on *compatible, interrelated,* and *comprehensive,* and not on individual items of information.

Among the outstanding needs are the following:

1. We need a better way of determining what basic quantitative information useful for statistical purposes should be stored in machine-

---
[*] Office of Statistical Standards, Bureau of the Budget, Washington, D. C.

readable form as permanent or semipermanent files so that they can be retrieved and used efficiently.

2. We need a better way of serving the needs of governmental and nongovernmental users of statistics in the analysis of both macro and micro relationships. This need is particularly important for comprehensive analyses that require the use of data files over time and/or interrelated files providing cross-section and longitudinal data for analysis of a microcharacter at a given point in time and over some span of time.

3. We need a continuing operation that will examine the current and prospective data files useful for statistical purposes to make certain that they are compatible and, where they have deficiencies, suggest steps that might be taken to assure compatibility of future files. This is a feedback effect for the future improvement of statistical information for recognized analytical uses.

4. We need a facility that can reduce duplication in the collection of quantitative information for statistical purposes by making better use of the information already collected by different agencies without sacrificing the privacy of such information so far as any individual or business unit is concerned.

5. We need an organization that can specialize in assisting users of statistics—both governmental and nongovernmental—in obtaining the special tabulations or data arrangements they require, whether this involves data from one or many collecting agencies. This should reduce the need for printing some of the more complicated cross-classifications of data that for many uses have to be put into machine-readable form for statistical processing.

6. We need a service that can facilitate checking whether the industrial classification of establishments or firms by different agencies is uniform and in line with the standard industrial or other classifications prescribed.

It is for these reasons that we have currently been examining the feasibility and propriety of establishing a federal (or national) statistical data center. We have been conscious from the outset of our investigations into these matters that a statistical data center can be a feasible way of meeting these needs only if we can maintain the long-accepted practice by statistical agencies of protecting the confidentiality of information that they collect from individuals or business units. Statistical agencies and the Bureau of the Budget have long been convinced that the U.S. statistical program enjoys a major advantage over the statistical programs of many other countries because of the greater willingness of businesses and

The Idea of a Federal Statistical Data Center

individuals to cooperate in providing information. We are also convinced that the ready cooperation in providing basic data for statistical purposes requires that it be used for statistical purposes only and that so far as the individual respondent is concerned it will not be used against him or be revealed with reference to him in any way.

The importance of well-organized and carefully designed quantitative information about the functioning of the social and economic institutions of our society is now well recognized. Demands for extensions of information of this type are mounting. In order to protect against duplication and unnecessary burden on respondents we must make fuller use of data already collected—whether these originally were collected for statistical or for other purposes.

Recent reactions to publicity about our investigations of the need for a federal statistical data center, and congressional and public discussion of the general problem of the privacy of individuals* have served to strengthen our conviction that a successful proposal for a statistical data center must offer substantial means of protecting confidentiality and forestalling invasion of individual privacy. More important, they have shown us improved ways of protecting privacy and have encouraged more attention to the solutions of privacy-protection problems.

I believe that many of our current and future requirements for a body of compatible and accessible statistics for interrelated analysis on both a micro and macro level could be materially advanced by a federal statistical data center. I also agree that such a center must not sacrifice confidentiality of reports for statistical purposes or the privacy of individuals.

It is important to bear in mind that statistical use of quantitative information does not require publishing or otherwise releasing information that can identify an individual reporting unit. It is necessary, however, that selected data about individual units be available within a processing center if important types of analysis are to be possible; for example, if we want to know the relationships between the incomes of individuals and their age, sex, color, marital status, level of education, geographic location, and the like, it should be possible to classify by

---

* The issue concerning the privacy of the inidvidual is of course much broader than the storage and use of information after it is collected. The issue in terms of the propriety of collecting information for behavioral research was reviewed by a distinguished panel established by the Office of Science and Technology. The report of this panel was published under the title *Privacy and Behavioral Research* (Executive Office of the President, Office of Science and Technology, February 1967; available from the U.S. Government Printing Office, Washington, D.C.).

these characteristics at any one time or over time. The analysis, however, can be performed within the privacy of the machine, and the relationships can be revealed in the form of coefficients of correlation, regression equations, or tables constructed so as not to show information about any individual unit.

A statistical data center must internally have access to data about individual units, but it can serve statistical purposes without revealing information about the individuals per se. In contrast, many other types of data centers can serve their purposes only if they are organized to reveal information about individuals. For example, if we want a center where a state highway department can find out whether one of its applicants for a driver's license has ever had a license revoked by another state the information must refer to a particular individual. Information centers of this type exist. A statistical data center is not of this type, as it should not be, and its data-organization arrangements should not be designed to serve such purposes.

Another point to be kept in mind is that data in (or accessible to) a statistical data center might have been collected for nonstatistical purposes and have fewer restrictions on what can be revealed about individual reports than if it had been collected for statistical purposes. A statistical data center would not release even this type of information about an individual unit. If such release is to be made, it would have to be by the original agency that collected the data in accordance with the provisions of law.

At this time no decision on a specific proposal for a federal statistical data center has been reached. All I can do here is share with you current thinking about the general principles on which a proposal should be based.

We believe that if a federal statistical data center is to be established, it must be clear that such a center will not make available to public or governmental agencies, or other bodies, any information about individual persons or businesses. This prohibition should be established by law, but in addition the organization of data files and the concentration of files in such a center should be so designed as to protect against abuse of the system even by high authorities.

We believe this means that center records should be selective and certain types of records should not be in the center at all. Examples of records we think should be excluded are the following:

1. Individual personnel records (letters of reference, performance ratings, test scores, etc.) of federal employees and applicants.

The Idea of a Federal Statistical Data Center

2. Military personnel records.

3. Files compiled by the FBI, by regulatory or other agencies as a result of investigations of individual persons, or by businesses or other organizations.

4. FBI fingerprint files and files on persons convicted of crimes.

5. Files of revoked driver's permits.

6. Medical records on government employees or applicants and patients of government institutions.

It seems obvious to us that since data of this type are largely useful in providing information about individuals per se, it has no proper place in a statistical data center, which, by definition, does not provide data about individuals.

We believe that it will also be necessary to take another step in restricting the files of a federal statistical data center. The files the center actually possesses should be restricted to samples so that no universe data would be in the continuing possession of the center. This will foreclose to a considerable extent temptations to organize files along individual dossier lines and will vitiate attempts to use the center to obtain information on individuals. However, if the center is to achieve its purposes, it must have authority to use universe data outside its own files under appropriate conditions and arrangements, and also to have some impact on the type of file maintenance of such data.

Just as important as these general principles is the need for providing a way of determining and authorizing what data files are to go into the center. It might be provided that transfers of data into the center could be only by direction of the Director of the Bureau of the Budget after consultation with appropriate advisory groups to the data center and to him. This could be arranged by supplementing the authority now vested in the Director under existing law.

I have not given any systematic attention to the mechanical aspects of the ways in which statistical data center files could be made less subject to inappropriate uses than is true of the current files of the collecting agency. I do not intend to dwell on this point, because, although considerable attention is now being devoted to promising technical devices, such devices must be proven. There are, however, two fairly obvious and currently available methods that should be used. First, it is well understood that machine-readable files are much less subject to abuses by dishonest employees than are man-readable files. An employee cannot go to a file cabinet and easily abstract a particular machine-readable file. Thus all but data-documentation information should be in machine-readable form only, and documentation information should have severely restricted access. Second, the machine instructions can be so developed as to bar printout of information on individual units. There are numerous other ways of restricting identifying codes so that, even within the center, identification of the units is restricted.

We believe that these types of arrangements supplemented by an annual report of the center's file inventories and the uses it has permitted could substantially provide the necessary protection of privacy. These arrangements would not significantly impair the usefulness of a center in making data and data services available and in improving the compatibility of different data files.

It must be remembered of course that the effective operation of a successful center could not be immediate. I estimate that the first two years would be required to determine what files are pertinent for center use; to edit them for storage and retrieval uses, and to arrange for their transfer or for access to them under appropriate safeguards when transfer seems undesirable.

The use of information about the present and the past to help solve the problems of the todays and the tomorrows is having, through the machine, a rebirth of promise. Can we collect and use information for social decision-making in a way that does not destroy valued individual privacy? Statistical methodology makes it possible to discover social and economic relationships without revealing the identity of the private individuals whose data are used. But, can we separate these statistical uses of information from other uses that we desire to relate to specific individuals—those who have committed a crime, are bad credit risks, or are undesirable employees? I think we can if we carefully distinguish the uses to which the data are to be put and do not champion a completely common data base for all purposes—even if machinery makes a common data base possible.

The privacy issues that some persons see in a federal statistical data center are largely associated with an assumption that a national, or federal, center would store all information known about every individual in dossier-type files. The assumption is that everyone would be given a number at birth. Some further assume that such a center would add all available information about individuals from birth to death. It should be obvious that such a system, even if feasible technically, could not be supported by any statistical requirements. Such an extensive system could of course be used to meet some statistical needs, but its costs and other burdens could be defended only on the basis of uses other than statistical. In fact such an all-encompassing system would not meet statistical needs well. The universe character of the data would make its accuracy suspect and would make the data expensive and cumbersome to use. Adequate samples are all that is necessary: accuracy is better with samples, and analysis is usually both less costly and more efficient with them.

My point in ending with these observations is to make it as clear as possible that the statistical data center envisaged is not an all-inclusive informaton system. An all-inclusve system would not meet well the present or future statistical needs. Such a system could only be defended on other than statistical grounds; it would pose the privacy issue in its most critical form. I personally do not believe that such comprehensive all-purpose recording of all data about everyone is defensible on any grounds even if technically feasible, and such an all-inclusive system is not technically feasible at the present time. It certainly in no way resembles the concept of a federal statistical data center that responsible government officials hold.

BIBLIOGRAPHY

Bowman, R. T., "The National Data Bank: Friend or Foe?", *Automation Magazine*, January 1967.

Dunn, E. S., Jr., *Review of a Proposal for a National Data Center*, Statistical Evaluation Report No. 6. Washington, D.C.: Office of Statistical Standards, Bureau of the Budget, December 1965.

Report of the Task Force on the Storage of and Access to Government Statistics. Washington, D.C.: Bureau of the Budget, October 1966. (available in mimeograph form).

Ruggles, Richard, et al., *Report of the Committee on the Preservation and Use of Economic Data to the Social Science Research Council*, Washington, D.C.: Social Science Research Council, April 1965.

U.S. House of Representatives Subcommittee of the Committee on Government Operations, *The Computer and Invasion of Privacy*. 89th Congress, 2nd Session, July 1966. (The Gallagher Hearings.)

U.S. Senate Committee on the Judiciary, Subcommittee on Administrative Practice and Procedure, *Computer Privacy*. 90th Congress, 1st Session, March 1967. (The Long Hearings.)

U.S. Congress Subcommittee on Economic Statistics of the Joint Economic Committee, *The Coordination and Integration of Government Statistical Programs*. 90th Congress, 1st Session, 1967.

Zwick, C. J., *A National Data Center*. Address to the Annual Meeting of the American Bar Association, Honolulu, Hawaii, August 1967.

Chapter Five

Federal Information Systems—Some Current Developments

Roye L. Lowry*

The terms "data base," "data bank," and "information system" have become a part of the general vocabulary. As a part of the generl vocabulary, each term has gathered about it a whole cluster of meanings that together tend to obscure any differences among them.

For the purposes of this chapter the term "data base" refers to the sum total of information collected for any particular purpose. The materials collected in the census of population are a data base; the price information collected by the Bureau of Labor Statistics constitutes a data base; the income tax returns filed with the Internal Revenue Service are a data base.

An "information system," on the other hand, refers to an ordered arrangement of information from one or more data bases. The Census

---

* Office of Statistical Standards, Bureau of the Budget, Washington, D.C.

Bureau's arrangement of materials for publication of the *Census of Population* is an information system; *The Consumer Price Index* is an information system; *Statistics of Income* is an information system.

Some information systems are constructed out of materials from a single data base. Others draw from several different data bases. Still others draw from a complex of different information systems or combinations of data bases and information systems.

In discussing federal information systems this chapter does not attempt to catalog all of the federal activities that develop data bases or lead to the formation of information systems. There has never been a comprehensive directory of all available federal statistical information, and this task is clearly beyond anything that could be done in one chapter of this book. Rather, this chapter describes some general lines along which developments are taking place and in particular considers possible implications that these developments may have for social science researchers.

Let us start by noting the most optimistic feature—the great interest in data bases and information systems. The words themselves have captured the popular imagination. There is almost no passing day that does not cast up some new proposal for an information system of some kind to serve some purpose or other. Whatever may be one's opinion of any particular proposal, the mere fact that ever broader groups are talking about or concerning themselves with matters relating in some way or another to the collecting processing, preserving and retrieving of information almost surely presages an expansion of information that will make the information explosion of the present seem like the popping of a champagne cork. When influential members of Congress, the top federal executive management, governors, mayors, and city managers all begin to evince a particular concern about the information available to them—whether as to quantity, quality, comparability, or form of presentation—the chances of bringing about change are considerably improved.

EXPANSION OF GRANT-IN-AID PROGRAMS

There are other harbingers of change that are of a more substantial character. Requirements in law associated with the expansion of federal aid programs in recent years have specified information requirements that must be met as conditions for establishing eligibility to receive grant-in-aid funds. This is a powerful force for focusing attention on problems relating to information; it is surpassed only by a more powerful force—

namely, the provision of financial assistance to enable applicants for federal aid to gather or otherwise provide the information needed to support applications for federal program assistance.

NEW BUDGETARY TECHNIQUES

The introduction of the concept of a planning-programming-budgeting system (PPBS) and its extension over the whole broad range of federal activities and into the realm of state and local governments is another powerful force that stimulates the development of information systems. Its influence has hardly been felt as yet. Potentially it can have an enormous impact on the development of information systems, because PPBS calls for an entirely different way of looking at governmental programs: it requires (1) that objectives be stated more explicitly, (2) that alternative means of achieving objectives be explored more explicitly in terms of alternative costs and benefits, and (3) that results and associated costs be quantified insofar as possible.

COMPUTER TECHNOLOGY STIMULATION OF INFORMATION SYSTEMS

The development of appropriate information systems to serve the purposes of expanded federal aid programs and the more sophisticated techniques of program planning, management, and evaluation relies heavily on the use of the computer. Thus computer technology and management are an important third force that is influencing recent developments in federal information systems.

The role of the computer in stimulating the development of information systems is plain to all. Public interest has been focused almost exclusively on the computer, its use, and its potential. Legislative and executive policy makers, administrators, and researchers alike have given much of their public attention to the computer. Relatively little public attention has been addressed to the other significant forces that exert an effect on the development of federal information systems.

INFORMATION SYSTEMS DESIGNED TO SERVE PROGRAM NEEDS

At the outset let us note that the word "system" implies purposeful organization. Two of the principal forces that are shaping the development of information systems at the present time are concerned with the organization of information on ways to improve the effectiveness of program planning, implementation, and evaluation. The information systems developed to meet these needs are not particularly designed to serve general purposes, even though they may use general-purpose information in quantity. The benefits that may accrue to social science researchers from the development of these information systems will be incidental to the main purposes of the systems themselves. Some of this potential fallout is, however, interesting, important, and worth noting.

PPBS and Projections

The advanced budgeting techniques associated with PPBS give new importance to the development of projections—of population, of economic and social developments. The PPBS techniques recognize that annual budgets are meaningful only as they are considered in the stream of time; that the basic problems that give rise to government programs are complex and not effectively resolved within the span of a single fiscal year; that costs and benefits do not end with the conclusion of a fiscal year; and that objectives and results for a given year must be measured against long-run objectives and take into account sunk costs.

Since most federal programs are designed to have an impact on the particular socioeconomic conditions that called them into existence, many programs start from the same or closely related basic sets of facts. If we are going to have consistency in planning-programming-budgeting efforts, it seems clear that we shall have to give some thought to developing a standard set of assumptions as to how the socioeconomic variables in today's basic facts may appear at some future point in time. Without common projections it is difficult to see how it would be possible to make the rational overall planning and programming decisions that are essential in the preparation of the Budget of the United States.

The present data base and existing information systems contain some of this kind of information. Projections of the population and of the labor force, the input-output projection to 1970, and the long-term growth econometric model to project labor force, employment, industry output, productivity and gross national product to 1970 are examples of tools already in our statistical locker. We may confidently expect that they will be more widely used and further developed in the future as the information systems required for the effective implementation of PPBS are more fully articulated. A handbook describing procedures for developing projections of manpower requirements by industry and occupation down to state and local levels under preparation in the Department of Labor is an example of the kind of development we might reasonably expect to see more of in the future. New developments of this kind help to expand the Nation's general-purpose statistical resources while serving federal program purposes. Social science researchers stand to gain from such increases in the stock of generally available information.

Regional Analysis

With some reasonable confidence we might expect the social science researcher who is interested in regional analysis to benefit from the development of information systems being designed to serve the needs of many of the new grant-in-aid programs. These programs are not only of a federal-state cooperative character; they are also programs that affect different parts of the country differentially; that is, the program operates at a higher or lower level in this or that part of the country, depending on whether particular specified characteristics exist to a greater or lesser degree—for example, the number of children under 18 in families whose annual income is under $2,000 or the rate of unemployment.

Community Profiles

The effect of this is to stimulate the development of information systems that attempt to describe how one area compares with another in terms of a number of specific variables. The continuing efforts by the Office of Economic Opportunity (OEO) to develop a "poverty index" to compare the severity of socioeconomic problems in one county with those of another is a case in point. For over a year the Office of Economic Opportunity has been working on the development of a "profile" for each county in the United States. The *County Profile* is a computerized textual and statistical report with a standardized format that includes materials on a broad range of economic and social conditions culminating in a series of "12 poverty indicators." These poverty indicators rate each county in comparison with all counties in the United States on a seven-position scale ranging from "extremely favorable" (ranks higher than 90–99 percent of all counties in the United States) to "extremely unfavorable" (ranks lower than 90–99 percent of all counties in the United States) and centering on "normal" (ranks no higher and no lower than 41–59 percent of the counties in the United States). The data in the system are drawn primarily from census materials and other existing general-purpose information systems.

The *County Profile* is, in short, an information system oriented to depict the relative economic and social position of each county in the United States. It is a source book of information that includes statistical data from many sources, together with some textual description and other simple analyses of the data presented. A critical examination of the *Profile* would quickly reveal a number of shortcomings. Its importance lies not in what it has actually achieved, but rather as an example of one trend in the current development of information systems in the federal government. This is not the only effort along this line. The Department of Housing and Urban Development has some metropolitan profiles, which draw together selected basic data from general-purpose statistics that describe individual metropolitan areas. The Department of Agriculture is working toward the development of a series of rural profiles: "... a system of measurement to provide a continuing series of rural economic indicators which would (1) provide basic information for policy and program planning, (2) serve as benchmarks for evaluating the progress and effectiveness of the set of programs and policies which operate in rural areas, and (3) provide guidance for the coordination of impacts of various programs conducted by agencies of this and other departments." This information system would provide a profile of some 200 subregions—each subregion being a collection of counties. Like the *County Profile*, the rural profile would draw its information from a wide variety of sources.

For a program agency the profile concept provides a description of how the problems with which it is concerned are spread about the country. As noted, the profile draws on existing information systems. Since it is thus limited by the availability of information already in existing systems, some program agencies are seeking to overcome this constraint by drawing on the data base generated by their own activities; for example, the Office of Economic Opportunity, is experimenting with ways of utilizing the data developed at the neighborhood centers of the various community-action agencies over the country in its county profiles as well as for other administrative purposes.

Other Programs

Quite apart from the development of profiles for the purposes of program agencies, there are also continuing efforts to define new kinds of areas in order to sharpen analysis of important socioeconomic problems through more effective use of materials from existing information systems. Such, for example, is the experimental work of the Bureau of the Census, which seeks to define "major areas of concentration of poverty" in large metropolitan areas and to provide a detailed picture of the socioeconomic characteristics of the population of these areas. Such, too, are the updating of 1960 census materials in such critical areas as Watts and Hough through large-scale surveys or special censuses.

On another front the Office of Business Economics is carrying forward a great deal of work on a "regional economics information system" that would develop considerable data on (1) personal income, (2) a demographic description of the labor force, (3) government revenues and expenditures, and (4) capital investment for a series of "functional economic areas." These data, drawn from census materials, social security records, and the like, are to be worked into a common pattern of information for 165 "functional economic areas" that the Office of Business Economics hopes to be able to make widely and publicly available.[1] Since this information system would store considerable amounts of information for individual counties, there appear to be potential opportunities for social science researchers to arrange for combinations of data organized according to configurations of counties that differ from those chosen by the Office of Business Economics.

Finally, we should note the increasing efforts related to the possible development of a system of social indicators to take its place alongside the national economic accounts. A structure of social indicators designed to focus attention on social conditions as the national economic accounts focus attention on the Nation's economy would almost surely call for a substantial new data base. Should a system of social indicators be developed, both the expansion of the data base and the development of a new information system to support the social indicators would be important advances for social scientists.

INFORMATION SYSTEMS ON FEDERAL PROGRAM EXPENDITURE

An information system that reports on federal expenditures by program, by agency, by county, city, or congressional district has long been desired by many political leaders, program administrators, and researchers. Some work along these lines has been done by individual agencies or for particular programs in the past, and on various occasions the Bureau of the Budget has attempted to develop information on federal expenditures by states, but systematic government-wide efforts are of recent origin. The most widespread information system of this type that is operational at this time is the so-called Federal Information System developed by the Office of Economic Opportunity under the aegis of the

Federal Information Systems 77

Economic Opportunity Council. This was originally an effort to get monthly reporting of expenditures by county, by program, by agency for every program in the OEO *Catalog of Programs for Individual and Community Improvement*. The original concept also included collecting information on the number of beneficiaries served by each prgram at the county level.

The financial records of federal agencies proved to be inadequate to support the system as originally conceived. By a series of successive compromises that cut down on the number of programs from which reports were required, reduced the amount of information provided, lengthened the time period to be covered in a single report, and modified various concepts originally specified, the Office of Economic Opportunity developed a report that, although unsatisfactory in many ways, does, on a systematic basis, attempt to report on the level of federal financial outlays by county for about 160 programs that accounted for about $30 billion in federal expenditures in fiscal year 1966.

The effort to develop a more satisfactory way of reporting federal government program expenditures by geographic areas is being actively pursued. Substantial problems have yet to be overcome, but most of them are not inherently impossible to resolve. Thus we may expect to see in the not too distant future a new federal financial information system that will report program expenditures by small areas according to consistent definitions and conventions; it will be considerably more comprehensive than the present OEO system.

Intergovernmental Aspects

Once this sort of information system becomes part of the federal financial reporting system, we can expect to see attempts to tie relevant parts of the federal system to various state financial reporting systems as governors seek to improve the executive management of state programs—both those that are financed in part from federal grants in aid and those financed entirely from state resources—in different parts of their states. An experimental effort that would tie together the relevant data from OEO's *Federal Information System* and data from the state financial reporting system is already under way in Tennessee. We can imagine the enormous problems involved in developing a clear, consistent, and meaningful information system on program expenditures out of the separate financial reporting systems of federal and state governments.

A somewhat different information system, which would utilize data from federal, state, and local sources, has been designed to serve the regional planning activities of the Economic Development Administration, whose mission is to promote the economic development of areas that have either (1) a substantially higher degree of unemployment than the Nation as a whole or (2) a median level of family income that is substantially below the median level of family income for the nation. The Economic Development Administration wants to know to what extent public investment has an impact on employment or income or both. It has given a charge to a private contractor to design an information system that would report, by county, all public investment—federal, state, and local. Investment is understood to mean both (1) investment in physical facilities and (2) investment in human resources (e.g., expenditures on education). The contractor has completed a design for such a system that is now being reviewed. Whether it gets beyond the drawing board will depend on an evaluation of prospective benefits in comparison with anticipated costs of installing and operating the system.

We can envision that the development of such expenditure information systems together with the previously noted profiles might substantially change not only the course of executive decision-making in the future but even the terms of political debate and policy-making. This is not farfetched. We have in our own time seen how the development and use of the information system we know as the national economic accounts has influenced policy-making in both the public and private sector in the past 20 years.

The interrelationships of the information systems that serve federal, state, and local governments have already become a matter of joint concern. As a result of expressions of concern by a committee of the Council of State Governments and after consultations with state and local governmental organizations, the Director of the Bureau of the Budget has recently appointed an intergovernmental task force on information systems. The task force has been asked to examine and recommend coordinated courses of action that might be taken by federal, state, and local governments to improve the flow of information within and among these governments.

USING INFORMATION SYSTEMS MORE EFFECTIVELY

Along with these developments of new information systems to serve management and policy-making needs, federal agencies are seeking to find new ways of making better use of existing information systems. Traditionally this has been accomplished through the development of special tabulations of already available materials. Now imaginative efforts are being addressed to finding ways by which individual researchers may address particular questions to computer-based information systems.

The work of the Bureau of Labor Statistics in developing a manpower information system has already been described.[2] Since the time of that description, the Bureau has made continuing progress in developing means by which an analyst may directly query the information system even though he may have no training in specialized computer languages.

The Bureau of Labor Statistics is not alone in its attempts to find ways of permitting easier access to computer-stored data. The Economic Development Administration is also engaged in a developmental effort to bring the analyst closer to its computer-based information system. By following extremely simple instructions, an analyst can query the information system and can request some simple forms of analysis of data without knowing a single word that is related in the slightest degree to computer technology or computer procedures. Both of these developments have particular significance to social science researchers because they address themselves to a question of compelling importance: can a way be found to permit researchers to make the fullest possible use of computer-stored information without requiring them to learn yet another specialty? Although many social scientists have become adept in the use of the computer today, it is reasonably safe to say that the development of new and easy ways of querying the computer without actually knowing anything about it will advance social science research significantly by making the computer available to many fine and perceptive minds who are unable to use it today.

A second consequence of this type of development is that existing information systems become much more flexible in that data may be rearranged in ways that are necessary or convenient to the particular lines of inquiry being pursued by individual social science researchers.

Greater flexibility will come from providing social scientists access to data bases themselves. The possibility of using the address register and the geographic coding system to combine information from different data bases opens many exciting possibilities. Similarly a federal statistical data center, which has been discussed a great deal lately, would do much to liberate social science researchers from the constraints imposed by the conventions and organizing principles of any information system. The many and difficult problems associated with more direct contacts between the social scientist and the federal government's data bases are being worked out, and current developments that affect federal government information systems will surely broaden the horizons of all engaged in social science research.

REFERENCES

1. "Personal Income in Metropolitan Areas," *Survey of Current Business.*
2. R. L. Bisco, *American Political Science Science Review,* **LX**, No. 1 (March 1966), pp. 93–109.

Part III Case Studies in the Development and Use of Complex Data Bases

This part contains two case studies about how elaborate data bases are put together and how their use involves whole systems of problems. The more complex the data base, the more complex must be the software and hardware, the more extensive must be the data-linkage capabilities, and the more difficult of solution the privacy-protection issues can be. In different ways these two chapters also demonstrate that the more complex the research problem, the more there may be a need for a complex data base.

A special benefit of these two chapters is that they show, in the context of ongoing research, the need for more attention to the problems dealt with in the subsequent parts.

Chapter Six

Working with Complex Data Files: I. Development and Analysis of Complex Data Files in a Regional Transportation Study*

Robert J. Miller and Noreen J. Roberts†

---

* The preparation of this report was financed in part through federal funds made available by the U.S. Department of Transportation, Federal Highway Administration, Bureau of Public Roads, and state highway funds made available by the State of California, Department of Public Works; and in part by an urban planning assistance grant from the Urban Renewal Administration of the U.S. Department of Housing and Urban Development under Section 701 of the Housing Act of 1954, as amended; and in cooperation with the Association of Bay Area Governments and the Bay Area Rapid Transit District. The opinions, findings, and conclusions expressed herein are those of the authors and not necessarily those of the State of California, the Bureau of Public Roads, or the Department of Housing and Urban Development.
† Bay Area Transportation Study Commission, Berkeley, California.

The collection of survey and inventory data was a major phase of the Bay Area Transportation Study Commission (BATSC) work program. As in all regional transportation studies, data from these sources are of basic importance in creating input to a series of comprehensive models for the prediction of future transportation and land use. In addition to its use within the study, these data form the base for a regional information system, available for use by state and local agencies. A basic premise of the study is that heavy involvement in data processing and, in particular, a well-designed software system are necessary for the completion of the complex task of translating data into methodology and plans.

In order to achieve the objectives of model and planning development a vast amount of data must be gathered, processed, and analyzed. It has been estimated that BATSC has handled over 20 million words of data to date. The majority of these data are in the form of complex files of mixed data structure. For meaningful and orderly analysis these files must be organized as part of an information system.

The Home Interview Trip Origin and Destination Survey is presented as a case study in the development and analysis of this form of complex file. About 1½ million keypunched data cards, containing approximately 10 million words of data, have been collected and processed, making this survey the largest single source of data in the BATSC information system.

It is the purpose of this chapter to discuss the problems associated with the collection and processing of these data files; the solutions adopted, with emphasis on the use of modern computer software and hardware; and recommendations for changes in the conventional methods of design and handling.

COMPLEX DATA FILES

Definition

Complex data files may be defined as files of mixed data structures; that is, *several* different record formats are organized in a logical or natural relationship within the file. In addition there can be a variable number of any one or all of these formats. This contrasts with a simple data file, which contains only *one* record format.

The Advantages of Complex Files

The major gains of handling data in complex form result from the ability to relate data items to information contained by a different form of entity. This capability can be duplicated in the expanded simple file, but only at the cost of considerable repetition. Originally simple files were used because of limitations in early computer and programming systems, but now methods of handling complex files exist. Some of the advantages of using complex files are the following:

1. No loss of data through factor aggregation.
2. Preservation of the natural relationship of the data.
3. Flexibility in analysis schemes.
4. Shortening of processing time.
5. Simplification of data collection, coding, and contingency checking.
6. Ease in handling missing data.
7. Ability to treat a single complex file as a source of data for multiple purposes.
8. Specification of analytic files can be done after preliminary analysis.

Traditional Simple Files versus Complex Files

In the past origin and destination trip data collected by personal interview have been processed in the form of either simple files derived from a single card format or a series of simple files derived from multiple card formats. The analysis of home interview data is traditionally performed at the aggregate level. This is largely due to an inability to handle missing data and the higher probability of error resulting from larger file size. Although we are not yet at a point where we can process extremely large files without corresponding high costs, the original conditions that led to the analysis of aggregated factored data no longer hold.

Handling data files at the complex level is more difficult than at the simple file level, but the advantages of doing so far outweigh the difficulties. The main reason for dealing with the household as an entity instead of separate trip files, household-characteristics files, job-history files, housing files, and employment files is that the data are interrelated. The individual simple file tends to destroy the hierarchical relationship of data and result in a loss of potential interactional analysis. Far too often files are split into the simple analytic files before the modeling effort is finished, only to find that certain combinations of widely divergent variables are needed. Since complex files require fewer physical files to be processed, there is usually a reduction in computer time. The initial file-preparation stages are shorter, even though the actual analysis runs may be longer. Traditionally simple files were usually created once during the initial processing phase. This resulted in a rigid and somewhat simplistic data analysis. Simple files must still be created as input to most statistical analysis programs. However, if all preliminary processing is performed on complex files, the creation of simple analytic files is more closely related to analysis runs and a great deal of flexibility is derived in the specifications of the necessary simple files. Many different files can be created at the time of analysis, depending on intermediate findings rather than using file structures defined before analyses begin.

Another constraint imposed by simple file structures occurs when expansion factors are used to produce estimates of population characteristics from sample data. Expansion factors, when applied to simple files, require that all factors be calculated, and this must wait until all file processing is completed. Complex file processing allows factors to be added to the entity record without waiting until all processing is completed. These files can be used to meet specific analysis requirements and utilized by analysts during the preliminary analysis. Expansion of simple files destroys the original entity form. In complex file factoring, however, the expansion factors are included as additional variables in each individual entity record. The original entity form is retained, and the factors can be applied or not as analysis warrants. Sequential factoring of complex files thus allows analysis at intermediate phases and allows the file analysis to parallel file operations.

SYSTEMS DESIGN IN COLLECTION AND PROCESSING

Handling large volumes of data in complex file format requires systematic work-flow operations in both data collection and file processing. During the collection phase accounting for individual entities of either sample unit or spatial unit becomes critical as the volume of data collected and the number of personnel involved increases. Involvement of computer hardware and software in all phases of these operations becomes mandatory not only for efficiency in collecting and processing but also for accounting purposes and management control. With a system designed to account for entities within each survey or inventory the current status of the process is readily available in detail. A parallel workflow in collection, coding, and file processing allows feedback on the status of each phase and enables problems to be recognized and solutions formulated while the phases are still under way. This is particularly true when comprehensive methods of quality control are incorporated as an integral part of the system design.

The Need for Systems Design

The physical handling of large volumes of data creates specific problems of inventory and locational control. Until such time as the data are in machine-readable form the sheer volume of paper involved creates problems with which hand record keeping can no longer cope. Although BATSC utilized a systems approach to the control of this volume of paper, it is clear that a much greater involvement would have been desirable. Once the data have been read onto magnetic tape, the problem of volume remains. In addition there are problems of complexity of format and those presented by subsetting and transforming original data files into analysis files.

These problems require a system design of documentation, inventory, and information retrieval in addition to the capabilities of file processing. In this area BATSC has made full use of advancements in information systems software, with a considerable saving of staff and computer time while retaining the flexibility of complex file formats.

Software Systems

A very important requirement in processing large data bases is a powerful file-processing system. The software should be capable of supporting the full range of file-processing tasks both on simple and complex file structures. It should also contain basic documentation aids and be easily learned by nonprogrammers. The system BATSC uses is the SPAN processing system developed by Vladimir V. Almendinger of the System Development Corporation.[1]

SPAN consists of a series of modules, each of which performs a basic file-processing task (see Figure 6.1 and 6.2). The modules are connected by common file formats, common conventions, and contain powerful transformation and stratification languages. The components of SPAN include a tape sort, file summary, collator, data abstractor, standard tabulation module, regression- and factor-analysis modules, graphic display, and the complex file processor MIDAS (*MI*xed *DA*ta Structures).[2]

Data documentation at BATSC is accomplished by means of the DATADOX system (developed by the System Development Corporation).[3] Reference data sets—that is, data about data—are stored as part

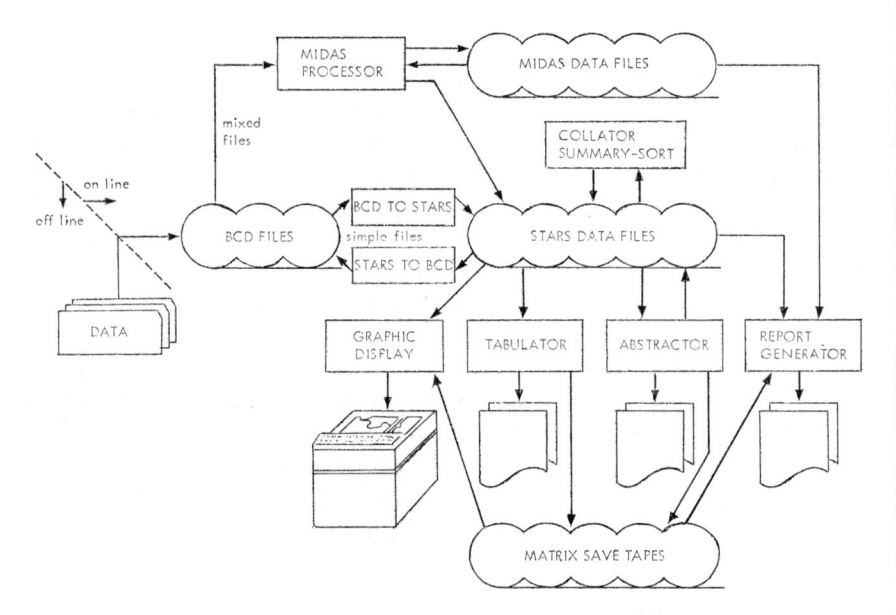

Figure 6.1 SPAN file processing and display.

of the data base. DATADOX, a set of MADAM (*M*oderately *A*dvanced *DA*ta *M*anagement) procedures utilizing the IBM 1401 computer, produces reference documents and dictionaries from the reference data sets.[4]

**THE HOME INTERVIEW TRIP ORIGIN AND DESTINATION SURVEY—
A CASE STUDY**

The home interview survey is a major information source in transportation analysis. It is comprised of interviews with families and individuals, recording their characteristics and the trips they make. Detailed descriptions of the traditional form of this type of survey covering sample design, variables collected, and the methods of collection are available in publications of the Highway Research Board, Bureau of Public Roads, and in manuals published by other transportation studies. Variations in these methods are outlined in a series of BATSC publications.[5]

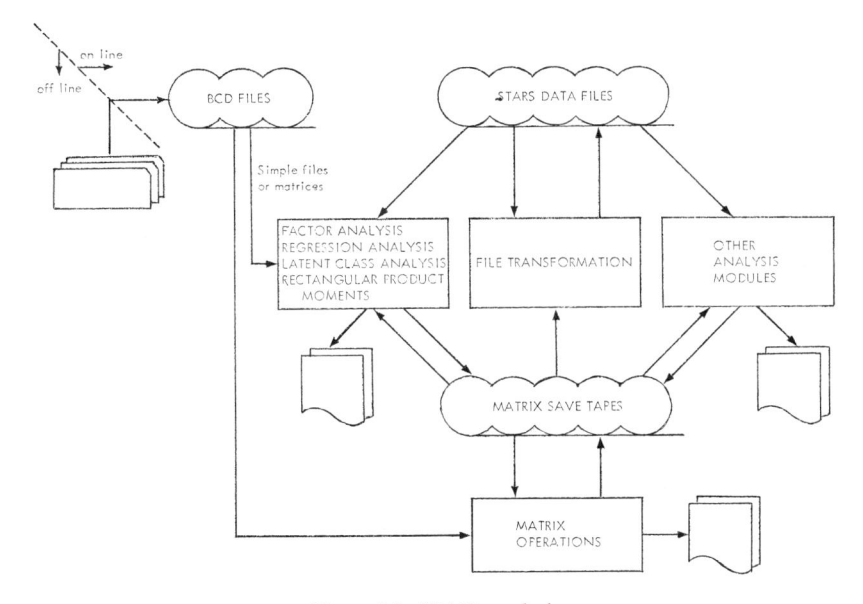

Figure 6.2 SPAN: analysis.

In recent years transportation planners have realized the importance of the socioeconomic characteristics of the region and its inhabitants, as they affect and are affected by transportation systems. To conduct concerted analysis in this area it has been necessary to collect more detailed information not only about the trips people make but also about the people themselves. This analysis requires the determination of the relationships within this complex data-collection format.

The transitional aspect of transportation planning is most clearly seen in the changing form of the origin and destination survey. This change is outlined in a paper by Prof. Norman Kennedy,[6] in which he refers to current metropolitan transportation studies as follows:

"These (metropolitan transportation) studies, extensions of the origin-destination surveys begun in American urban areas soon after the end of the war, are yielding much very useful information. The earlier origin-destination surveys were focused on collecting data mainly for highway planning. Beginning with the Detroit study in 1953, the scope and purpose of the origin-destination study have been expanded to include collection of data pertaining to all travel within the metropolitan area, regardless of mode, and to see if relationships could be established between use of land and its transportation requirements. From this study and others since initiated, transportation engineers and planners are beginning to find quantitative evidence of the relationship between land use and the kind and amount of transportation required to sustain that use.

As useful as these studies are, as they are now conducted, they are really only the starting point in our search for better understanding of the fundamental nature of transportation and its interrelationship with society and economy.

The Home Interview Complex Data Files

The BATSC survey is a later form of this traditional origin-destination survey. Its large and varied content was handled by using a complex file format. The schematic representation of the home interview short-form MIDAS file (Figure 6.3) is an example of the combination of census-type survey data into an interacting complex format. Each completed interview contains information on the following:

1. The household—housing type, market or rent value, income, members, drivers, vehicles available, etc.
2. The people in the household—age, sex, relation to head, education, employment, whether drive, vehicles owned, etc.
3. The trips made—origin, destination, mode of travel, purpose, land use at origin and destination, parking costs, transit times, time of trip, blocks walked, etc.

The file is arranged in this manner: Each household record (cards containing data on the household itself) is followed by a sublist of data on the head of household, then by a set of records of all trips made by the head. These data lists are followed by the data record of the second person in the household (if there is one), then by all the trips made by this person. These data lists are in turn followed by a variable number of such sets of person and trip information, depending on the number of people in the household and the number of trips made by each.

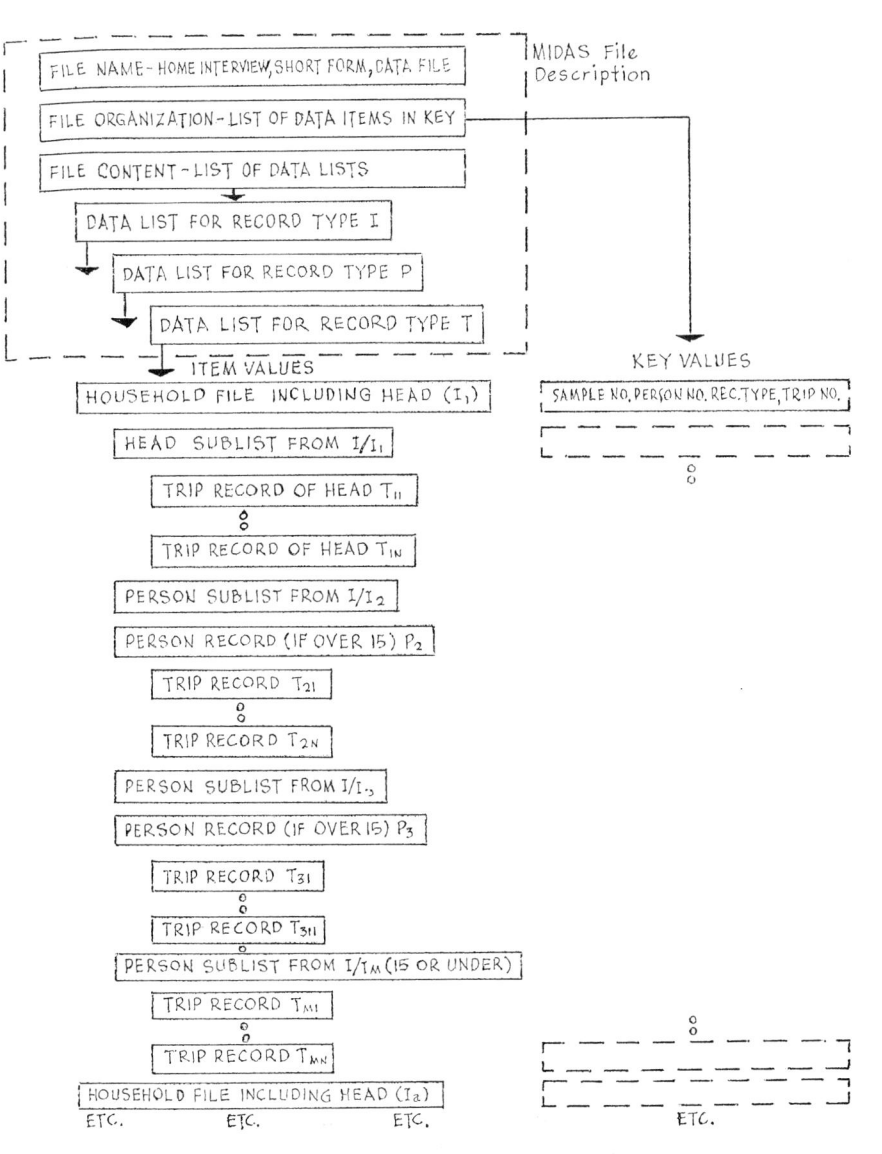

Figure 6.3 Schematic of home interview short form MIDAS file.

An Example of the Use of Simple versus Complex Files—Trip Linking

Trip linking is a normal phase of transportation analysis and consists of evaluating individual trip entities and combining or collapsing these entities into a simple file of new trips that have a dominant mode or purpose. The combinational operation is usually a straightforward process involving a series of logical tests.

However, the result reflects a set of conditions that may not hold for all purposes and, further, usually destroys some information in order to create a simple file. The natural form of the linked trip should be complex. The new entity is a combined trip containing a variable number of component parts. In this form it is possible to retrieve information about any component of these linked trips without the loss of other information; for example, the linked trip with three input trips and the linked trip with two input trips can be handled with equal facility. In fact except for large-file-size considerations, analysis could proceed directly from the original MIDAS home interview file.

Basic Problems—Sources and Solutions

As transportation planning evolves to a more and more complex form of analysis, so does the volume and diversity of data being collected and processed. Many new problems occur, and solutions must be found. In this transitional phase from simple to complex and interacting model input developments in computer hardware and software become increasingly important. BATSC has utilized these developments in all phases of collection and processing. Experience indicates the need for an even greater involvement in information systems.

Basically problems occur because large volumes of data are being handled in a complex format. These problems begin with the sample design and continue through the collection, coding, contingency checking, geographic coding, factoring, and file-processing operations.

Sample design

The home interview sample design and size was specified by the Bureau of Public Roads. This design was originally formulated for zone-to-zone trip end expansion as input to an iterative growth model (Fratar). The sample design is a function of an area system and sample size as determined by the size of the metropolitan area under study, on the assumption that the area system is a function of this size. However, iterative growth models are no longer generally used, and new models have made this form of sample design obsolete.

The new transportation models require individual sample designs. Where a data intersect between models occurs, of course, the sample can be combined. These individual samples will be small in size and, when summed, could be appreciably smaller than the present area-wide sample for the same level of product reliability.

However, as specified by the Bureau, the BATSC home interview sample was a random-probability sample stratified by the area (sector). A subset of this sample, random but unstratified and still area dependent, was selected for in-depth interviewing. This subset most clearly shows the transitional aspect of the data collection. Data from the in-depth interviews contain seven unique but interacting files that have multiple uses in model analysis. The sample design attempted, under the above area constraints, to bridge the transition from simple files and simplistic analysis to a form of complex multipurpose files. The main sample (short form of the questionnaire), although in multicard format, is primarily three interacting, but essentially simple, files of trip, person, and household characteristics. Although they are based on a simple sample design, these files must be used for multiple purposes.

Stage One—Transportation Models

Trip Generation

Entity Input	*Model*
	Nine trip purposes
Person trips	Person trips
Auto driver trips	Auto driver trips
Public-transportation trips	Public-transportation trips

Trip Distribution

Entity Input	*Model*
Person trips	"Gravity" trip-distribution models by purpose
Auto driver trips	
Public-transportation trips	
Time/distance matrix	
Person trips	"Growth" trip-distribution models
Auto driver trips	
Public-Transportation trips	
Time/distance matrix	

Stage Two—Transportation Models

Trip Generation

Entity Input	Model
	16 trip purposes by household type or other
Person trips	Person trips
Auto trips	Auto trips
Vehicle trips	Vehicle trips
Public-transportation trips	Public-transportation trips
Truck-taxi trips	Truck-taxi trips
External trips	External trips

Trip Distribution

Entity Input	Model
Same as for trip generation above	"Gravity" trip-distribution model for above purposes

Model Split

Entity Input	Model
Trip record	Modified demand model
Travel time	Household-type split model (captive versus choice)
Cost values (transit/auto)	
Parking costs	

Regional Models—Population-Demographic

Entity Input	Model
Person records	Population-to-household conversion model
Household records	

Locational Models—Residential-Employment

Entity Input	Model
Household record	Modified Herbert-Stevens model
Household record from in-depth sample	Submodel analysis

Multipurpose Uses of Home Interview Data as Input to BATSC Models

The following is a listing of the types of new transportation models used at BATSC and a listing of the entity input required for each. It can be clearly seen that the diversity and complexity of these models require complex data input, and to obtain these data at an acceptable level of reliability requires that individual specific sample design meet the requirement of each model.

Collection and Coding

The collection and coding of large volumes of survey and inventory data are the most time-consuming and costly factors in the establishment of an information system. Since most studies operate within a severe time constraint, it is essential that these operations be run parallel to avoid costly lapsed time. It is also desirable to use statistical quality-control procedures on data as they are being processed to check the reliability of the data being collected and coded, and to determine the performance of interview and coding personnel. Current information on the quality of the data and the problems encountered in the collection can be used in a feedback mechanism while the collection-and-coding processes are still functioning.

Batch processing is the usual form of control in this type of survey. However, there is a certain amount of lapsed time while a batch is being collected/coded. For this reason BATSC utilized an individual-interview-processing concept in the collection-and-coding phase. Each sample address and the resulting disposition of the interview was treated as an entity.

The problem of administering the collection and coding of 53,000 interviews and the problem of accounting for each interview was resolved, utilizing an IBM 1401 and the software system MADAM, developed by the System Development Corporation. Two forms were designed to control the collection-and-coding process: the interview schedule (BATSC form 02-15) and the coding schedule (BATSC form 02-16).

As each sample address was selected it was written on tape. From these tapes were printed listings of sample number, address, and travel day, on multipart paper for use as master control lists. Self-adhesive labels were also printed containing the same information for use at the various dispatch points.

Immediately after sample selection a home interview permanent operation-flow file was produced. This file contained all sample numbers in the home interview and their status. It was updated periodically from the working operation-flow file. In this way the permanent operation-flow file gave a complete overview of the status of the survey.

The working operation-flow file was created when labels were printed for a particular sector. All sample numbers when released to the field office were put on a standby basis. As the sample numbers were activated, an 02-15 form was dispatched to the data-processing section. The sample number thus went from standby to scheduled status. At each subsequent step in the interview procedure the prior status of the interview was replaced by the current status on the working operation-flow file. This procedure was followed with both the 02–15 and 02–16 forms until the sample number had received a final disposition; that is, either a nonresponse form had been filed or the completed coded interview had been dispatched for keypunching. The working operation-flow file was updated each day from cards produced from the 02–15 and 02–16 forms. These cards were processed through a computer contingency check for accuracy and logic before they were used for updating.

The procedure outlined was operational at BATSC and eventually provided a complete record of the disposition of each sample. The system was not as efficient as it should have been. It should, in theory, have provided a daily report on the current status of each interview, interviewer, and a summary of the entire collection process. It should also have eliminated the need for detailed hand record keeping. Unfortunately this did not occur. It requires persistent effort to obtain current and accurate information from field personnel. It was noted that there was a strong resistance on the part of field personnel to the use of computer processing, due primarily to a lack of understanding. There was also little understanding of the concept of "work-flow," or "assembly-line," processing in parallel. A good computer systems design must be backed up by those administrating the process.

File Assembly

The file-assembly phase consists of converting the interviews into checked and formatted machine-readable input. This phase of ordering the data cards, checking for missing cards within the interview, checking the data for errors, and producing the final complex data file is the largest file-processing job of the survey. Unfortunately there is very little published work on the methodology of such activities.

Although there is a severe need for general data-assembly and checking routines, none of those available at the time were capable of handling a truly large-scale, complex-file-processing job. Coupled with this was the fact that none of the existing programs handled missing data correctly. As interviews grow in length and complexity, the probability of a complete set of answers decreases, and missing data usually can be classified as a form of answer and will be significant for analysis. Thus missing data should be preserved and be identifiable.

With these problems in mind the programming staff at BATSC developed a system of IBM 1401–based programs to handle the file-assembly task. Figure 6.4 illustrates the operational work flow. As soon as 600 interviews were keypunched, the cards were batched together and sorted into interview and card order. The generator checked the cards for proper order, duplication, and missing cards. Samples that were in error were identified for later correction and deleted from the batch. Correct card sets were combined into a more compact data format and were written as a batch tape.

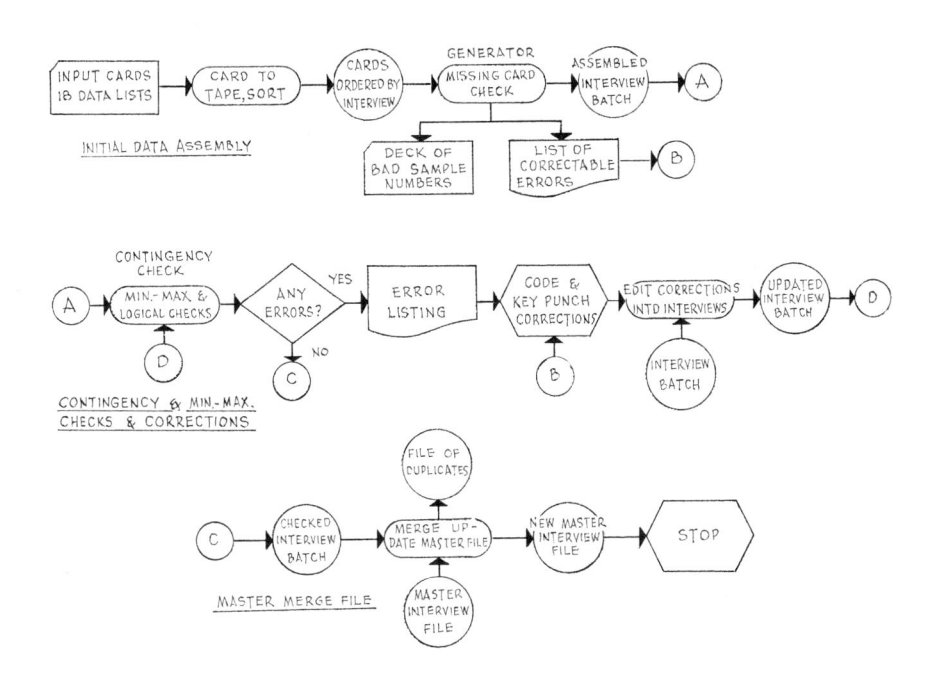

Figure 6.4 Home interview data file assembly and checking.

The next phase, the contingency check, checked each data item to see that its value fell within the range of possible values (min-max check) and checked variables that were dependent on each other for a particular coding set (logical or contingency check). The entire batch was copied while flagging interviews in error. A listing of errors for each interview giving the location of the error and the reason for error was sent to the coding section for correction. The corrections were coded directly on this listing, and it was returned for keypunching. The punched error corrections were edited into the batch of interviews, which was then rechecked. This checking and correcting process was repeated until the batch was considered to be clean; this usually required three passes. The cleaned batch was then merged into the master sector files. The generator errors from the first step were held until the bulk of the processing was finished, then batched together and corrected in the same manner.

The advantages of this method are twofold: processing of batches completes overlap of processing time in that all phases of the data assembly are asynchronous and that computer efficiency is maximized, as is the clerical work. The more time-consuming nonparallel-operation method forces the overall process to wait as each step is executed in sequence, resulting in a lengthening of processing time and an inefficient use of machinery and personnel.

Geographic Coding

In line with the desire to preserve data at the entity level and in view of the areal component of the data, the household address, trip origin and destination addresses, and the employer's address were coded to their unique geographical location. The areal system decided on for this unique location was a combination of census tracts and blocks. Geographic coordinates were used as data items rather than as an areal system.

As part of the inventory and survey collection a street index was created. This index listed all numeric street addresses and all intersections in the nine-county region, along with the related census blocks and tract numbers, and the city and county codes. In addition traffic generators—that is, place names, public buildings, etc.—most frequently referred to by place name, were added to the index with their census block and tract numbers as they were encountered in the coding process. The index, when completed, contained about 300,000 records and was used to code all survey and inventory addresses to a geographic location code.

The STAMMER system (*ST*reet *A*ddress *M*atch *MER*ge) was written by BATSC programmers for the IBM 1401.[7] These programs matched the addresses within the data files to the street index and added the corresponding census tract and block number to the data. Addresses that did not match were returned to the map coding section along with the reason for nonmatch. Either corrections were made to the survey address or additions were made to the street index. The match rate averaged about 80 percent, and in all about 700,000 addresses from the home interview were geographically coded in this manner.

It is possible to subset the data files based on any coding scheme by using either the census tract and block scheme or by using the actual coordinates of the data. This example of adding data to a complex file utilized the complex file structure to the fullest.

The main problem encountered in geographic coding was a duplication of processing runs. At the time that the street index was available for coding, the various analysis zones had not been defined. Thus it was necessary to produce a correspondence table (ICORR) between the street-index census block and tract numbers, and the related analysis zones and their geographic centroids. All address data had to be processed again, and the analysis zone numbers and coordinates had to be merged into the files. Considerable processing time could have been saved if these zone numbers had been incorporated into the street index prior to the initial processing.

Documentation: DATADOX

The information system must, as a fundamental requirement, expose the contents of the data base to the user. These complex data files will have many users, not all of whom will be associated with the data collection and basic file preparation. This is particularly true when the data base is used by external agencies. The information system must provide the user with accurate and timely documentation on the availability of particular data observed over particular sets of entities and on the characteristics and location of these data. Many programming systems were developed to assist in the massive data collection of the study. The development and implementation of the information system is a joint BATSC/SDC (System Development Corporation) project.

The following is a list of the reports available within the DATADOX information system:

Case Studies in ... Complex Data Bases

Data-Documentation-System Reports

DDS-1	Data inventory	DDS-8	Physical storage media directory
DDS-2	Data dictionary		
DDS-3	Data directory	DDS-8T	Tape volumes directory
DDS-3A	Data directory (condensed)	DDS-8C	Card volumes directory
		DDS-9	Maps directory
DDS-4	Data list layout	DDS-10	Computer Programs directory
DDS-5	Variables list layout		
DDS-6	Codes list layout	DDS-11	Data file description (added by BATSC)
DDS-7	Data-sets director		

This system has worked well at BATSC. It is difficult to imagine how complex data files can be user oriented without a similar system of documentation.

It has been found necessary to have a data librarian to operate and control the system. This librarian controls documentation, the tape library, and the data-set storage. She provides instructions in documentation and data-item-retrieval methods, and assigns and controls the use of variable and file labeling.

The DATADOX system is only as useful as the information supplied to it. Documentation supplied to the system must be current, complete, and accurate. Since analysts and programmers have a tendency to avoid documentation whenever possible, the librarian has the responsibility and the authority to insist on current and complete documentation. This aspect is essential to full utilization of the system.

Since the DATADOX system is well documented elsewhere,[8] we should mention that certain adaptations have been incorporated. One major adaptation has been the inclusion of the data file description report (DDS-11). Whenever an analyst has created or intends to create a new file, tabulation, graphic output, and the like, he completes a copy of BATSC form 04-14 and submits the form to the data librarian, who checks to insure that the file has not already been created or is in the process of being created. These data file descriptions are summarized weekly to provide an updated report for staff and administrative information, indicating what files, tabulations, etc., are available for use.

Definitions of codes and variables are included in DATADOX. Some of these definitions are quite long and are usually included in the collection or coding manuals of the various inventories and surveys. When this occurs, it has been found advisable to include a reference to the pertinent manual in the DATADOX definition so that the entire definition is not duplicated.

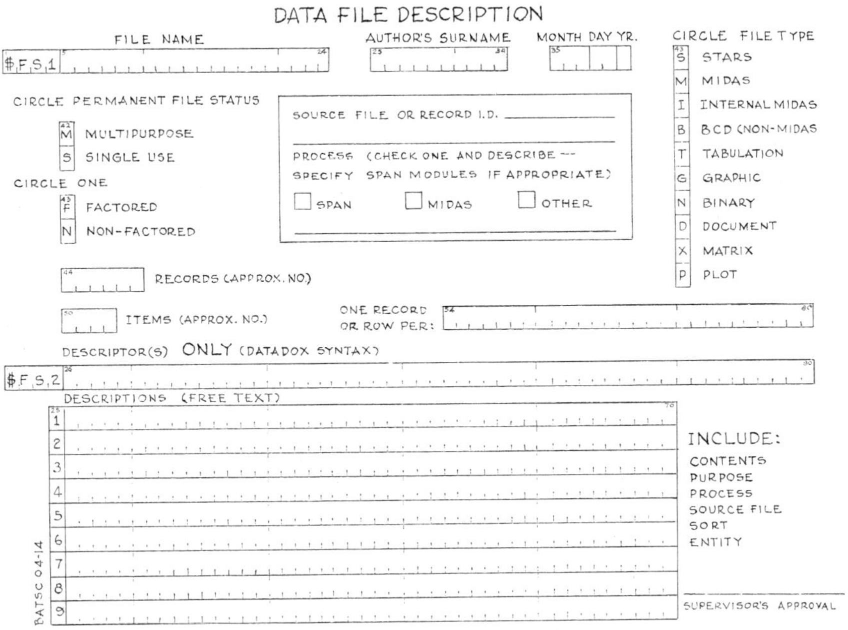
DATA FILE DESCRIPTION

FILE NAME $F,S,1 — AUTHOR'S SURNAME — MONTH DAY YR.

CIRCLE FILE TYPE: S STARS; M MIDAS; I INTERNAL MIDAS; B BCD (NON-MIDAS); T TABULATION; G GRAPHIC; N BINARY; D DOCUMENT; X MATRIX; P PLOT

CIRCLE PERMANENT FILE STATUS: M MULTIPURPOSE; S SINGLE USE

CIRCLE ONE: F FACTORED; N NON-FACTORED

SOURCE FILE OR RECORD I.D. ______

PROCESS (CHECK ONE AND DESCRIBE — SPECIFY SPAN MODULES IF APPROPRIATE) ☐ SPAN ☐ MIDAS ☐ OTHER

RECORDS (APPROX. NO.)

ITEMS (APPROX. NO.)

ONE RECORD OR ROW PER:

DESCRIPTOR(S) ONLY (DATADOX SYNTAX) $F,S,2

DESCRIPTIONS (FREE TEXT) 1 2 3 4 5 6 7 8 9

INCLUDE: CONTENTS PURPOSE PROCESS SOURCE FILE SORT ENTITY

SUPERVISOR'S APPROVAL

BATSC 04-14

Figure 6.4 Home interview data file assembly and checking.

Factoring

Factors to expand the sample home interview data were calculated in sequential stages. Initial analysis of trip files required only trip expansion factors, but later analysis requires a complexity of factors, such as ratios to occupied dwelling units, by census tract, by structure type; adjustments for missing data items; adjustments for nonresponse; and adjustments for seasonal variation. The flexibility of the processing system enabled the inclusion of expansion factors as additional variables in the individual records.

There are two major advantages to this approach:

1. The data remain in their original unexpanded form. Records containing missing data items are retained in the file and identified. A variable number of expansion factors can be added to the original record.

These factors can be applied for a variety of analyses alone or in combination by using the transformation capabilities of the SPAN system. They can also be ignored if analysis requires original unexpanded data.

2. Preliminary analysis of the data files can begin with the original data. As factors are calculated and entered as part of the data records, analysis can continue on expanded data in sequential levels of detail. Thus the flexibility of the system permits considerable time saving in that finalized expanded files are not required before analysis can begin.

File Processing at the Analytic Level with SPAN

The version of SPAN used at BATSC is the tape-based SPAN 7094. SPAN functions as a user-oriented file-processing system that can be used by nonprogrammers to conceive and implement file-processing and analysis jobs of a striking level of sophistication. The analysis staff, some 20 at BATSC, has been trained in SPAN in a series of short lectures combined with practical working examples. This extent of user participation has allowed BATSC to use only four programmers for basic file processing. These processing jobs are necessary for file building and require an intensive background in programming and data processing. Once a file is prepared, the analysts are given full rein to carry out their analysis without being dependent on the programming section.

There are multiple advantages to such a system. The analysts are much closer to the data and quickly perceive the nuances of data interaction and the problems of interfacing a work program and data systems; this results in an overall gain in efficiency and in using the data base. Another obvious gain is that the programming staff is much smaller than would be expected because most of the analysts may be considered to be part-time programmers. Also, the common feeling that analysts should analyze and programmers should program is erroneous. A large amount of an analyst's time is traditionally spent in describing the files and machine runs he needs. He must conceive the problem, transmit it to a superior, who then transmits it to the data-processing section where finally it filters down to a programmer. The programmer then executes the job, at which time the analyst may find that certain changes should be made. The problems of communication are tremendous, and the level of overall efficiency is low. With SPAN, the analyst describes the job in the simple and uniform notation of SPAN and then executes the job, usually within one day. This contrasts vividly with the week or so time lag in the traditional job-oriented file-processing shop. The fact that everyone working within the data base knows and uses SPAN results in a higher level of communication, which helps reduce the duplication of effort that is so

Working with Complex Data Files: I 103

common. Also, anyone's work can be checked or finished by others, since there is no need to learn someone else's notation and methods. Finally, the modular structure of SPAN aids in decomposing a complex job into the logical series of simple steps, each of which then can be executed in a straightforward manner. Considering the difficulty of programming most file-processing tasks, even for a trained programmer, an analyst solving a typical problem in SPAN can do in an hour what a programmer could do in a week, writing and checking a program while using twice as much machine time.

As stated before, not all jobs are best done with simple files. The complex file structure is important in many jobs. The complex-file-processing function within SPAN is performed by MIDAS, which operates on a data set (file) containing a series of logically connected data lists (record types) that comprise a data entity. MIDAS provides for many of the basic file-processing tasks; among them is the capability of reducing complex files into simple files, either in binary coded decimal form for transposing to other systems or in STARS format for operation within SPAN. The ability to subset, merge, or update files, and the report-generator feature of MIDAS make possible the generation of formatted tabulated reports.

Nearly any file that can be described logically can be considered as a MIDAS file. The simple file is a special case of the general complex file. Since a complex file can be organized in many ways, one of the most important functions of MIDAS is to take an unorganized file or files and order it to produce a rational file.

An example of the need to organize a file in several different orders is the use of the in-depth subset of the home interview. This interview contained 24 different card formats and collected data on person trips, household and housing characteristics, the employment history of the head of the household, the locational history of the household, the migrational characteristics of the household, and the changing composition of the household. MIDAS is being used to produce these seven unique but interlocking data files for analysis. The total amount of MIDAS programming effort required, beyond that which is needed to specify what data items are to be used in each of the files, amounts to less than 20 hours a week. Contrast this with the 100 to 150 man hours and 4 weeks that would be needed to produce the minimal amount of unique programming to produce the same results.

Processing the Home Interview with SPAN and MIDAS

The MIDAS processor of SPAN was used to process the complex files into both simple analytic files and new subsets of complex files. Figure

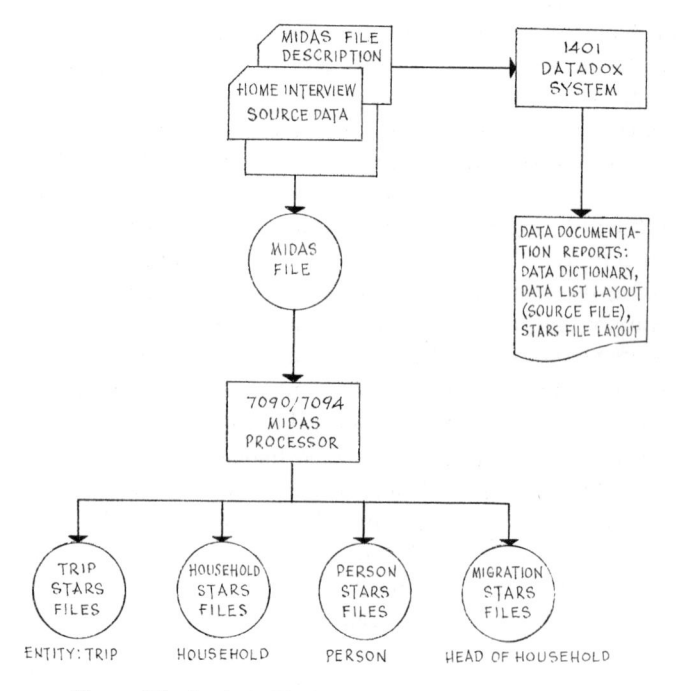

Figure 6.5 Analysis file data flow (MIDAS to STARS).

6.5 illustrates how MIDAS produces the four main analytic files. The trip file contains all person trips for the region, along with the related household and person information repeated as needed. This is the largest file and contains 250,000 entities. The household file exists at the interview or household entity level. The person-file entity level is that of the individual person within the household and some related household and trip information. Finally, the migration file has as its entity structure each location of the household, as reported by the head, for the past 10 years.

The structure of these files was derived after considerable preliminary analysis covering the whole complex file. Factoring and geographic coding were done as the derivative files were prepared.

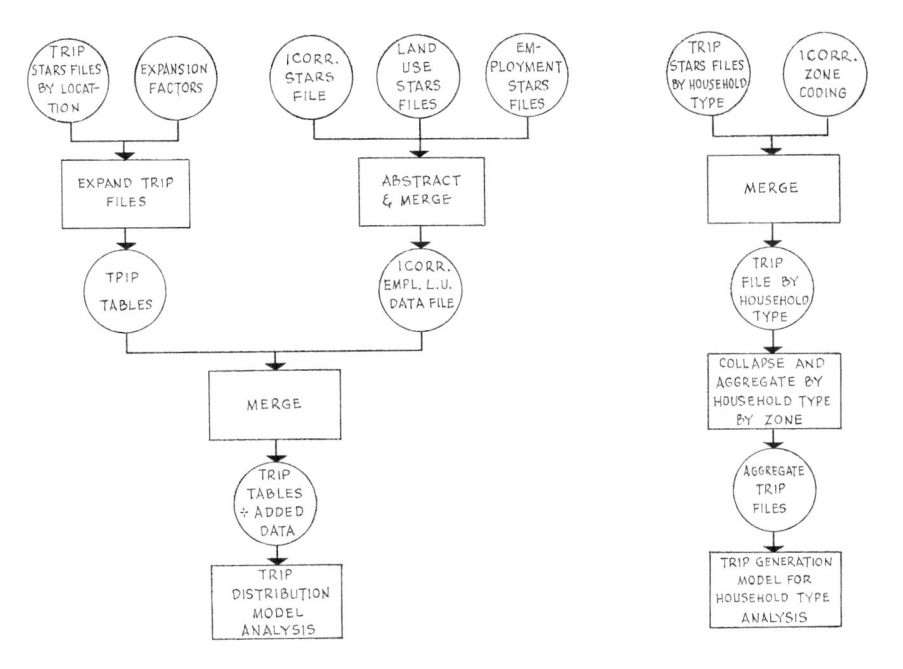

Figure 6.6   File merging and processing input for model development.

Figure 6.6 shows how the data files from other surveys and inventories are combined with the home interview to serve as input to the models.

An Example of the Use of MIDAS in Creating a Home Interview File

The person file of the home interview consists of a record for every person in the 33,000 households interviewed (approximately 98,000 persons). Each record contains information about the person's educational background, his employment status and occupation, his vehicle ownership, and a summary of his trip-making characteristics. Also included with each household member's data are the corresponding data of the head of the household. As described, each record contains more than 1000 characters of information.

The input file contained three different file types: an I record (A) DATA), which contained household and head of household data;

a P record (B) DATA), which contained data on up to five household members over 15 years of age in each tape record; and a T record (C) DATA), which contained data on up to six trips made by the household members in each tape record. The number of P and T records could vary from zero to as many as needed to describe the person and trip characteristics of the household.

Thus the output file contained subsets and accumulations of data from all three data lists. In addition to subsetting and accumulating data, 39 new variables were created as transformations of input variables.

The IDLIST and VARIABLES specifications indicated what data items were to be included in the output file. The letter prefix indicated the data region, and the number indicated the position within the data region. Data items with a D prefix were the results of the data-transformation operations. The transformation operations in Figures 6.9 and 6.10 produced the 39 new variables.

The majority of the program was written by a programmer-analyst while instructing a nonprogramming sociologist in the concepts and processes of MIDAS. This nonprogrammer then wrote the remaining data transformations he desired, performed all of the required program checkout, and monitored the actual production runs. The home interview was divided into 11 subgroups to facilitate operations. The machine time spent on the MIDAS phase was 15 hours of IBM 7094 computer time. The 11 output files were then merged into one region file with an expenditure of an additional four hours. This process required about 40 man-hours to design, write, check, and complete the file-reduction task. Writing and checking a comparable task-oriented program for the IBM 1401 computer would require about 100 hours of programming time and 20 hours of an analyst's time to specify a file and check the results.

This fairly simple example indicates the great time savings a complex file processor such as MIDAS can produce. Although it is not immediately apparent, the simplification of the file-processing activities required results in great gain in operational efficiency because a complex file form was used. A useful sidelight is that the input file specifications (the $DLF cards) were used to produce the required file documentation and record layouts by the DATADOX programs. Also, the output file was self-describing, and with the aid of other DATADOX programs tape layouts were produced and distributed to the analysis staff with little additional processing.

Since a sizeable series of data-reduction and file-processing programs were not necessary, such uses of MIDAS allowed the staff to concentrate on the analytic model programming.

Working with Complex Data Files: I 107

Processing Large Files

A problem with the current state of the art in large-scale file processing is the very real one of file size. It is quite easy to generate files that require more than one magnetic tape. The trip file from the home interview now covers 20 reels of tape. Since nearly all computers are severely restricted by the speed of the input/output devices, multireel files require an inordinate amount of computer time in relation to the actual amount of work done. For example, to read the entire trip file on an IBM 7094 computer at maximum tape speed would require about 90 minutes. This time becomes particularly important when only part of the file is needed.

Since magnetic-tape files are sequential—that is, to find one record requires reading all those that precede it—machine costs become particularly important as a limit to the amount of analysis done. One solution is to fragmentize the file into many shorter files in the expectation that one or two of these shorter files will suffice for any given task. The fragmentation approach leaves much to be desired. If only a few files are prepared, the overall work program is limited because the data base is too restricted. On the other hand, if many subset files are prepared, the file-processing costs begin to climb. Often several files must be combined to form an analysis file.

Such problems with large data files will be solved as more use is made of the new mass-store devices such as disk files and bulk core. An entirely new approach to file processing will be possible—that of random access. With a random-access file the user has immediate access to any data item, providing he knows where it is located. Work on methods of data retrieval is under way in many locations, and the problems of mapping the contents of data files are being solved. The proposed SPAN/360 programming system will provide for such use of random-access mass-store devices as well as the sequential-access tape files.

RECOMMENDATIONS

If this presentation were to make one salient point and one specific recommendation, it would be this: that data collection and processing is too complex and too costly an operation to continue in its present evolvement without *concerted system design*. The collection of data in a transportation study or in a regional information system—they are becoming synonymous—requires not only file-processing systems design, which is mandatory at this point, but also sample and collection systems design, which has been less than adequate.

108   Case Studies in ... Complex Data Bases

Some of the solutions to processing problems adopted by BATSC may prove to be useful in the collection and processing of other types of complex data. The following recommendations are not specifically oriented toward transportation studies but apply to the collection and processing of any complex data required by a large information-system project.

Changes in Sample Design

One overall sample design based on an areal system is completely inadequate for multiple-purpose input to a series of models. Much work needs to be done in specifying a series of interlocking, small subsamples designed for very specific purposes or for multipurpose use. This design in turn depends on a more specific definition of the models for which these data are input. The current aggregative or semiaggregative models, whether descriptive or optimizing, require inventory and large sample data in a simple format that can be geographically aggregated. The trend toward "behavioral" models, whether they imply optimization or not, will require individualistic data in depth in a complex interacting format and individual sample design.

Predesign of Collection and Processing

The collection and processing of complex data are so involved that a thorough systems approach to the design of collection, coding, and data-assembly phases must be provided. It is imperative that the entire operational work flow be designed and checked before data collection begins.

1. More time should be provided for predesign of data collection and processing systems.

2. Software systems such as MIDAS and MADAM should be an integral part of the predesign.

3. Parallel collection, coding, and file processing are necessary if time and costs are to be held to a minimum.

4. Parallel operations allow quality control of data and a feedback mechanism to field operations.

5. A system of area coding should be finalized before coding to location begins to avoid duplication of runs.

6. If staffing of experienced field personnel is not possible, subcontracting of data collection and coding should be considered, providing

that complete statistical control over the data is retained by the study. Census-type survey data are sufficiently similar, regardless of their purpose, to make the use of experienced and qualified survey-research or market-research personnel quite feasible.

Required Software Systems

An extensive software system is essential to all operations from data collection through processing.

The work done at BATSC has shown that a uniform user-oriented file-processing language can be used at a high level of efficiency. There were several deficiencies in this information system, but they were worked out as experience in using an interacting data base and information system was obtained. The SPAN/DATADOX interaction was not automatic and placed most of the burden of documentation on the file creator. It would be of greater use if the file-processing system would provide the necessary file documentation from the program specifications. Also, the documentation and the file creation runs were made on different computers, which resulted in a lag between creation and documentation. The original design of SPAN included the documentation processor, but time constraints forced the use of MADAM to provide the documentation programs. A better system would be one in which the programmer is given the ability to produce file documentation.

Interaction Among Data Bases

Since the whole concept of the complex-file-processing system has worked well, more groups should sponsor research, generalize the concepts of complex file processing, and provide the operational procedures. Also, more attention should be paid to the general dissemination of current findings. Further work must be done in file organization, data-item retrieval, documentation systems, and file-processing methods. Much money is being spent on urban data systems, and we need operational methods to operate on the data banks or data bases being created. Because many different groups are working with federal funding, a common file-processing system would allow greater understanding of what is being done and greater interaction among these groups. Standardization for the sake of standardization is not desired, but a common language that would allow communication among the several data bases in the country is needed immediately.

SUMMARY

This chapter has attempted to outline some of the aspects of complex file processing as it relates to a regional transportation study. As in most research, there is an evolutionary process in transportation planning. Each new transportation study analyzes and accepts or rejects the new techniques used by previous studies. In addition advancements in methodology from other areas of research are incorporated. The concepts used at BATSC reflect this transition, particularly in the use of the systems approach. The problems BATSC has encountered in the collection and processing of complex data files are not necessarily unique. The solutions adopted, although often pragmatic, indicate the adaptability of modern hardware and software systems.

Solutions to some of the more basic problems could not be implemented within the study. These basic problems are primarily ones of design and concept and require considerable changes in the conventional design and handling of transportation-study data.

REFERENCES

1. See the following sections of the *SPAN Reference Manual*, Santa Monica, Calif.: System Development Corporation: V. V. Almendinger, "SPAN: Introduction and General Description," TM-1563/000/00, November 27, 1963; V. V. Almendinger, "SPAN System Operation," TM-1563/010/02, December 1, 1965; V. V. Almendinger, "SPAN Data-Transformations and Stratification Capability," TM-1563/014/03, July 29, 1966; V. V. Almendinger, "Data Files Manipulation and Processing," TM-1563/021/02, December 1, 1965.
2. V. V. Almendinger, E. W. Franks, and K. A. Hinman. "Mixed Data Structures (MIDAS) Processor and Report Generator," TM-1563/023/01, November 17, 1966; and J. I. Chess, "Span Graphic Display System," TM-1563/025/00, March 31, 1966. *SPAN Reference Manual*. Santa Monica, Calif.: System Development Corporation.
3. V. V. Almendinger and J. M. Kibbee, *Bay Area Transportation Study Commission Information System: Data Description and Documentation*. Santa Monica, Calif.: System Development Corporation, TM-2690, December 1965.
4. V. V. Almendinger and J. M. Kibbee, *BATSC Support MADAM Library*. TM-(1)-2689, December 1965; W. O. Crossley, *The MADAM System*, TM-2198/002/00, December 1965. Santa Monica, Calif.: System Development Corporation.
   Davidson, Susan T. "BATSC Data Documentation System (DDS) Procedures Manual." BTR 050/01/00. Bay Area Transportation Study Commission, Berkeley. February 1966.
5. G. W. Fairman, R. G. Drosendahl, and Kathleen M. Grady, *Home Interview Manual*, November 1965; Noreen J. Roberts, *Home Interview Expansion Factors and Final File Preparation*, BTM 215/00/00, October 1966; F. T. White and Helene L.

Stephenson, *Home Interview Coding Manual,* November 1965. Berkeley, Calif.: Bay Area Transportation Study Commision, Berkeley.
6. Norman Kennedy, *Transportation Hubs and Concentration of Man,* Institute of Transportation and Traffic Engineering, University of California at Los Angeles Conference on Man and His Total Environment, March 1967.
7. W. P. Hackett, *STAMMER (STreet Address Match MERge),* BTM 214/00/00. Berkeley, Calif.: Bay Area Transportation Study Commission, September 1966. Noreen J. Roberts, *Electronic Data Processing in Survey Design and Information Systems,* BTM 212/00/00. Berkeley, Calif.: Bay Area Transportation Study Commission, September 1966.
8. James Wigle, "Matrix Operations System (MOPSY)," TM-1563/022/00, May 1967; and "Point-in-Polygon Assignment (POLYGO), TM-1563/024/00, July 1967. *SPAN Reference Manual.* Santa Monica, Calif.: System Development Corporation.

Chapter Seven

Working with Complex Data Files: II. The Wisconsin Assets and Incomes Studies Archive

*Richard A. Bauman, Martin H. David, and Roger F. Miller**

---

* The authors are a Project Supervisor and Professors of Economics, in that order, who are currently in charge of supervising the development of the data archive described at the Social Systems Research Institute of the University of Wisconsin. Financial support for this data development has come from the Brookings Institution, the National Bureau of Economic Research, the Social Security Administration, the National Science Foundation, and, through the University of Wisconsin Graduate School Research Committee, from the State of Wisconsin and the Wisconsin Alumni Research Foundation.

We could hardly begin to list (much less fully acknowledge) the many other individuals who made personal contributions in time and effort to development of these data. On an organizational level, however, we wish to recognize the invaluable cooperation of the personnel of the Wisconsin Department of Taxation, The Social Systems Research Institute, and the Wisconsin Survey Research Laboratory. Finally, for his unfailing encouragement and initial backup support, we acknowledge a great debt of gratitude to Prof. Guy H. Orcutt.

It is a commonplace that the inability to conduct controlled experiments (amongst other things) makes the social sciences more difficult fields of scientific inquiry than the physical and even the medico-biological fields. It has only relatively recently become recognized that this can be overcome, with modern statistical analysis, provided that a sufficient number of significant variables is available for analysis. As yet it is almost exclusively the professional social scientist (who wishes to analyse such data) who recognizes the implications of these statements, whereas those in a position to provide these data are largely ignorant or unconcerned about these implications.

If it can be said that the survey is the social scientist's test tube, then surely the vast bodies of data on human behavior that exist in the files and administrative records of governmental and business organizations can be regarded as the social scientist's cyclotron—or perhaps the survey is comparable to an electron microscope, whereas administrative sources represent a varied assortment of reflecting and refracting visual telescopes, radio telescopes, spectrometers, etc. These analogies are particularly apt in that they distinguish investigative methods that concentrate on many aspects of microunits in great detail from those that look at a relatively few aspects but look at the same objects of analysis repetitively to observe their uncontrolled variations. The other sciences utilize these methods in conjunction with one another, but this has proven to be a stumbling block for social scientists: it is extremely difficult to assemble a variety of data about individuals from various sources in a manner that allows the required analyses.

One of the difficulties involves a matter of policy; that is persons are shy about revealing their personal data and thus insist on its confidentiality even when they are required by law to provide the data. This type of difficulty is discussed at length in a separate section of this book. In this chapter we wish to concentrate on a distinct difficulty or set of difficulties. These are technical and technological in nature, and although our experience of them may not be unique, we feel they carry special weight because the difficulties are found in the new context of a vast, multifile archive of great complexity and because of the logistics associated with a large data-collection operation that is distributed over a long period of time. It is especially pertinent experience in view of current proposals to do on a national scale what we have been doing with respect to Wisconsin taxpayers.

It was roughly five years ago that we began collecting data on a large sample of individuals from their Wisconsin individual income tax returns for the years 1946–1960. At that time it was contemplated that the usefulness of the tax-return data could be vastly enhanced by the addition of data on these same persons from other sources and by extending the data by continued collection of tax records. So far we have been successful in gathering these additional data into our archive's files and have even performed some integration of the data from the various files. Some of the analyses being undertaken by members of the Wisconsin Assets and Incomes Studies (hereinafter WAIS) staff involve intertemporal income patterns, the effects of tax averaging proposals, changing incomes from retirement, and realization of capital-gains income.*

Nothing in this chapter should be construed as an advertisement for general distribution of the data. Not only are the files not yet ready for general distribution, we have no license to distribute the data. We have an implicit understanding with the Wisconsin Tax Department that tax records may be used for bona fide research; it has not been made clear how far the data may be rediffused to others. Data on name, address, and other identifying numbers would not in any case be released to other researchers in order to protect the individuals involved and the agencies through whom we secured the data. Finally, an important part of the data files, obtained from records of the Social Security Administration, was made available to us only for specific research objectives in connection with a research grant. They were made available under restrictions that safeguard the confidentiality of the data and prevent disclosure of information pertaining to any identifiable individual to any unauthorized person. Therefore these portions of our total collection of data files are not part of the WAIS archive per se. When the research objectives have been completed, the data are to be returned to the Social Security Administration. No release of data for individuals from social security records and no violation of our contractual commitment to the Social Security Administratin is intended or implied.

---

* In addition selected observations have been made available to a member of the National Bureau of Economic Research staff for analysis of the averaging effects of business loss-carry-over tax provisions.

BASIC FILES

The eight basic WAIS data files are the following:*

1. Master tax-record file.
2. Property-income file.
3. Social security benefit file.
4. Social security earnings-records file (805).
5. Personal-interview survey file.
6. Household-assets diary file.
7. Identification file.
8. History-selection file.

Subsequent sections of this chapter are concerned with the data archive resulting from the integration of these basic files. Descriptions of the contents of each basic file follow.

Master Tax-Record File

The master file contains summary data from tax records that were available in the archives of the State of Wisconsin for the period from 1946 to 1960. The basic tax-year records were collected by taking a 1 percent alphabetic sample of names in 50 clusters. The clusters were chosen randomly from the 1958 Wisconsin income tax rolls. Clustering maximized the possibility that a particular individual (with a given first name and surname) could be identified with a *series of records* supplied to the tax department over this period, so that we could collect the time series of data for each individual in the sample. (Misfiled returns were included automatically in the sample unless the misfiling resulted in a record being placed physically outside the name clusters. Also, the files were in 12 separate locations around the state by person in each of three subsets of years, for four geographic subdivision, or "tax districts" and an individual could have had one return in each location). Cluster sampling made it possible to find them all.

The summary data included in the master file for every individual in the sample is of four types:

1. Coded demographic data, such as place of residence, occupation, marital status.

---

* In addition we have available such files as Standard and Poor's Compustat, which provides additional data on other aspects of the data contained in these files. Similar ancillary files were developed for companies whose data were not already obtainable from Compustat or similar sources.

2. Summary income data—for example, income by major source categories (wages, interest, etc.), total income from all sources, adjusted gross income, net taxable income.

3. Summary deduction, tax computation, and tax data—for example, standard deduction, deductible interest paid, personal exemption allowance, net normal tax.

4. Computed data—for example, standard deduction (this had to be computed to find net taxable income for taxpayers who could use a tax table to calculate their tax), and discrepancy indicators (see "Processing," p. 1).

For many individuals, then, the master file contains essentially a computerized image of their tax records. Detailed data covering certain sources of income that are not reported by all taxpayers are contained in the property-income file, which is described below.

The basic unit for the master file is a tax return or an individual record for one year. Approximately 135,000 taxpayer-year records are included in the file.

Property-Income File

The property-income file also contains data from the tax returns for these same persons; it is a file of detailed transactions that produced property or business income for a taxpayer. Hence the basic unit in the property-income file is an asset-taxpayer-year. The file contains approximately 147,000 such records, and includes separate entries for dividends on different stocks; for capital gains received from the sale of stocks or other properties; and for different items of rent, interest, or business income. The identity of the asset source of the property income (e.g., the name of the corporation paying dividends) was coded into the data for each source that could be identified. An ancillary file of firm-identification systems in sources such as Compustat was developed to facilitate portfolio estimation. This file was also used to identify assets found in the household-assets diary file.

Social Security Benefit File

The social security benefit file was collected from benefit-payment records at each of the Social Security Administration's benefit-payment processing centers throughout the United States. As noted earlier, this file and the earnings-record file were loaned to specific senior WAIS analysts by the Social Security Administration under restrictions safeguarding confidentiality. Uses of these data were restricted only to specific studies. The benefit file contains data on the benefit status and monthly benefit payments to beneficiaries of the social security accounts of taxpayers in the master-file sample. Some beneficiaries (primarily wives and dependent children of taxpayers) of these accounts do not appear in the master file because they did not file tax returns during the period 1946–1960. The monthly payment data have been aggregated for beneficiaries, so we have as basic units, beneficiary-year records, comparable to units in the master file. (The original data received from the Social Security Administration report *all changes* in monthly payment amounts; in this form the data could not be easily integrated with tax-record data on an annual basis.)

Social Security Earnings-Records File

The second file obtained from the Social Security Administration, the 805 earnings records, contains quarterly information on the amount of all earnings on which social security payroll taxes were paid since the year 1951, as well as age, race, and administrative data. This file contains data for every individual who correctly reported a social security account number on any of his tax records. Another ancillary file, the supplementary age and death file, was created when we discovered that approximately 15 percent of the individuals in our master file did not provide valid social security account numbers. By cooperation with the Wisconsin Motor Vehicle Department (driver's license records) and the Wisconsin Board of Health (birth and death records) we were able to supplement our data on ages and deaths for this group. More than half of the individuals without 805 records are included in the supplementary file.

Personal-Interview Survey and Household-Assets Diary Files

The interview file contains coded data obtained from approximately 1300 personal interviews made in 1964; a stratified subsample of the taxpayers in the master file was obtained. Stratification permitted more than a proportional number of interviews with high-income taxpayers, taxpayers with income from property, and taxpayers with a long filing experience in our sample. The interview elicited data on occupational history, education, housing, and attitudes toward portfolio management. At the time of the interview an assets diary was left with certain members of the interview sample to obtain reports of the portfolio holdings and recent portfolio changes of these members of the sample.* Those data are recorded separately as the household-assets diary file. Attrition in the return of diaries results in an asset-data file of 1100 diaries, approximately 200 less than in the personal-interview file.

Identification File

The identification file is primarily for administrative convenience. It contains identification numbers associated with the tax-record sample and social security account data. It also contains a fixed-format coded version of the taxpayer's most recent address and his birth year. The file is used to merge tax records from different years, to ensure that appropriate social security data are merged with the tax record even when multiple account numbers occur, etc.

History-Selection File

An abstract of key information from each of these seven files is recorded in a single history-selection file, which serves as a link among the major files. It provides coded explanations of missing records for an individual whose time series is interrupted or otherwise incomplete. The logic behind creating such a file is explained in the section on "File Maintenance and Document Handling."

PROCESSING

The basic processing of data included in the file can be illustrated by the procedures that are currently being used to add tax-record information for 1960–1964 to the existing file of tax-return data for persons in the same clusters. The flow chart of the operations is shown on the left-hand column of Figure 7.1. Records in the alphabetic segments are microfilmed. Positive images are then compared to the list obtained from the existing identification file to determine whether the individual has an existing identification number or should be assigned a new one. After the records have been identified basic demographic data and information on continuity of tax filing, marital status, and the like are encoded.

Coded data together with income amounts on the tax form are then

---

* When no diary was left the household was asked to complete the same schedules at the time of the interview.

Working with Complex Data Files: II

keypunched in predetermined formats and verified. Each card is then checked for illegal punches and logically impossible combinations of codes to provide a basic record edit. Upon completion of single-card edits a multicard image of the original record is created on tape. At this point the encoded version of the identification file becomes available. The additions to the file can be checked against the original file to eliminate illegally assigned identification numbers and to integrate records for an individual that were inadvertently established as records for two individuals.

Consistency Checking and Machine-Error Correction

Upon completion of identification number checks and any remaining checks on the characters in the image each tax record can be processed through a consistency program that uses the basic logic of the tax form to correct errors of transposition of digits, omission of ciphers, decimal points, etc.[1] Finally, as the last stage in processing, income amounts that run over the size of the field provided in the basic card formats can be inserted into the file to produce a final edited version of the file.

Processing of files 2 through 7 is very similar to the illustration for processing the master file. Development of the property-income file, for example, actually begins at the coding step, since the source documents and identification numbers are those used for processing the master file, and is carried through all of the following steps. Files derived from source documents other than microfilmed tax records (e.g., social security benefit and personal-interview survey files are processed by steps almost identical to those shown in Figure 7.1.

A multiple-file archive also requires some sort of interfile consistency as well as intrafile consistency. This second stage of processing is illustrated in Figure 7.2.

For simplicity Figure 7.2 shows checking for interfile consistency of only two files: the master tax-record and property-income files. Each is checked first for the existence of records implied by fields or records on the other file; for example, a nonzero "net rent" field (master file) implies a detailed rent record (property-income file). Secondly, amount comparisons can be made, the summary "net rent" field (master file) should equal the sum of "net rents" on all detail cards (property-income file) for that individual year. Since records are often derived from different sources, one additional feedback, called discrepancy decription in Figure 7.2, may develop in the consistency checking of several related files. If a discrepancy is discovered on the source documents, it may be impossible

Master-File Processing

Feedback and Correction

Microfilm and produce positive copies ← — — — — — — — — — — { Missing-record check / Illegal-identification check

↓

Assign identification numbers

↓

Code ← — — — — — — — — — — — — — — { Data edit / Logic check

↓

Keypunch and verify

↓

Card edit — — — — — — — — — — — — — —

↓

Multicard-record image ← — — — — — — — — { Error indications from consistency check

↓

Illegal character and identification-number check

↓

Consistency check — — — — — — — — — — — —

↓

Over-the-field cases

↓

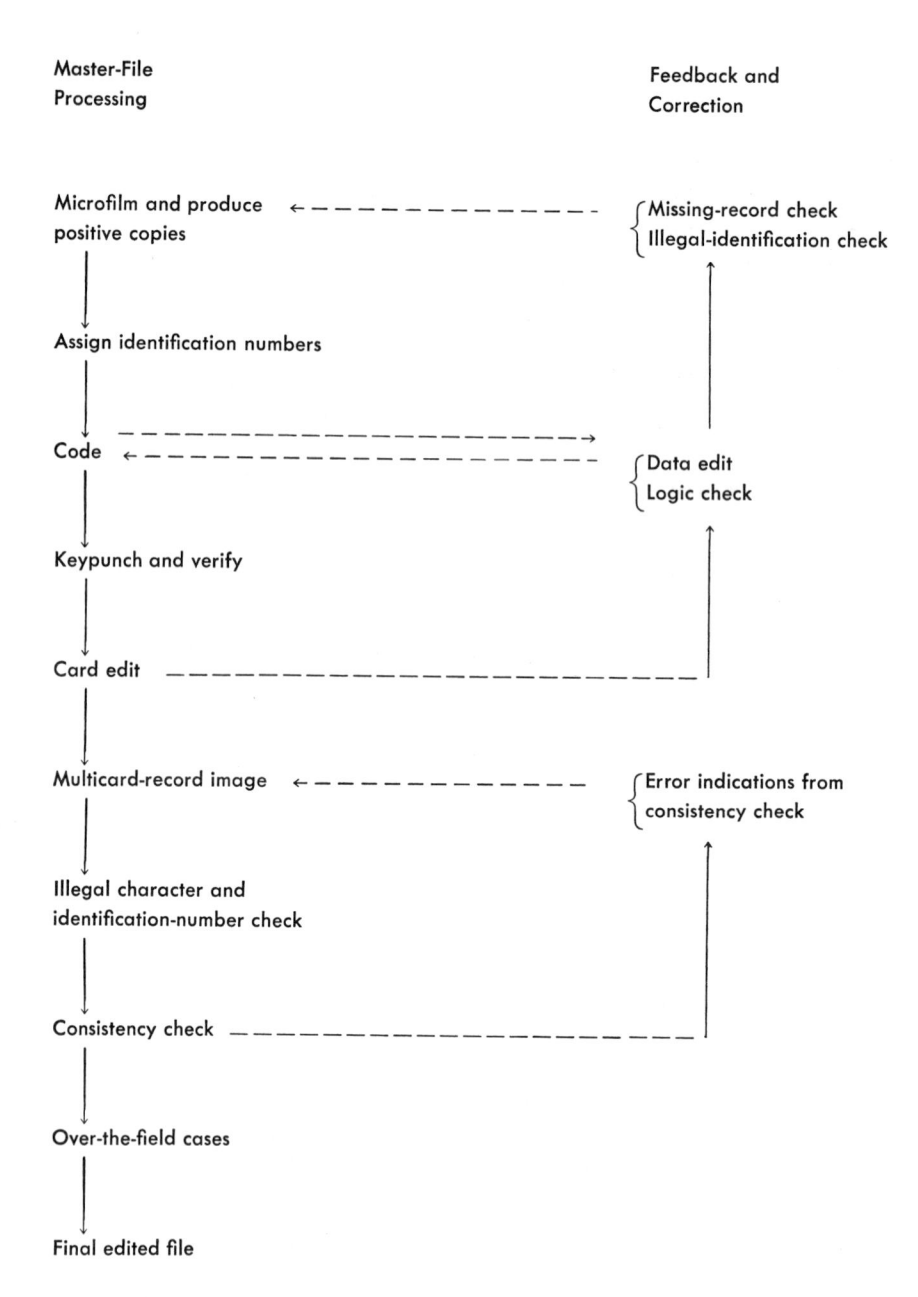

Final edited file

Figure 7.1 Flow of operations for updating the master tax-record file.

120

to ascertain which number is in error. The discrepancy is then left standing, but both records receive coded indications of the type and amount of the discrepancy.

It should be pointed out that these "discrepancies" may result from (internally) *consistent* files. An example of the problem and its "solution" should make this point clear. Suppose that for a certain taxpayer in a certain year we find a total net rent in the master-file source field of $1000 and net rent as derived from the detailed amounts in the property-income file of $700. If no "errors" have been made in the transcription of the data from source documents to tape records, the discrepancy and its algebraic sign are recorded or coded in each record. At least three possible causes of such a discrepancy can be suggested. The taxpayer may have made an error of minus $300 in both the net rent and either the gross rent or expenses figures on his rent schedule that was not *also* entered in his source of income schedule, thus making both sets of figures internally consistent; or he may have made an error of plus $300 on his source of income and total of sources of income schedule that was also not entered on his rent schedule; or a supplementary schedule describing an additional rental property may have been lost somewhere in the taxpayer-tax department-WAIS files flow. Other information could be used to ascertain the *probable* cause (e.g., detail rent data for the same taxpayer in adjacent years) but it remains inherently impossible to determine the *actual* cause of the discrepancy.

Obviously more complicated forms of discrepancies can and do occur. Suppose that the taxpayer in the preceding example had recorded a total of sources of income that was $200 less than a computed total based on his given sources of income. The result is an inconsistent master file as well as an interfile discrepancy. The following section describes some of the procedures used to find and correct intrafile errors.

CONTROL ON THE PRODUCTION OF DATA

Let us return now to Figure 7.1, several features of which bear note.

Physical Selection of Returns

The method for filing returns in the state archive was responsible for the following two special considerations in microfilming the returns:

1. When returns were being audited by the state tax authorities the

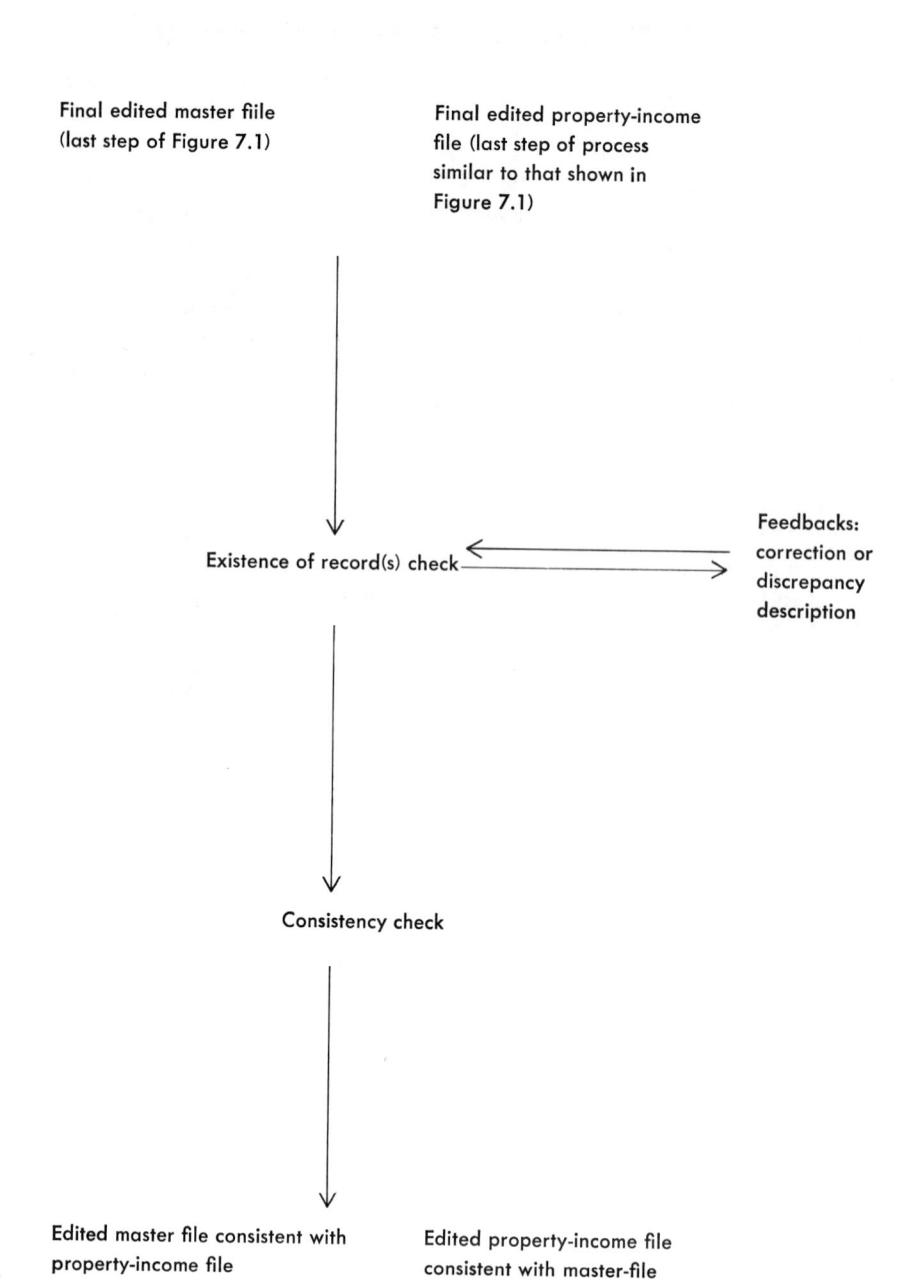

```
Final edited master file            Final edited property-income
(last step of Figure 7.1)           file (last step of process
                                    similar to that shown in
                                    Figure 7.1)
              │                                │
              │                                │
              ▼                                ▼
                                                        Feedbacks:
         Existence of record(s) check  ←──────────      correction or
                                       ──────────→     discrepancy
                                                        description
              │
              │
              ▼
         Consistency check
              │
              │
              ▼
Edited master file consistent with    Edited property-income file
property-income file                  consistent with master-file
```

Figure 7.2 Interfile-consistency checks.

current file for an individual was removed from the file. (The current file contained four or five recent-tax-year records; older returns were kept in separate archives.) If the individual's name was in the sample, his returns for those years could not be microfilmed at that time. Two procedures were used to ensure that returns for these persons were included in the sample. First, we rechecked the files for replaced folders at the end of our microfilming process; second, we returned to the files 12 months after our original microfilming operation to photograph returns of persons whose file had in the interim been replaced.*

2. Returns filed by married women since their last marriage, if any, are filed in the state archive with the returns of their current spouse. These returns were included in the sample. Thus some of the individuals in the tax-return sample are not in the name-group sample for some of the year records, those for years prior to the year of marriage. For most purposes these records effectively "replaced" those for a group of sample women who married persons outside the sample.

Identification

Since tax records from a number of years must be assembled to produce the income history of a taxpayer, it is extremely important to have positive and accurate identification of an individual. Bitter experience has taught us that redundancy in identification is the only way in which a positive check can be maintained on the accuracy of file integration; that is, in cases where we have a taxpayer's full name, his address, age, and social security account number we are able to determine that two successive tax-year records belong to the same individual. The identification of a person by social security account number corroborates the name, address, and age as identifying one person. If any one of these items is missing, errors in the reporting of social security number, age, variations in the manner of reporting the name (full name, first name and initials, initials only, etc.), or changes of address may make it impossible to integrate individual-year records that belong to a given taxpayer.

Keypunching

During the years 1946–1960 seven major changes were made by the State of Wisconsin in its forms for reporting individual income taxes, because

---

* This procedure was also used to pick up files that had been previously misfiled or returned from a special (inaccessible) archive used for taxpayers who had recently died (the tax records were returned after probate).

124 Case Studies in ... Complex Data Bases

of changes in the tax law and attempts to improve and simplify the reporting. Also, in most years different forms were available; both "short" and "long" forms for husbands (or single persons) and for wives. Although a single format for keypunching the returns might have facilitated later processing steps, it would have complicated the keypunching step itself considerably. Twenty-five or so separate formats seemed complicated, too. Five card formats were actually used (three for "long" forms and two for "short" forms), one for each group of years in which the forms were similar enough to enable keypunchers to punch the data with a minimum of searching on the returns. Assembly of single cards into records of a fixed format was postponed to the multicard-record-image creation step in which the various formats could be interpreted by the computer.

Feedback for Error Correction

The right-hand sides of Figures 7.1 and 7.2 indicate that each stage of the processing operation entails feedback of information to an earlier stage in the processing. The procedures used provide corrections to records that were incorrectly processed and check the adequacy of the original data-collection process.

One of the most interesting features of our data-checking systems was the use of the information in the tax record to diagnose and electronically correct certain kinds of systematic errors in the underlying reported data. A greatly simplified version of the logic of the tax form appears in the following set of equations:

$$\Sigma x = A, \tag{7.1}$$

$$A - (D, D_s)_{\max} = T, \tag{7.2}$$

$$D_s = \min, (0.09A, 450) \tag{7.3}$$

$$L = f(T) - P. \tag{7.4}$$

Individual income sources x are summed to arrive at adjusted gross income A. If itemized deduction D are not claimed, the standard deduction D_s must be equal to some amount based on the total amount of income. Taxable income T is computed as the difference between adjusted gross income and deductions. A tax function $f(T)$ is applied to the amount of taxable income to determine the gross tax liability. Lastly personal credits P are deducted to arrive at the net tax liability L. If any one of these conditions is violated by the numbers actually present on the form, the record is inconsistent. However, it may be that the logic of the form can reveal the underlying error; for example if the amount A was incorrectly transcribed from a computation sheet, Equation 7.2 could be satisfied by substituting the computed sum of sources (i.e., substitute for A in Equation 7.2). If the substitution produces a true statement, it is highly likely that an error of the type described has actually occurred. Alternatively, if Equation 7.2 is not valid because the amount D has been recorded without a correct decimal point, it may be possible to use Equation 7.3 to recalculate the appropriate deduction and determine that the taxpayer had made an error in computing his standard deduction. With this type of logic the consistency-checking program was able to reduce the number of records in which data were inconsistent by half, or from about 10 to 5 percent of all records. Indications of the size and nature of inconsistencies were kept so that the foibles of error-prone taxpayers could be studied.

Inter-personal and Inter-temporal Validation

Another type of consistency check was made possible by coded responses to questions asked of the taxpayer on the returns. Three of the questions were (1) "Did you file a 19— (preceding year) return?" and "If not, explain"; (2) "Spouse's name" and "Does spouse have separate income?"; (3) "If marriage took place in 19— (current year), give full name and address of spouse before marriage." Fourteen types of inter-year- and interperson-record inconsistency were checked for, using the coded responses and existence of returns. One such check was, "Wife says husband has separate income, husband's return not present." About 600 cases (0.6 percent of the total number of records) of this inconsistency were found. Some 200 resulted from data-transcription errors. The remaining 400 were a mixture of "missed" returns and errors or misinterpretations made by the taxpayer.*

FILE MAINTENANCE AND DOCUMENT HANDLING

In order to maintain the file we have developed a series of special-purpose programs that display the record in each file on call. We also are

---

* Some inconsistencies seemed to transcend the traditional bounds of social science research. Ronald O. Durant, who devised a scheme for checking these codes, described one case as "dead husband resurrected." This resulted from a spouse-died code (in year t), a spouse-present code (in $t+1$), but no marriage (during $t+1$). Thirty-eight resurrections were discovered. To our additional surprise one taxpayer was resurrected once a year for 11 consecutive years. Further investigation revealed that all of these resurrections were errors in transcribing the coded data onto the tape records.

able to correct any part of each basic file when errors are discovered by means of standard techniques.

Editing Program

The usefulness of the program is extended by a general program that assembles data from several records in a file or in several files to provide input for the card edit. This program was particularly useful in checking individual detail cards against individual summary cards in the social security benefit file. It is also useful for checking detailed items of property income against corresponding aggregates in the master file.

In the processing of our files we have found it necessary to maintain a double-entry bookkeeping system that accounts for the flow of all records through the processing operation and makes it possible to provide positive checks on the number of records accurately assembled into the file, the number waiting for correction, and any residual ones that may not yet have been processed. A similar system of bookkeeping for errors located in editing cards and tapes is also desirable.

Correction of Identification Numbers

An aggravating problem that developed in the processing of the file concerns numerous cases in which identification numbers had been incorrectly assigned. The problem can be most easily understood if one considers the problem that we now face in updating the master file for 1960–1964. Additional tax-year records must be assigned to the correct individual or else two non-over-lapping time series of income for two individuals will appear in the master file rather than one integrated series of years. If an incorrect assignment is detected, changing the identification number clearly implies that some procedure must be available for sweeping through the entire library of eight basic files described above and changing the identification number for a given person in all files. The change is accomplished by encoding a standard set of instruction cards, which are kept as part of our permanent files. The cards indicate the original and the revised identification numbers to be encoded on each individual's file entries in the different files. A pass of these identification-number-correction cards against any of the basic files results in either the elimination of duplicate or invalid records or a change in the identification number on certain records. The corrected records can then be resorted and merged with the unchanged records in identification-number and year sequence.

In the earlier data processing the problem of incorrect identification numbers arose from the use of the number as a device for integrating records belonging to all individuals in the same household. Sometimes individuals were not correctly grouped into households at the time of the original identification number assignment. In some cases such errors were detected as a result of finding (1) duplicate records for a given year, (2) inconsistencies between the identification number and sex or age data, or (3) incompatible address information. We are not attempting such an integration in updating the file, beyond identifying husband-wife pairs.

Units and File Integration

One of the major mechanical problems in dealing with such a large and diverse set of data files is that each of the first seven basic files contains a different number of "observations," thus several records in one file may correspond to one record in another file (several years of tax records in the master file correspond to one entry identifying a person in the identification file, and so forth). In order to facilitate the integration of these files a history-selection file of basic data on the information available about each person was extracted. The history-selection file contains all pertinent identification numbers and enables the user to cross-index data available on a given individual. By using the entry recorded in the history-selection file it is possible to select people by social security account number or by the identification number that we assigned. It is also possible to determine whether entries exist for persons in the tax-record file, in the property-income file, or in the social security benefit file, etc. The history-selection file thus provides a link between identification numbers and between records based on different units of analysis and different data-collection techniques. The links provided are illustrated in Figure 7.3. Further record-selection capabilities incorporated into the history-selection file are described subsequently.

ANALYSES OF THE ARCHIVE

So far the archive has been subject to limited analyses, restricted because only portions of the archive were in a form suitable for manipulation. From the preceding discussion it should be clear that difficult and time-consuming operations are necessary before a complex data file is suitable for analysis. However, a number of projects that take advantage of the multifile aspects of the archive are well into the planning stage. Some of the existing publications are discussed below.[2]

128   *Case Studies in . . . Complex Data Bases*

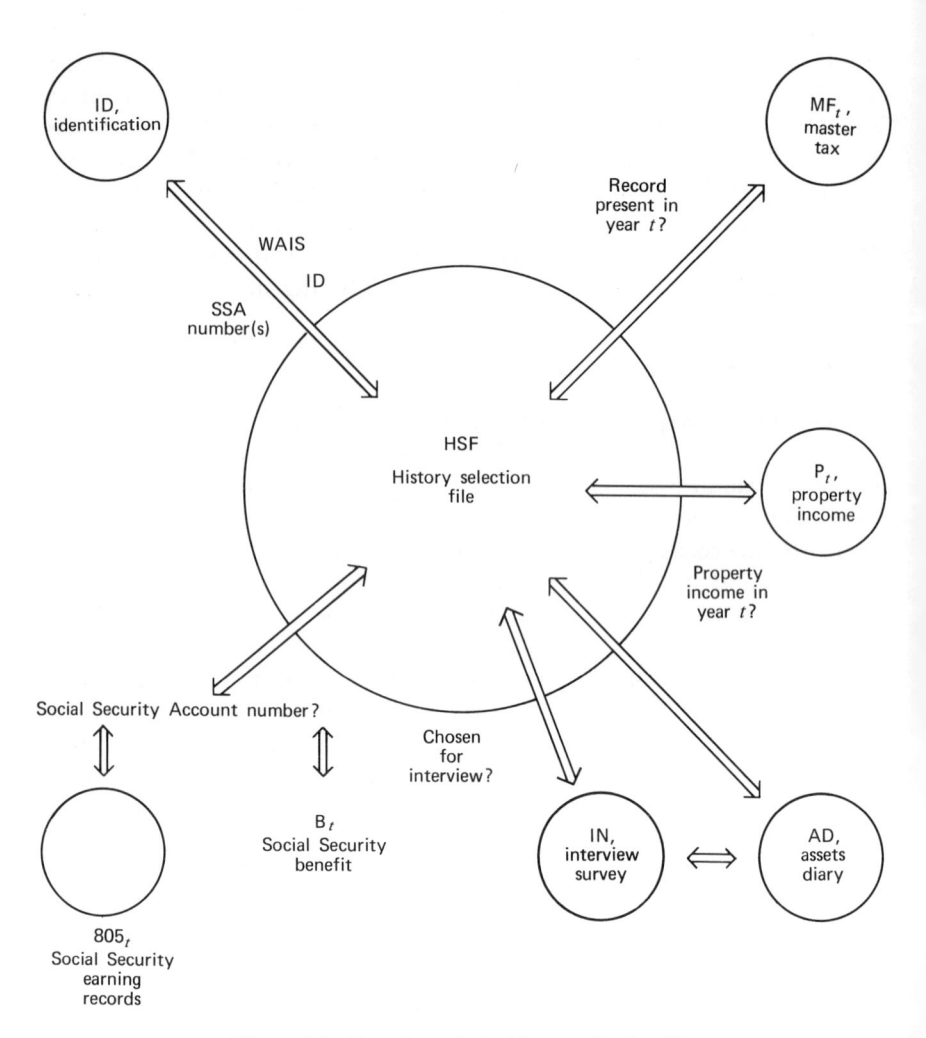

Figure 7.3 Functions of the history selection file.

File-Validity Studies

File-validity studies have two aspects. In the first place the files are regarded as samples from the population of Wisconsin taxpayers, and estimates of certain magnitudes for this population based on the archive data can be compared with comparable magnitudes derived from other sources to examine the extent to which differences exists. Where the comparable magnitudes are the actual population values, we obtain from this an estimate of the degree of "bias" involved in utilizing the sample data. These estimates can then be used as weights or correction factors.

The second aspect of the file-validity studies involves adding information to the file to permit generalization to populations other than the Wisconsin income-tax payers. To some extent this procedure involves the expansion of the file by inferences from the data that have been already collected. (See pp. 118–123.) The data concerning filing in prior years or filing by the spouse form at least a crude basis for inferring whether a taxpayer was in the Wisconsin population in years for which no tax return is present. Inclusion of such missing observations will make it possible to go some distance toward expanding the sample to the adult population of Wisconsin. Data from the social security benefit file can be used to the same end.

In addition the weights attached to the records may be modified so that they may be reinterpreted as samples from the population rather than samples of taxpayers. Basically this simply is an extension of the procedure described above, with the comparable magnitudes being derived from population as a whole. There are some very interesting theoretical questions raised by this procedure of population switching, which we hope to analyse and test in the near future.

A beginning toward such validity studies was undertaken by M. Eugene Moyer.[3] This study was primarily concerned with the analysis of various income distributions from the master file, from the state population of state tax returns, from the estimates of federal tax returns in Wisconsin *(Statistics of Income)*, and from the 1960 Census.

Other studies of file-validity are under way or planned. The most advanced is that for personal-interview survey file (which will also apply to the household-assets diary) because the great stratification of this subsample (together with nonresponse) made the development of weights an obvious necessity, and a first report of results (mailed to respondents) was a high-priority item.[4] A number of internal memoranda have been generated with regard to the validity of this file.

Property-Income Studies

Property-income studies concentrate on the income-earning assets that people hold, the detailed data being the content of the household-assets diary for interviewees and the property-income file for everyone in the sample reporting such income, as well as some less specific data included in the interview and master files. These are to be used with files having detailed price and income information (such as the Lori-Fisher data and Standard and Poor's Compustat) to reconstruct the individual portfolios that people hold, through time and by person. This will in turn be utilized with our income and demographic data to study portfolio-management behavior. Of particular interest is a study of the realization of capital gains. The above studies have generated a sizeable file of internal memoranda, which is being steadily expanded as we grapple with the problems involved. A model of portfolio behavior has also been developed.[5]

Another study utilizes the person-Interview file to examine whether or not the acquisition and holding of some assets in broad categories are independent of one another—and, if not, which type of relationship exists (complementary or substitute). This is the work of James A. Geffert for his Ph.D. dissertation. In it he is trying to discriminate amongst models of asset choice that are strictly random, random but lumpy, and deterministic.

Longitudinal Income Studies

Sources of Income Variability for Male Individuals in Wisconsin, 1947–1959,[6] by the authors of this chapter, represents a first look at the data on incomes in the master file. Exploratory models of the inter-temporal behavior of individual incomes are estimated, and the distributions of the parameters about their theoretical values are examined.

Expansion of these models to include analyses of husband-wife unit inter-temporal income patterns and analysis of information on nonfiling individuals is planned. Studies of income fluctuations by source and the development of relevant models are also under way.

An analysis in progress of the behavior of incomes at retirement from the labor force makes use of our data on social security benefits. The relation of preretirement to postretirement earnings is of particular interest, and we plan to investigate this relationship by using integrated data from our master and social security benefit files.

One study involving the inter-temporal behavior of the wage earnings of male Wisconsin taxpayers has been completed.[7]

Simulation of the Effects of Changes in the Tax Law

Computer simulation of the effects of the 1964 Tax Averaging Law on a subsample of persons included in our master file was successfully completed in early 1966 in a project financed by the U.S. Treasury Department. The effects of varying the definition of income, the definition of persons eligible for averaging, and several parameters in the 1964 law were tabulated by income classes and by selected demographic variables so that comparisons could be made of the effects of possible changes in the law. Further analyses of tax averaging are planned for both different averaging schemes and different analysis years (the simulation carried out was for the years 1954–1958).

Some plans have also been made for simulating the effects of changes in regulations concerning various deduction items, such as medical expenses.

SPECIAL DATA-PROCESSING PROBLEMS IN PARTICULAR SUBSTANTIVE ANALYSES

Several interesting problems have arisen in putting the data into a form suitable for the analysis of specific substantive problems. One such difficulty surrounded the translation of basic data on social security claims into a form that could be integrated with master-file income information. Such an integrated file would be essential to our studies of the relationship between preretirement and postretirement incomes. Social security claims data were presented as a record of the changes in the payment amount month by month. This record was inserted into a matrix of calendar months, and a record of actual payments in each month was reconstructed from the available information on changes in benefit payments. Subsequently monthly benefit payments were aggregated into calendar years to create a benefit-year record that could be integrated with tax information in the master file. However, such integration could not be achieved by merging records according to social security account number; for example, a widow could be receiving benefits from her husband's account, so that the benefits would be identified by his account number, and in that case it would be necessary to integrate benefit-payment information with the income-tax information supplied by the wife rather than the deceased husband. Thus an analysis of who received benefit payments and the determination of his or her identification number in the master tax file was necessary before benefit-year information could be integrated with other income information.

The existence of numerous gaps in the master tax file affords another example of the kinds of difficulties that arise in integrating data for analysis. No tax return appears in the file for persons who were out of state, unemployed, not working, or working and receiving incomes below the legal filing limit. In each of these instances gaps appear in the master file. Although the file represents the characteristics of taxpayers, it does not represent characteristics of the statewide adult population.

Nonfiling is a particular problem with respect to wives who do not work and with respect to the aged. Many wives never appear in the tax archive. Most of the aged cease filing tax returns after they retire. In an effort to expand the master file to account for such gaps we are analyzing data included in questions on the first page of the tax form concerning the filing of returns. Those questions provide cross references to the tax record obtained in the proceding and the tax record of the taxpayer's spouse. In many instances use of this cross-referencing system enables us to infer that records of spouses or records of earlier years should have appeared in the file and are not available. In other cases we can infer that such records should not exist and income in the year in question is small or zero. By using such data it is possible to extend the file and to obtain a far more interesting picture of, say, the income patterns of intermittently working wives. Coded indicators of the explanations for record gaps are derived and inserted into the history-selection file so that gap-plugging records can be imputed and analyzed along with existing tax-year records. This is the file-expansion procedure mentioned previously in connection with validation of the data.

MORE GENERAL PROBLEMS

This project has been enormously time consuming and expensive, but it has also been highly rewarding in many ways. Some of the rewards are just appearing in the form of substantive studies, and we feel that this ultimate payoff will repay the cost many times over. Even without this substantive payoff, however, there have been rewards of another sort.

From one point of view WAIS has been a tremendous educational experience and a valuable pilot project for similar data collection and integration projects such as that proposed for a federal statistical data center.[8] (See chapter 4.) Like all learning experiences, ours have often been painful, and as good educators we pass along the things we think others should beware of to spare them needless frustrations.

Some of our most exasperating difficulties have been associated with the fact that we are embedded in a university in a time of great technological change. One aspect of this is the need to pursue independent financing on a piecemeal basis. The fact that we initially substantially underestimated the costs involved exacerbated this difficulty, and a disproportionate amount of the energies of the principals (particularly the present authors) were devoted to the fund-raising task. What really is needed is a continuing commitment from some foundation that will recognize the value of these data and provide long-range support for their collection and processing. A university, particularly a state university, finds it difficult to shoulder this burden when it is in a constant struggle to find adequate financing for its strictly educational purposes and must distribute its limited free research funds among many competing groups with worthwhile projects.*

The lack of assured continuity of financing has prevented us from building a substantial staff of experts in the various data-processing skills. Indeed we have had considerable fluctuations in the number of persons on the staff and turnover of personnel typical of the part-time graduate staff available in a university setting. In this respect we were fortunate to be associated with an excellent university and we were able to recruit students who also had short time horizons (although some of them had their horizons extended by their involvement with WAIS). They were intelligent and they tended to have a high learning capacity; some had been already partially trained as programmers. On the other hand, as our project progressed and became more complex, it required an increasing investment to train new personnel. We now feel that we have reached the point at which the usual pattern of hiring, training, and utilizing personnel is very close to the point of zero returns—by the time they are trained and fully informed as to our file structure and its interdependencies, many of our staff are close to leaving! Our response is to hire persons with technical backgrounds that make them more fully pre-trained, more quickly trainable, and much more expensive.*

A related difficulty is the constant change and modification of computer equipment and its associated software with which we have been faced. Formats and codes easily interpreted by IBM 1410 are unacceptable to the CDC 3600. An excellent Autocoder (1410) programmer finds himself at sea in FORTRAN (3600). The intervening CDC 1604 and the yet-to-arrive Burroughs 8500 are added complications to a project that had only an IBM 650 available at its inception! This is complicated by

---

* We think that the support we have received from the University of Wisconsin has been extraordinary in this respect. It has maintained the effort at critical stages in the research.

* At this point, however, we run up against two new problems. The university has an established pay scale for students, and as a state university we are subject to civil service regulations and pay scales for nonstudents. In addition the best qualified students get fellowships and cannot be hired!

the necessity to choose between one-shot special-purpose programs and more generalized and repetitive programs. Will the language of the general program survive the next change in computer technology? And what does it matter if extract routines are generalized but financing is about to expire? The bias here has been toward special programs, but we are aware of the long-run sacrifice involved, although some of our file-maintenance programs are generalized. Hopefully, the decision to make all University of Wisconsin machines compile both COBOL and FORTRAN will alleviate this situation and make us machine independent.

Another problem with the maintenance of a "permanent" and growing set of files such as ours only recently came to light in connection with another large-scale project (though not as complex as WAIS) in which one of the authors of this chapter was engaged. In this case four identical binary coded decimal tapes were developed and sent to and stored in four separate locations: the University of Wisconsin in Madison, the IBM Service Bureau Corporation in Chicago, and the Federal Reserve Board and Department of Justice in Washington. Within two years *all four* of the tapes had deteriorated to the extent that they were *unusable!* Fortunately in this instance the IBM Service Bureau Corporation (which had generated the original tapes) was able to reconstruct the tapes because the deterioration-caused read errors were never in the same locations on two of the original tapes. However, it takes little imagination to realize the terror that this news struck to the hearts of WAIS's principal investigators, who had tremendous *personal* and intellectual investment in WAIS's tapes, including our sacrosanct backup tapes, which were to be used only in case of an error that might damage our working tapes.*

PROBLEMS OF CONFIDENTIALITY AND DATA RELEASE

One of the most difficult obstacles to the establishment of a national data bank concerns the extent to which it involves an invasion of the privacy of individuals.[9] The similarity between the proposed federal statistical data center and the WAIS files makes our own experience in this respect of some importance, although by tradition (if not by temperament) Wisconsin is not typical of the United States as a whole.

The first element in our protection of confidentiality is to keep actual identifying information in separate, inaccessible, and unreleased files. The

---

* As a result Wisconsin's Data and Program Library Unit, a cooperative data archive, has instituted procedures for continual checking and renewal of its files on new tapes.

reproduced tax forms are stored in locked files in rooms that are locked when not in use. The identification tape files are similarly protected. The remaining data files contain our identification number for cross-referencing. We are obligated to make some of the data files available to other social scientists on a marginal cost basis, primarily the master and property-income files. When doing so it will be necessary to remove identifying information contained in the records (other than our identification number, of course). Clearly the social security numbers of the individuals represent one such nonreleasable datum.

The possibility will still exist of course that the person's set of "nonidentifying" data itself may in fact reveal his identity. Without prohibitively expensive investigation no one could ever be absolutely sure that this would not occur unless the variables were recorded into classes in such a way that every possibly distinguishable cell in a cross tabulation would necessarily contain several (at least three) observations. The loss of significant detail involved in such recoding would be extreme, as can be realized when one considers that it would have to be applied to the entire set of years and not just to any one year.[10] Although we have not fully resolved this issue, our present thinking is that suitable restrictions on the *use* of the data, as opposed to access to the data, can be implemented in such a way as to protect individuals from disclosure of their personal data.[11] Naturally we feel constrained at present to prevent access to any of the data that are potentially revealing, until restrictions on use are more fully explored and a protection system is implemented.

Obviously the greater the detail about any person, the more potentially revealing the data are. This is one of the difficulties with providing access to such supplementary data as the personal-interview and household asset diary files.* Given appropriate restrictions on use, however, no new problems are raised by such access.

A somewhat different problem arises in connection with the social security benefit and wage-earnings-record files. These are strictly nonreleasable due to the contractual terms under which they were obtained. For these files, therefore, no confidentiality or release problem exists (at least from our point of view).

In the interest of wide and thorough analysis of both the data archive and selected data from the Social Security Administration files it is our hope that a nonsensitive release of those data can be developed by responsible officials of the Social Security Administration.

---

* A subsidiary problem here is that these files were never properly financed, so that somewhat more than purely marginal cost may have to be charged for them.

REFERENCES

1. See S. J. Farber, "Changes in Annual Wage Credits as Workers Age—A Cohort Analysis," *American Statistical Association: Proceedings of 1963 Annual Meeting.*
2. See also J. Geffert, "Computerized Error Correction Applied to Tax Returns," *The Tax Executive,* October 1966; and M. E. Moyer, *The Processing of Data from a Multi-Year Sample of Wisconsin Tax Returns,* WAIS Monograph 2, Madison, Wisc., 1966.
3. M. E. Moyer, *The Validity of Income Distributions from a Multi-Year Sample of Wisconsin Income Tax Returns,* WAIS Monograph 1, Madison, Wisc., 1966.
4. Wisconsin Survey Research Laboratory and WAIS, *A Report on the Economic Study.* Madison, Wisc.: University of Wisconsin, 1967.
5. R. F. Miller and H. W. Watts, "A Model of Household Investment in Financial Assets," in *Determinants of Investment Behavior,* Universities–National Bureau Conference Series No. 18, National Bureau of Economic Research, 1967, pp. 357–380.
6. M. David, R. Miller, and R. Bauman, *Sources of Income Variability for Male Individuals in Wisconsin, 1947–1959,* presented to the Universities–National Bureau Conference on Income and Wealth, March 1967 (obtainable as Research on the Economic Behavior of Households Workshop Paper No. 6704, Social Systems Research Institute, University of Wisconsin, Madison).
7. R. O. Durant, *An Analysis of Earnings Dynamics of Wisconsin Taxpayers for the Period 1948–1960,* Ph.D. dissertation, University of Wisconsin, 1965.
8. See, for example, E. Glaser, D. Rosenblatt, and M. K. Wood, "The Design of a Federal Statistical Data Center," *The American Statistician,* 21, No. 1, (February 1967), pp. 12–20.
9. For extended discussions of these problems of confidentiality and release of personal data see E. S. Dunn, Jr., "The Idea of a National Data Center and the Issue of Personal Privacy," *The American Statistician,* 21, *No.* 1 (February 1967), pp. 21–27; and R. F. Miller, *Confidentiality and Usability of Complex Data Bases,* Systems Formulation and Methodology Workshop Paper 6702. Madison, Wisc.: Social Systems Research Institute, University of Wisconsin, May 1967.
10. A general discussion of the efficacy of recoding for nondisclosure is given by R. F. Miller, ref. 9. A particular application is contained in R. F. Miller, "The Recoding of the Federal Reserve Board Business Loan Surveys of 1955 and 1957."
11. Again see R. F. Miller, ref. 9, for a general discussion of restrictions on use and on access.

Part IV Computer Systems for Managing Complex Data Structures

Developing computer systems for handling large, complex data bases is not something the individual researcher or small analysis project is likely ever to undertake. Designing, implementing, testing, documenting, and maintaining such a system for modern computers requires a complex social organization and tens or, more accurately hundreds, of thousands of dollars.

Chapters 8 and 9 describe two computer systems for handling complex data structures. There is surprisingly little technical detail, as both authors concentrate on showing what a user can do with a set of commands for creating, maintaining, destroying, merging, and doing other things with computer-stored data files and sets of such files. The Castleman chapter describes an interactive system, whereas the Braddock chapter summarizes batch-process-oriented facilities.

The described systems were developed by commercial organizations, and there is a secondary message in that.

Chapter Eight

Data Management Techniques for the Social Sciences*

Paul A. Castleman†

The general-purpose data-management system described here has been in operation for over two years. It is used to store and retrieve automatically information in complex-structured data files. Several of the system's file-structure, input, and retrieval techniques are particularly useful for social science data management. Beyond the internal mechanics of this system, its interface between the computer and the human problem solver illustrates techniques for delivering a data-management tool directly to noncomputer professionals. The first section describes the

---

* Work reported here was performed at Bolt Beranek and Newman, Inc., Cambridge, Massachusetts, under contract PH43-62-850 with the National Institutes of Health, Public Health Service., U.S. Department of Health, Education, and Welfare.
† Bolt Beranek and Newman, Cambridge, Massachusetts.

140   Systems for Managing Complex Data Structures

functions of this data-management system and its human engineering provisions. Then, after a discussion of specific data-handling techniques, an actual example is presented.

THE DATA-MANAGEMENT SYSTEM

The system runs on a time-shared computer, servicing up to 64 users simultaneously. At scattered Teletype terminals users interact directly with the central computer. Because the system is shared and all data are continually on line, a user can manipulate his private files and also participate in maintaining a shared data base.

The language of the system is a conversational English dialogue. The computer asks questions and the user supplies answers that specify his data structure, input restrictions, retrieval population selectors, and output format. One advantage of the language is that computer laymen use the system without professional programmer intermediaries. Another advantage is that the language is nonprocedural; while the data-management programs remain in procedural control user-type responses specialize or modulate the predefined procedures, and improper user answers are immediately detected and corrected. The debugging step necessary in directly programming algorithms and procedures is eliminated. These points should become more clear in the later illustrations of system operations.

There are three phases in the information-handling cycle of the data-management system: the description of the data structure and format, the introduction of data into a user's file (according to the description), and the selective retrieval of data from the file. Each phase is performed by a separate program, which interacts with the user at his Teletype. The user runs the description program once to establish his file; thereafter he can run the input-and-retrieval program many times.

The file-description program sets up the structural skeleton for a user's file and specifies the format of data to be assimilated. By running the description program the user in effect "writes" the input program for his file. A file is a collection of structurally identical entries, or records. Each record comprises pieces of data, or fields. Files, records, and fields are of variable length. Internally the fields within a record have a two-level tree structure, which can have any number of branches. The file structure of the data-management system is illustrated in Figure 8.1. With the file-description program the user specifies the following

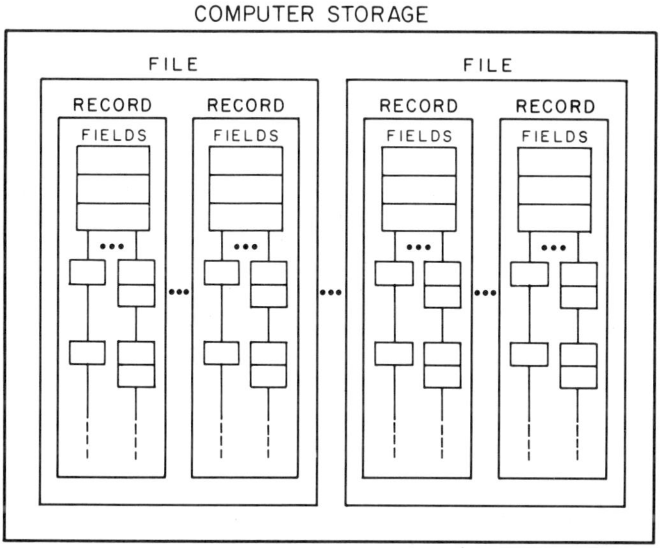

Data Management Techniques for the Social Sciences   141

Figure 8.1 Data-management-system file structure.

properties of each field: name (e.g., ID NUMBER, BIRTHDATE, SEX), position in the record's tree structure (single- or multi-valued field), data type (integer, decimal number, date, or text), input location on punched cards, and configuration of acceptable values.

Using the card-input program a social science researcher can easily assimilate into his file large volumes of keypunched data from a variety of different sources. Another program accepts Teletype input for file updating.

The retrieval program prints out either all fields or selected fields from the population of records of interest to the user. The program can also compile interrecord summations of field values for samples of interest within the retrieval population. The summations for each field are printed in a two-dimensional matrix.

In addition to the three primary informational-handling functions there are several ancillary programs in the data-management system that index records in a file, restructure the data in a file, preserve a file on magnetic tape, and perfrom algebraic operations via a JOSS-language interpreter.[1]

The next section describes the file structure and input techniques

142 Systems for Managing Complex Data Structures

for building useful social science data files. Features in the retrieval program that allow meaningful searches and interpreting of encoded information are also discussed.

DATA-MANAGEMENT TECHNIQUES

When a user defines his file structure with the description program he describes the information fields that will constitute the records in his file. The description of each field specifies what the information will look like and where it will come from during the input phase. Initially the user defines different input-card types. Then, to identify the source of each field, he specifies a card-column location on a particular card type. This card-column location has several uses for building a social science data base.

If a researcher has related punched card data from several sources in different formats, he can easily merge the data into single computer file by identifying the format of each distinct group of input cards as a different card type. The card-column location can be used as a selector

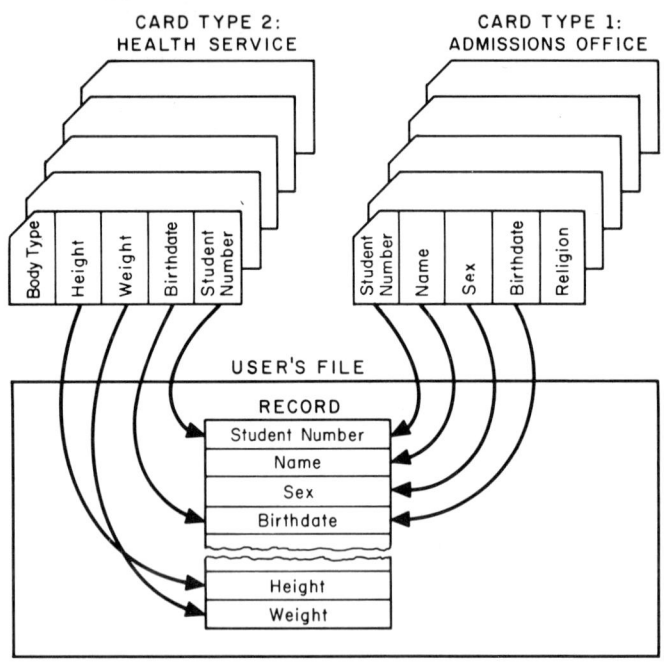

Figure 8.2 Merging different card types.

Data Management Techniques for the Social Sciences   143

to glean portions of existing data on cards into the research file; for example, as illustrated in Figure 8.2, only certain fields are extracted from the input cards. Data in columns not included in any card-column location are ignored. In Figure 8.2, religion data from the admissions office cards and body-type data from the health office cards are not included in the file.

The card-column location can also be used for introducing the same field from two or more card types and cross-checking the duplicated information at the same time. For example, a university researcher may be constructing a file of student records, merging two existing types of data cards. If the student's birthdate appears on both card types, the researcher may specify the origin of the birthdate field as particular column locations on both card types. Note that in Figure 8.2 birthdate is entered into the file from both card types. At input time whichever card type is encountered first for the student supplies the value for the birthdate field. When the second card type is encountered its birthdate value is compared to the first. If it disagrees, its value is rejected by the input program, and a message noting the disagreement is printed immediately at the user's Teletype. After verifying the discrepancy the user can correct the value that was entered in the file, if necessary, with the Teletype input program.

Another effect of the user's specifying the card type and column location for each field is that the information on every input card is uniquely earmarked to be read by the input program. The cards can be input in any order; no particular card type need precede another, and, in fact, the input cards can be accidentally shuffled. Different card types can even be entered at separate times. The card types in the first input batch will partially fill the data base, and the remaining card types will later complete it.

Using the description program the user also defines the acceptable configuration of values for each field. The configuration is specified as an edit picture, or syntax definition, of the field.[2] Input data that do not conform to the syntax definition for the field are rejected. The user also specifies one field common to all input cards, which identifies the record. All cards with the same record-identifying field are merged into a single record. In Figure 8.2 the student number is the record-identifying field.

If a researcher has a large body of input data, he can incorporate a subset of the data into his file by applying a selective syntax definition to the record-identifying field. For example, a card file exists in which each record is identified by a five-digit number. A researcher

144 Systems for Managing Complex Data Structures

may want to construct a file containing only records whose identifying numbers begin with the digits 65. Clearly the cards could be mechanically sorted and only the relevant cards submitted as input to the computer. In this case the syntax definition for the record-identifying field would accept any five-digit number. However, the researcher could specify only the desired subset of cards—that is, identifying numbers beginning with 65—as the syntax definition for the record-identifying field. In this case all the cards could be retained intact and submitted as input; only the desired cards would be absorbed into the file.

Another feature that is especially useful for handling complex social science data is employed during the input phase. Using this feature a researcher may construct a file by entering a small body of input data and then augmenting it with pertinent information extracted from a larger set of cards. The file structure is defined to include fields from both sources. Then the smaller group of data is entered. Note that, if all the data were entered together, the records for which there were cards in both input groups would be completed, but many partially filled and extraneous records would be generated by the remaining cards in the large input group. Consequently the input program offers an *update-only* option by which fields are added to the file only for already existing records. When the large group of cards is entered by using update only, only the cards corresponding to the records established by the small input group are accepted. For example, a university researcher maintains a file of student records. The file is initially created with student-admissions data from the School of Engineering; however, provision is made in the file structure for health information on each student. The health office data contain the medical information for all university students. The pertinent data—namely, the cards for engineering students—are mingled with the health data of nonengineering students. Using update only the input program extracts from the large body of health office data only cards for existing records—that is, health information on engineering students. In Figure 8.3, a schematic illustration of the update-only process, student numbers 65002, 65005, and 65007 are engineering students.

In the retrieval phase the user selects a subset (or population) of the data base for retrieval and specifies either full or abstracted output records. Users write descriptor statements to define their retrieval populations in terms of the field values of desired records. For example, the descriptor SEX-MALE is a criterion for retrieving

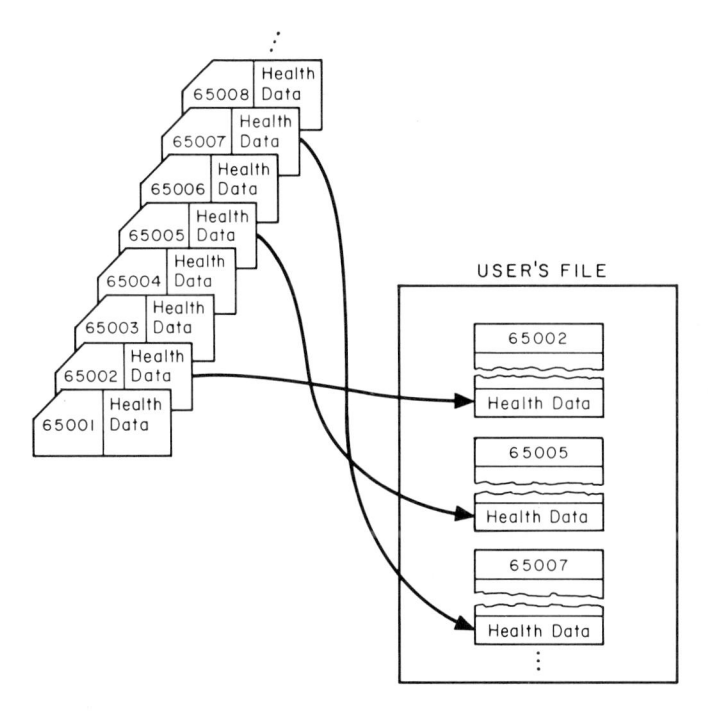

Data Management Techniques for the Social Sciences 145

Figure 8.3 Adding health data, using update only.

all the records in which MALE is the value of the data field called SEX. Simple descriptors may be combined by using Boolean operators to construct more discriminating descriptors such as, for example, SEX-MALE AND AGE < 18 AND REMARKS CONTAIN "HOSTIL" Note that descriptors can use the text-handling operator CONTAINS in addition to algebraic operators.

The retrieval program can also summarize the values of selected fields in the retrieval population of records and can compile an output matrix of the summations. Fields can be summed over the entire retrieval population or over samples of records within the population. The summation matrix is defined by a field-value descriptor for each row and column. Each element in the matrix is the sum of the specified field values for a sample defined by the intersection of its row and column descriptors. For example, a researcher has a file of student records in which each record contains the student's grade average and family income. The researcher wants to count the number of students who come from high-income families and who have high, medium, and low averages. The matrix is constructed with three rows and two columns. The field-value descriptors for the rows specify high, medium, and low grade averages. The descriptors for the columns specify high income and other income. The student count in the output matrix then has the following configuration:

High average and high income	High average and not high income
Medium average and high income	Medium average and not high income
Low average and high income	Low average and not high income

Some data (e.g., regional codes) are often punched in coded form instead of text. The data-management system has a facility for interpreting pre-encoded information at retrieval time. If a researcher accumulates social science data containing encoded information, he can enter the original data into his file but produce output reports that contain English equivalents of the original codes. The mechanism for output code conversion is a dictionary lookup by the retrieval program. The dictionary is created by the user and stored in the computer. It contains the text equivalents for coded information. Dictionaries are independent of specific user files. A dictionary may be created before or after a file exists. A single retrieval of a file may reference multiple dictionaries; separate retrievals of a file may use different dictionaries each time to interpret the same codes. When the user specifies the fields from each retrieval record to be abstracted into the output report, he indicates which fields should be looked up and references the appropriate dictionary. The retrieval program extracts from the dictionary the text corresponding to the specified field-value codes and prints the text.

SAMPLE PROBLEM

The following example is a hypothetical complex-data-base problem that illustrates the data-management techniques described above. A social scientist is conducting a study of student achievement for the engineering admissions office of a university. A file of student records is constructed for engineering students in the class of 1965. Input to the file is obtained from three sources: admissions office, health service,

Data Management Techniques for the Social Sciences 147

and registrar's office. The admissions office data consists of two types of cards for each student: one card contains background information; the other contains the preadmission interviewer's remarks. These cards are not arranged by class but in some other order (e.g., alphabetical) and include the engineering classes of 1964–1967. Only the cards for the class of 1965 are relevant to the study. The arrangement of information on the engineering admissions office cards is shown in Figures 8.4a and b. The health service data consist of one card for each student, shown in Figure 8.4c. There is one health service card for each student in the university; therefore not all these cards will pertain to engineering students. The registrar's office data, shown in Figure 8.4d, comprise one card for every course taken by an engineering student. Like the admissions office cards, these cards pertain to the classes of 1964–1967.

Describing the user's file is the first step in creating the data base. The "conversation" with the file-description program is shown in Figures 8.5a–d. At his terminal the user types answers to the numbered questions printed by the program. For clarity, user answers are illus-

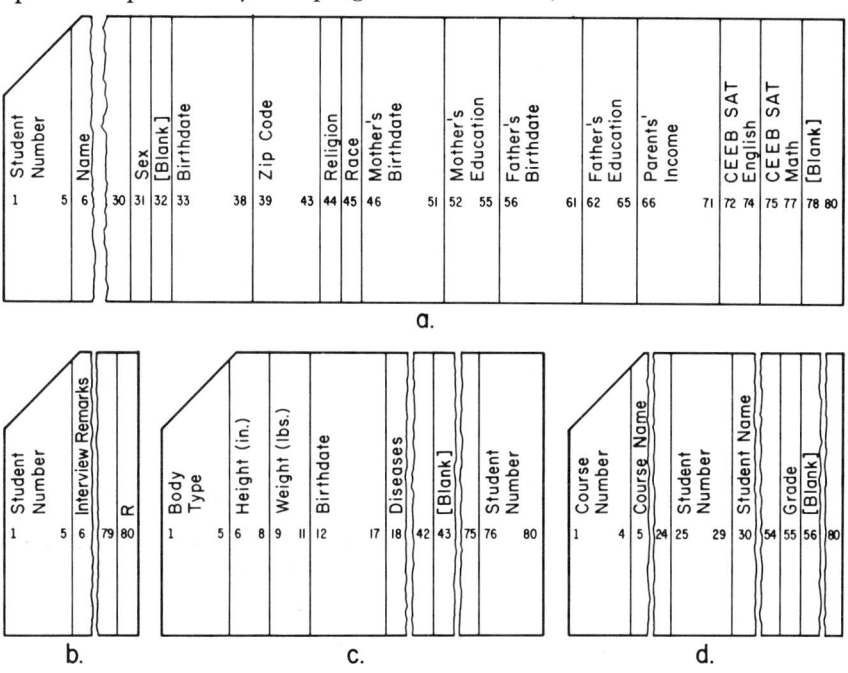

Figure 8.4 Input cards. (a) Admissions office—card type 1. (b) Admissions office remarks—card type 3. (c) Health service—card type 2. (d) Registrar's office—card type 4.

148 Systems for Managing Complex Data Structures

```
1:39 PM 6/9 BBN12-12
RISDES SGT
FILE FORMAT DESCRIPTION


0A  →/L
0A FILE TITLE: STUDENT ACHIEVEMENT
0B CONFIDENTIAL CODE:  BBN
0C NO. OF CARD-TYPES:  4
   0C1 DEFINING COLUMNS FOR TYPE # 1: 33-38,79-80
      0C1A SYNTAX DEF: 999999##
            TRY ME:   092345   ...OK.
            TRY ME:   09WW42   ...NOT OK.
            TRY ME:   03245698...NOT OK.
   0C2 DEFINING COLUMNS FOR TYPE # 2: 1-5
      0C2A SYNTAX DEF: AAAAA
            TRY ME:
   0C3 DEFINING COLUMNS FOR TYPE # 3: 80
      0C3A SYNTAX DEF: "R"
            TRY ME:   R...OK.
            TRY ME:
   0C4 TYPE # 4 IS ASSUMED TO BE ALL THE OTHERS.
1 FIELD # 1 NAME: STUDENT NO.
 1A UNIQUE TO RECORD? Y
 1B TYPE: →HOW TYPE INTEGER, DECIMAL NUMBER, DATE, OR REGULAR.
 1B  R
 1C CARD TYPE: 1,3
 1D COLUMNS: 1-5
 1E CARD TYPE: 2
 1F COLUMNS: 76-80
 1G CARD TYPE: 4
 1H COLUMNS: 25-29
 1I SYNTAX DEF:  "65"999;#####
           TRY ME:
2 FIELD # 2 NAME: STUDENT NAME
 2A UNIQUE TO RECORD? Y
 2B TYPE: R
 2C CARD TYPE: 1
 2D COLUMNS: 6-30
 2E CARD TYPE:
 2F SYNTAX DEF: XXXXXXXXXXXXXXXXXXXXXXXXX=<T>
           TRY ME:
```

Figure 8.5 (a) File-description program.

trated in red. In questions numbered $\emptyset$C3–$\emptyset$C4 four different input-card types are defined,* corresponding to the four card layouts illustrated above. (Data from all four card types are merged into the file during the input phase.)

After the card types are defined the user establishes the structure and format of each record by specifying the characteristics of each field. The first field described in Figure 8.5 is student number. Its characteristics are name (question 1), position in the record's tree structure (1B—note user's request for directions), input-card locations (1C–1H),

---

* Admissions office cards (type 1), health service cards (type 2), admissions office cards (type 3), registrar's office cards (type 4).

```
 3 FIELD # 3 NAME:SEX
 3A UNIQUE TO RECORD? Y
 3B TYPE: R
 3C CARD TYPE: 1
 3D COLUMNS: 31
 3E CARD TYPE:
 3F SYNTAX DEF: "M";"F";#
         TRY ME:
 4 FIELD # 4 NAME:BIRTHDATE
 4A UNIQUE TO RECORD? Y
 4B TYPE: DATE
 4C CARD TYPE: 1
 4D COLUMNS: 33-38
 4E CARD TYPE: 2
 4F COLUMNS: 12-18 NO. OF COLUMNS MUST
BE THE SAME AS IN OTHER TYPES FOR THIS FIELD.
 4F 12-17
 4G CARD TYPE:
 4H SYNTAX DEF: 99I"/"99I"/19"99;######
         TRY ME:  092345...OK....FILED AS:   09/23/1945
         TRY ME:  022965...OK.    BUT ITS NOT OF THE TYPE INDICATED.
...FILED AS 02/29/1965
         TRY ME:  022865...OK....FILED AS  02/28/1965
         TRY ME:
 5 FIELD # 5 NAME:HOME
 5A UNIQUE TO RECORD? Y
 5B TYPE: R
 5C CARD TYPE: 1
 5D COLUMNS: 39-43
 5E CARD TYPE:
 5F SYNTAX DEF:  99999;#####
         TRY ME:
 6 FIELD # 6 NAME:CEEB ENGLISH
 6A UNIQUE TO RECORD? Y
 6B TYPE: I
 6C CARD TYPE: 1
 6D COLUMNS: 72-74
 6E CARD TYPE:
 6F SYNTAX DEF: XXX
         TRY ME:
 7 FIELD # 7 NAME:CEEB MATH
 7A UNIQUE TO RECORD? Y
 7B TYPE: I
 7C CARD TYPE: 1
 7D COLUMNS: 75-77
 7E CARD TYPE:
 7F SYNTAX DEF: XXX
         TRY ME:
```

Figure 8.5 (b) File-description program (continued).

and format criteria (1I). The other fields are similarly described. As in the simple example of Figure 8.2, some data are not assimilated into the file from cards (e.g., religion, race, and parents' birthdates on admissions office cards). Other fields are selected from more than one card type; for example, birthdate is taken from admissions office (4C) and health service cards (4E). The field containing student number is derived from all four card types. This is the identifying field for each record and is so defined in question 16. The first two digits of each

```
 8 FIELD # 8 NAME: PARENTS' INCOME
 8A UNIQUE TO RECORD? Y
 8B TYPE: DN
 8C CARD TYPE: 1
 8D COLUMNS: 66-71
 8E CARD TYPE:
 8F SYNTAX DEF: XXXXXX
        TRY ME:
 9 FIELD # 9 NAME: INTERVIEW REMARKS
 9A UNIQUE TO RECORD? N
 9B TYPE: R
 9C CARD TYPE: 3
 9D COLUMNS: 6-79
 9E SYNTAX DEF: <T>XXXXXXXXXXXXXXXXXXXXXXXXXXXXXXXXXXXXXXXXXXXXXXI"  "
        TRY ME:
10 FIELD # 10 NAME: COURSE NAME
10A UNIQUE TO RECORD? N
10B TYPE: R
10C CARD TYPE: 4
10D COLUMNS: 5-24
10E SYNTAX DEF: XXXXXXXXXXXXXXXXXXXX
        TRY ME:
11 FIELD # 11 NAME: COURSE NO.
11A UNIQUE TO RECORD? N
11B TYPE R
11C CARD TYPE: 4
11D COLUMNS: 1-4
11E SYNTAX DEF: XXXX
        TRY ME:
12 FIELD # 12 NAME: GRADE
12A UNIQUE TO RECORD? N
12B TYPE: I
12C CARD TYPE: 4
12D COLUMNS: 55
12E SYNTAX DEF: X
        TRY ME:
13 FIELD # 13 NAME: HEIGHT
13A UNIQUE TO RECORD? Y
13B TYPE: DN
13C CARD TYPE: 2
13D COLUMNS: 6-8
13E CARD TYPE:
13F SYNTAX DEF: XXX
        TRY ME:
```

Figure 8.5 (c) File-description program (continued).

student number denote the class year. Because the admissions office and registrar's office data span several classes, the syntax definition for the record-identifying field will select only cards with student numbers beginning with the digits 65 (1I and 16G).

Question 17 defines course name, course number, and grade as a group of related fields. This further refinement in the record structure establishes a logical relation between the fields for retrieval purposes. For example, a retrieval descriptor to select records in which course name contains physics and grade equals 4 will include in the population only records containing the grade 4 for a physics course. If these fields were not grouped, the same descriptor would include in the population records

Data Management Techniques for the Social Sciences 151

```
14 FIELD # 14 NAME: WEIGHT
14A UNIQUE TO RECORD? Y
14B TYPE: I
14C CARD TYPE: 2
14D COLUMNS: 9-11
14E CARD TYPE:
14F SYNTAX DEF: XXX
        TRY ME:
15 FIELD # 15 NAME: DISEASES
15A UNIQUE TO RECORD? Y
15B TYPE: R
15C CARD TYPE: 2
15D COLUMNS: 18-42
15E SYNTAX DEF: <T>
        TRY ME:
16 FIELD # 16 NAME: RECORD-IDENTIFYING FIELD:
16A CARD TYPE: 1,3
16B COLUMNS: 1-5
16C CARD TYPE: 2
16D COLUMNS: 76-80
16E CARD TYPE: 4
16F COLUMNS: 25-29
16G SYNTAX DEF: "65"999
        TRY ME:
17 GROUP NAME: REPORT
17A FIELDS IN THIS GROUP: 10,11,12
18 GROUP NAME:


         16  STUDENT ACHIEVEMENT   (SGT)    1:39 PM 6/9/1967
2:02 PM
```

Figure 8.5 (d) File-description program (continued).

containing any grade in a physics course in addition to a grade of 4 in any other course.

Input is the next data-handling phase. In this particular data-management problem input is performed in two steps. In the first step the admissions office and registrar's office data are entered into the user's file. The interaction between the researcher and the input program is shown in Figure 8.6. Both groups of cards were stored together as images on

```
2:10 PM 6/9 BBN7-7
RISCDIX SGT

CARD INPUT
1 REEL NUMBER? 423
2 NUMBER OF FILE ON TAPE? 1
3 STARTING CARD? 1

1 FILE: 16  STUDENT ACHIEVEMENT (SGT)   1:39 PM 6/9/1967
  1A CONFIDENTIAL CODE: SGT   FIX
  1A IBM   FIX
  1A BBN
1 UPDATE ONLY? N

2:44 PM
```

Figure 8.6 Card-input program.

```
2:50 PM 6/9 BBN7-7
RISCDIX SGT

CARD INPUT
1 REEL NUMBER? 423
2 NUMBER OF FILE ON TAPE? 2
3 STARTING CARD? 1

1 FILE: 16   STUDENT ACHIEVEMENT (SGT)   2:10 PM 6/9/1967
1A CONFIDENTIAL CODE: BBN
1 UPDATE ONLY? Y

CARD 621 COL 12

3:25 PM
```

Figure 8.7 Card-input program (second run).

magnetic tape. The syntax definition that the researcher established for the record-identifying field selects only information from cards in which student number begins with 65. Consequently the records for engineering students in the class of 1965 are partially created from the two groups of input cards. The health-service cards are not included in the first input step. Although the health service cards all have student numbers that begin with 65 and therefore satisfy the definition for record-identifying field, they include numbers for nonengineering students. If all the health service cards were absorbed into the file, the cards for students not in the school of engineering would create records for which no engineering admissions office and registrar's office data are present or even desired. Health service data are therefore entered in the second input step, using update only (Figure 8.7).

The error message at the bottom of the printout in Figure 8.7 indicates that data beginning in column 12 of the 621st card conflicted with information already in the file and therefore were not entered. On health service cards the birthdate field begins in column 12. Card 621 has student number (record-identifying field) 65112. When the researcher checked the admissions office card for student 65112, he found that the student's birthdate had been erroneously entered in the file as 3/28/43. The value punched on the health-service card, 2/28/43, was in fact correct.

The researcher then called the Teletype input program (Figure 8.8) to enter the correct birthdate into record 65112. First the user committed a typographical error (question 5) and typed 2/29/43. The program recognized that this value was not a legitimate date (because 1943 was not a leap year), printed FIX, and reasked the question. The user then entered the correct birthdate.

Data Management Techniques for the Social Sciences   153

```
3:40 PM  6/9  BBN7-7
RISTTI SGT

TELETYPE INPUT

1 FILE: 16   STUDENT ACHIEVEMENT (SGT)   2:50 PM 6/9/1967
  1A CONF. CODE: BBN
  1A REC-ID: 65112 (OLD)
2   STUDENT NO.:
3   STUDENT NAME:
4   SEX:
5   BIRTHDATE: 022943 FIX
5   022843
6   HOME: -NR
  1A REC-ID:

3:43 PM
```

Figure 8.8 Making corrections with Teletype input program.

Once the data base is created, the retrieval program is used to print out records and summation matrices. Two typical applications of the retrieval program are illustrated in Figure 8.9a–c. The first application is a retrieval of abstracted student records belonging to some population of interest. In the hypothetial example one phase of the study is to examine in detail the records of male students (1) from high-income families, (2) whose college grades were poor, and (3) who furthermore appeared aggressive at their preadmission interview.

The retrieval program can use existing data fields to derive new fields for each record. The researcher derives a field containing the student's grade average from the grade field in each record (2A–2C). To abstract the records of aggressive low achievers from high-income families the researcher sets up a retrieval descriptor (3C) that specifies grade average less than 2.1. He also defines field-value descriptors that specify male students (3A), parents' income greater than $20,000 (3B), and interview remarks that contain words beginning with "aggressi" or "asserti" (3D–3E). In question 4A these descriptors are combined to define the retrieval population. Questions 5A–5H specify which fields to abstract from each record for the output report. The field called HOME (which was introduced from the admissions office card) contains the zip code of the student's home town. Prior to this retrieval the researcher stored a dictionary in the computer that relates each zip code to the text name of the associated city. The dictionary's name is ZIP/CITY, and it is assigned the number 113. In question 5D the researcher specifies that the field called HOME should be printed in the retrieval report but that the contents of the fields should also be decoded, using dictionary number

154 Systems for Managing Complex Data Structures

```
3:45 PM  6/9  BBN77-77
RISERCH SGT

SEARCH
1 FILE:  16   STUDENT ACHIEVEMENT (SGT)    3:40 PM  6/9/1967
 1A CODE:  BBN

1 DICT →/L
1 FIELD DICTIONARY?  NO
DERIVED FIELDS
   2A   FREQ GRADE  :  NUM
   2B   SUM GRADE   :  TOT
   2C   TOT/NUM     :  AV
   2D   FREQ STUDENT NO.  :  CNT
   2E
DESCRIPTORS
   3A   SEX = M  :  MALE
   3B   PARENTS' INCOME > 20000  :  HIINC
   3C   AV < 2.1  :  LOAV
   3D   INTERVIEW REMARKS CONTAINS "AGGRESSI"  :  AGGRES
   3E   INTERVIEW REMARKS CONTAINS "ASSERTI"   :  ASSERT
   3F   AV > 3  :  HIAV
   3G
SEARCH LIMITS
   4A  POPULATION BOUNDS  MALE AND LOAV AND (AGGRES OR ASSERT) AND HIINC
   4B  MAX NO OF RECORDS
   4C  MAX NO IN POP
   4D  MAX NO IN SAMPLE
FIELDS TO PRINT
   5A   STUDENT NO.
   5B   STUDENT NAME
   5C   PARENTS' INCOME
   5D   →D113,HOME  ZIP/CITY   (SGT)   1:45 AM 6/9/1967
   5E   CEEB ENGLISH
   5F   CEEB MATH
   5G   AV
   5H   INTERVIEW REMARKS
   5I
      5I1  PRINT INDET POP
FIELDS TO SUM
   6A
ROW SPECS
   7A  R1   SAMPLE
 8 STUDY TITLE AGGRESSIVE LOW ACHIEVERS FROM HIGH INCOME FAMILIES
 9 OK TO SEARCH Y
```

Figure 8.9 (a) Retrieval program.

113. The retrieval program responds by printing the name of the dictionary. The same zip-code field can be decoded by other dictionaries in other retrievals; for example, another dictionary may be created to associate zip codes with text descriptions of each city's population. Two of the abstracted records resulting from the search are printed in Figure 8.10*b*.

The other application is illustrated in Figure 8.9*c*. The researcher redefines the retrieval population as the records of all male students. Instead of printing portions of records he elects to count the number of records in the income/grade-average samples discussed earlier. The sum-

Data Management Techniques for the Social Sciences 155

```
3:56 PM 6/9/1967
AGGRESSIVE LOW ACHIEVERS FROM HIGH INCOME FAMILIES




STUDENT NO.              65112
STUDENT NAME             JONES, TIMOTHY P.
PARENTS' INCOME                 37500
HOME                     02181: WELLESLEY HILLS, MASS.
CEEB ENGLISH                    730
CEEB MATH                       645
AV                              1.6

INTERVIEW REMARKS

THE CANDIDATE SEEMED WELL QUALIFIED, ALERT, AND INTELLECTUALLY CURIOUS.
HE SEEMED SOMEWHAT AGGRESSIVE AT THE OUTSET, THEN RELAXED
SLIGHTLY.  HE IS VERY WELL-READ, PARTICIPATES IN SPORTS.




STUDENT NO.              65703
STUDENT NAME             SMITH, SAMUEL S.
PARENTS' INCOME                 24000
HOME                     98665: VANCOUVER, WASH.
CEEB ENGLISH                    620
CEEB MATH                       650
AV                              1.9

INTERVIEW REMARKS

HE HAS HIGH EDUCATION GOALS, IS ESPECIALLY INTERESTED IN MATHEMATICS.
HE SEEMS SERIOUS AND HIGHLY MOTIVATED TO WORK WITH ADOLESCENTS.
HE SEEMED TO DISPLAY HIS AGGRESSIONS IN CONVERSATION.




RECORDS SEARCHED    217
RECORDS SELECTED     13
RECORDS INDETERM      0
SAMPLE SELECTED       0
SAMPLE INDETERM       0
9 = 4A, 5A, 6A, 7A
```

Figure 8.9 (b) Retrieval program (continued).

mations are presented in an output matrix containing the number of records in the samples defined by each row-column-descriptor intersection.

CONCLUSION

After two years' experimental use the data-management system has demonstrated valuable information-handling techniques for complex-

```
4A POPULATION BOUNDS MALE AND LOAV AND (AGGRES OR ASSERT) AND HIINC
/MALE
5A     STUDENT NO.
6A     CNT:INC
6B
7A R1  SAMPLE  LOAV
7B R1  LABEL LOW AVERAGE
7C R2  SAMPLE NOT (LOAV OR HIAV)
7D R2  LABEL MID AVERAGE
7E R3  SAMPLE HIAV
7F R3  LABEL HIGH AVERAGE
7G R4  SAMPLE
COLUMN SPECS
8A C1  SAMPLE HIINC
8B C1  LABEL HIGH INCOME
8C C2  SAMPLE NOT HIINC
8D C2  LABEL OTHER
8E C3  SAMPLE
9 STUDY TITLE INCOME/GRADE AVERAGE MATRIX
10 OK TO SEARCH Y


4:30 PM 6/9/1967
INC MATRIX


                HIGH INCOME    OTHER
LOW AVERAGE          3           19

MID AVERAGE         10           41

HIGH AVERAGE         5           25
```

Figure 8.9 (c) Retrieval program (continued).

structured data bases. The shared-computer concept not only has made the data-management system more widely available but also has permitted research on common data. The interactive language has allowed non-computer professionals to use the system easily and at the same time to specify the building and searching of their data bases with considerable flexibility. As computer systems become increasingly used by social scientists these and other techniques will provide data-management tools equal to the complex information problems of the future.

REFERENCES

1. J. C. Shaw, "JOSS: A Designer's View of an Experimental On-Line Computing System," *Proceedings of the AFIPS FJCC,* **26** (1964), pp. 455–464.
2. P. A. Castleman, "User-Defined Syntax in a General Information Storage and Retrieval System," in *Information Retrieval: The User's Viewpoint—An Aid to Design,* Fourth Annual National Colloquium on Information Retrieval, Philadelphia, 3–4 May, 1967, (to be published).

BIBLIOGRAPHY

Allen, S. I., Barnett, G. O., and Castleman, P. A., "Use of a Time-Shared General-Purpose File-Handling System in Hospital Research," *Proceedings IEEE*, 54, (1966), p. 1641.

Castleman, P. A., et al., *Information Storage and Retrieval Cycle*, Hospital Computer Project Memorandum 6–D. Cambridge, Mass.: Bolt Beranek and Newman, Inc. (to be published).

Castleman, P. A. and Robinson, S. U., III, "Backus Normal Form Compiler/Interpreter for Medical-Record Editing," *Proceedings DECUS Biomedical Symposium*, New York, 1967.

Castleman, P. A., and Teitelbaum, S. G., "On-Line Management System for Massachusetts General Hospital," *Proceedings of the Second Symposium on Computer-Centered Data Base Systems*. Santa Monica, Calif.: System Development Corp., TM–2624/100/00, 1965.

Chapter Nine

The Informatics MARK IV File-Management System

Fred Braddock[*]

The title of this chapter will perhaps elicit two different questions from two different kinds of people. Those who know only a little about computers ask, "Why do we need a file-management system?" Those who are thoroughly familiar with computers, and particularly file management ask, "Why do we need *another* file-management system?" The answer to both these questions lies in considering the evolution of computers and the use of computers to handle large data bases.

File management is a self-descriptive term; the managing of files. There is nothing new about files. Large quantities of paper and the filing cabinet have been around for a long time. However, the quantity of data that was necessary to be stored began to increase exponentially to an astronomical amount during and after World War II. Fortunately at about this time there was a giant step forward in technology, and the

---
[*] Informatics, Inc., Sherwood Oaks, California.

The Informatics MARK IV File-Management System

electronic digital computer arrived. The computer promised the ability to store large quantities of data, to be highly accurate, to be almost infallible in handling the data, and to provide rapid retrieval of information. With these promises in mind much time and effort were spent in transferring data to computer memories and the forms of auxiliary storage such as magnetic tape, drum, and disk. At this point the disadvantages of the computer began to show. It was true that the computer was accurate; it was true that it could "remember" or file a vast quantity of data, but the promise of rapid retrieval contained some very fine print that read, "provided you can train or program the computer." With the old filing cabinets it was easy to say to a secretary, "Get me the Higginbotom file." The secretary knew to which filing cabinet to go, which drawer to open, which subdivision was required, and would retrieve the appropriate file. The computer knew nothing and could assume nothing. It had to be laboriously told every step, rather like telling a secretary to, "Stand up, step forward. Are you there? No? Well, step forward again," and so on. This task of training, or programming, a computer takes considerable time and effort. As a result retrieval, far from being rapid, took several months. Worse still, the users of the data bases had to learn a new and complex discipline.

The first step in aiding the user was to develop the file-management language. This enabled the user to state his requirements with English-language-type statements that were relatively easy to learn. The file-management language reduced retrieval to the order of two or three days.

Although file-management languages made the computer a more realistic tool for the manipulation of large data bases, certain drawbacks remained. It was necessary to learn the language, rather like a tourist learning a few basic verbs of a foreign language and trying to stutter out few sentences. Just as the tourist confuses the native with an incorrect grammatical structure, so the file-management-language user could confuse the computer. The languages still required the user to learn the disciplines of programming. This limited their use to users of the system who were above average intelligence and robbed these people of time that would have been better spent devoted to their own science. Programming errors were made and took valuable time to correct. To relieve the user from the task of programming, from the necessity of debugging or getting the errors out of his program, and to enable him to delegate the task of retrieval from the data base to a subordinate, Informatics Inc. has developed the MARK IV file-management system.

What then is the MARK IV file-management system? What it is *not*, is a computer language. For all visible appearances to the user, be he a social scientist without computer training or a professional programmer, the system is a series of check lists on simple structured forms. To use the system the user simply has to check what is required following rules easier to learn than canasta or contract bridge.

MARK IV is a general-purpose file-management system that provides, in addition to efficient day-to-day operation, quick response for special reports and other critical one-time requirements. It is a proprietary software package that simplifies computer solutions to many business-data-processing problems.

In brief MARK IV is a program that operates on the IBM system/360. Using the check lists that are input to MARK IV the user may

1. CREATE files from data on punched cards, magnetic tapes, and direct-access devices.*

2. MAINTAIN files by performing changes, additions, and other update actions.

3. READ a master file and as many as three related files simultaneously for updating, processing, and output.

4. SELECT records from files that contain data which meet specific qualifications.

5. EXTRACT data items from the selected records.

6. COMPUTE results for use in printed output, subfiles, updating of master files, and in further record qualification and additional computation.

7. ARRANGE output by sorting, sequencing, and grouping.

8. FORMAT printed reports containing such elements as preface, page title, page number, column headings, line numbers, detail entries, summaries, averages, and other details that make a printed report or document informative and attractive.

9. SUMMARIZE data to as many levels of totals and subtotals as required.

10. PRINT reports with wide flexibility in format and content on standard computer paper, special size output (labels, 3×5 cards, etc.), preprinted forms (paychecks, invoices, journals, etc.).

11. PRODUCE new files, parts of files, combinations of files, and audit files on magnetic tape, direct-access devices, and cards.

---

* MARK IV files may be on magnetic tape, cards, and direct-access devices. They may contain fixed- or variable-length records and may be processed sequentially or indexed sequentially.

The Informatics MARK IV File-Management System

EMPL. NO.	NAME	JOB TITLE	CLASS	DIVISION	DEPT.	GROUP			Level 1 Segment 1
HIRE DATE	SALARY	DEPEND.	SOC. SEC. #	COUNT FIELDS: Schools, Jobs					

| SCHOOL #1 | ADDRESS | YEARS | HONORS | DEGREE COUNT | REMARKS | Level 2 Segment 2 |

| DEGREE | GPA | DATE | Level 3 Segment 3 |

| SCHOOL #2 | ADDRESS | YEARS | HONORS | DEGREE COUNT | REMARKS | Level 2 Segment 2 |

| PREVIOUS EMPLOYER #1 | ADDRESS | TITLE | REF. COUNT | SALARY | TERM. DATE | START DATE | Level 2 Segment 4 |

| REFERENCE #1 | TITLE | YEARS KNOWN | EVALUATION |

| REFERENCE #2 | TITLE | YEARS KNOWN | EVALUATION |

Level 3 Segment 5

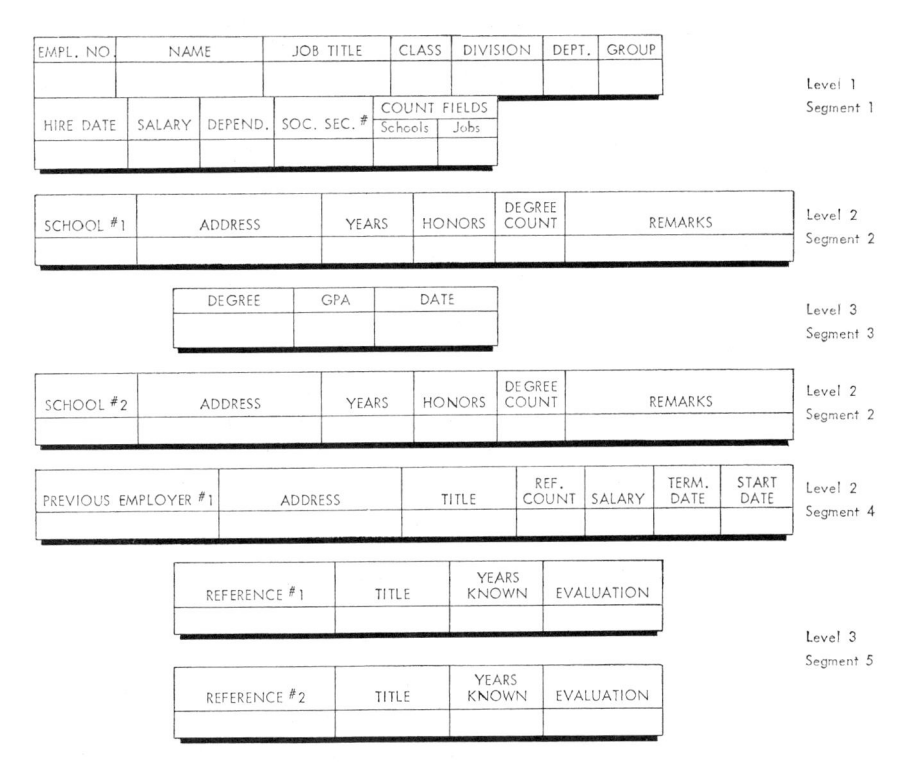

Figure 9.1 Typical MARK IV record.

The design of MARK IV has two underlying principles: (1) to keep the system simple and easy to use and (2) to be oriented toward user requirements.

In orienting MARK IV toward user requirements it is necessary to ask what kind of files the user has and what he wants to do with them. MARK IV is designed to process files containing records that can be considered to be in a hierarchical structure. That is to say, there is a prime, or level 1, segment, consisting of several data fields, with several subsegments, or level 2 segments. The level 2 segments themselves may have subsegments, or level 3 segments, and so on. At each level there may be several segments with different structures but equal importance in the hierarchy. Segments of identical structure at the same level are called repeated segments, whereas segments of different structures at the same level are called sibling segments. A typical record is illustrated in Figure

Systems for Managing Complex Data Structures

9.1. The two "school" segments constitute repeated segments; the "previous employer" is a sibling segment. Any record that can be expressed as a hierarchial structure, whether it contains just one segment at level 1 (in other words, a fixed-length file) or the permissible maximum 99 segments scattered through the nine allowable levels, can be processed by MARK IV.

The second aspect of user orientation is to determine, within limits, the form that his output may take. MARK IV is primarily designed to generate simple reports of a columnar nature with the ability to include titles and column headings, sort data, and take automatic summary information. A typical MARK IV report is shown in Figure 9.2.

To make the system easy to use a series of simple forms have been devised. The user is required to supply only the absolute minimum necessary information. In designing these forms consideration was taken of the three basic functions that the user wishes to perform: file definition, updating, and retrieval.

ANALYSIS OF EMPLOYEES WITH OVERSEAS RESIDENCE
30 JUNE 1967   PAGE 1

	COUNTRY OF RESIDENCE	YEARS RESIDENT	NAME	AGE	ANNUAL SALARY
	ENGLAND	12	EDWARDS	20	$ 7,000
		5	ANDREWS	32	12,000
			JONES	27	10,000
			DONOVAN	23	9,000
		1	CLARK	18	6,000
			HOWE	26	8,000
			MARTIN	29	11,000
COUNTRY AVERAGE.....................				25	$ 9,000
COUNTRY MAX					$12,000
	FRANCE	16	GESTE	34	$11,000
		4	BONES	51	15,000
			INK	37	16,000
			LOWE	30	10,000
COUNTRY AVERAGE.....................				38	$13,000
COUNTRY MAX					$16,000
	GERMANY	20	KLAUS	36	12,000
		16	FRITZ	34	13,000
COUNTRY AVERAGE.....................				35	$12,500
COUNTRY MAX					$13,000

Figure 9.2 Typical MARK IV report.

The Informatics MARK IV File-Management System

Line Number	Field Name	Delete?	Segment No.	Level No.	Field Location	Field Length	Field Type	Decimal Places	Output Edit	Column Heading Text
L	1 EMPL NO.		1	1	1	4				EMPLOYEE▽
L	2 EMPL NO.									NUMBER▽
L	1 NAME		1	1	5	20				NAME▽
L	1 JOB TITLE		1	1	25	20				JOB TITLE▽
L	1 CLASS		1	1	45	1				CLASS▽
L	1 DIVISION		1	1	46	15				DIVISION▽
L	1 DEPT		1	1	61	2				DEPT▽
L	1 GROUP		1	1	63	2				GROUP▽
L	1 HIREDATE		1	1	65	4	J			HIRE DATE▽
L	1 SALARY		1	1	69	6	Z		$	SALARY▽
L	1 DEPEND		1	1	75	2	Z		Z	NO. OF▽
L	2 DEPEND									DEPEND▽
L	3 DEPEND									ENTS▽
L	1 S.S.NO.		1	1	77	11				SOC. SEC▽
L	2 S.S.NO.									NUMBER▽
L	1 JOBS		1	1	88	2	Z		Z	JOBS▽
L	1 SCHOOLS		1	1	90	2	Z		Z	SCHOOLS▽

Figure 9.3 File definition.

File definition is the requirement that the user describe the structure of his records to the system. This is the blueprint of the record, and, like a blueprint, it contains such information as number of decimal places, position in the segment, and type of eld. In this form is concentrated all the information that is necessary for the processing of the record together with the type of information that need be defined once only. Thus subsequent users are relieved of the tedium of supplying the same information each time a run is made. Information such as the text of column headings falls into this category. The file-management definition form is illustrated in Figure 9.3. This simple form is the most complex of all MARK IV forms to fill out because it requires knowledge of how the data are stored on the file. This form is usually completed by data-processing personnel, and this is a one-time only operation, the information being stored by MARK IV for subsequent use. When a file definition is made to MARK IV a glossary is generated for the user. This glossary contains all the information that the user requires when using the file for subsequent processing. A typical glossary is shown in Figure 9.4.

The second function that the user wishes to perform on his file is that of file updating. This operation, which may consist of adding records to a file, segments to a record, or simply changing fields within a segment, is the type of action that is performed several times. However, frequently the updating action is the same and only the data differ. For example, on a payroll file every week an employee's year-to-date salary and the amount of income tax withheld are updated. The same action is performed each time, and only the numbers involved change. The term "transaction" is used in the MARK IV system to describe the action or set of actions performed at the time of a file update. Just as there is a file-definition form, so there is a form in which the structure of a transaction is described. Essentially the information entered on this form tells MARK IV where to find the data, with which field it is to be associated, and what particular action is to be performed (e.g., add, subtract, replace, etc.). It is only necessary on this definition to provide the field name of the field that is to be updated; MARK IV can obtain all the other necessary information from the file definition. Each transaction must have a transaction identifier, so that a user may request several different kinds of transactions on the same file. Thus a "1" in column 3 of a card may trigger off the inclusion of a new employee in the personnel file, the remainder of the data on the card being used to create the record. Alternatively a "7" in column 15 may cause the employee's weekly salary to be updated.

Once the transactions have been defined, it is necessary only to supply the data. Each transaction, and there are probably only a few of them, is defined only once. Again MARK IV remembers the transactions.

The third function the user wishes to perform is the retrieval of information and the preparation of reports. These operations are those most frequently performed by all users, therefore it is the simplest function of MARK IV. The function of creating reports is further subdivided into three groups: the basic Information request, the extended request, and the cataloged request.

The basic information request consists of one form. Simple logical record-selection criteria, together with the names of the fields that are to be printed, are entered on the form.

With the sample personnel-file structure, as shown in Figure 9.1, a special request can be entered to select employees who formerly were presi-

The Informatics MARK IV File-Management System

APRIL 19, 1967   PAGE 1

MARK IV FILE MANAGEMENT SYSTEM
GLOSSARY
FOR
FILE NAME — EMPLOYEE

FIELD NAME	LOCATION	LENGTH	EDIT CODE	COLUMN HEADING
EMPL NO.	1	4		EMPLOYEE NUMBER
NAME	5	20		NAME
JOB TITLE	25	20		JOB TITLE
CLASS	45	1		CLASS
DIVISION	46	15		DIVISION
DEPT.	61	2		DEPT.
GROUP	63	2		GROUP
HIRE DATE	65	4		HIRE DATE
SALARY	69	6	$	SALARY
DEPEND.	75	2	Z	NO. OF DEPENDENTS
S.S. NO.	77	11		SOC. SEC. NUMBER

Figure 9.4 Typical glossary.

dents of their own firms (Figure 9.5). The output from this request is shown in Figure 9.6. This search can be conducted on any type of field (e.g., physical characteristics or size and weight limitations to find persons who can work in cramped quarters in automobile assembly lines or to find specific work experience to bring together a team of certain skills).

The selection criteria can be suppressed from printing and only the desired information printed. The sequence of output can be by alphabetical order, or by seniority, or ascending order on weight, height, or in various combinations. Employees who are accident prone can be processed in a variety of ways to find certain characteristics of interest to social scientists or plant-safety officials.

The selection criteria may be simple or complex. MARK IV will accept any complex selection expression down to nine logical levels. At the other end of the scale, when every record in the file is involved and there is no logical expression, then none need be supplied; for example, assuming all that is required (from a personnel file) is a telephone directory, then the request would look as in Figure 9.7 and the resulting report, as in Figure 9.8.

Figure 9.5 Transaction data.

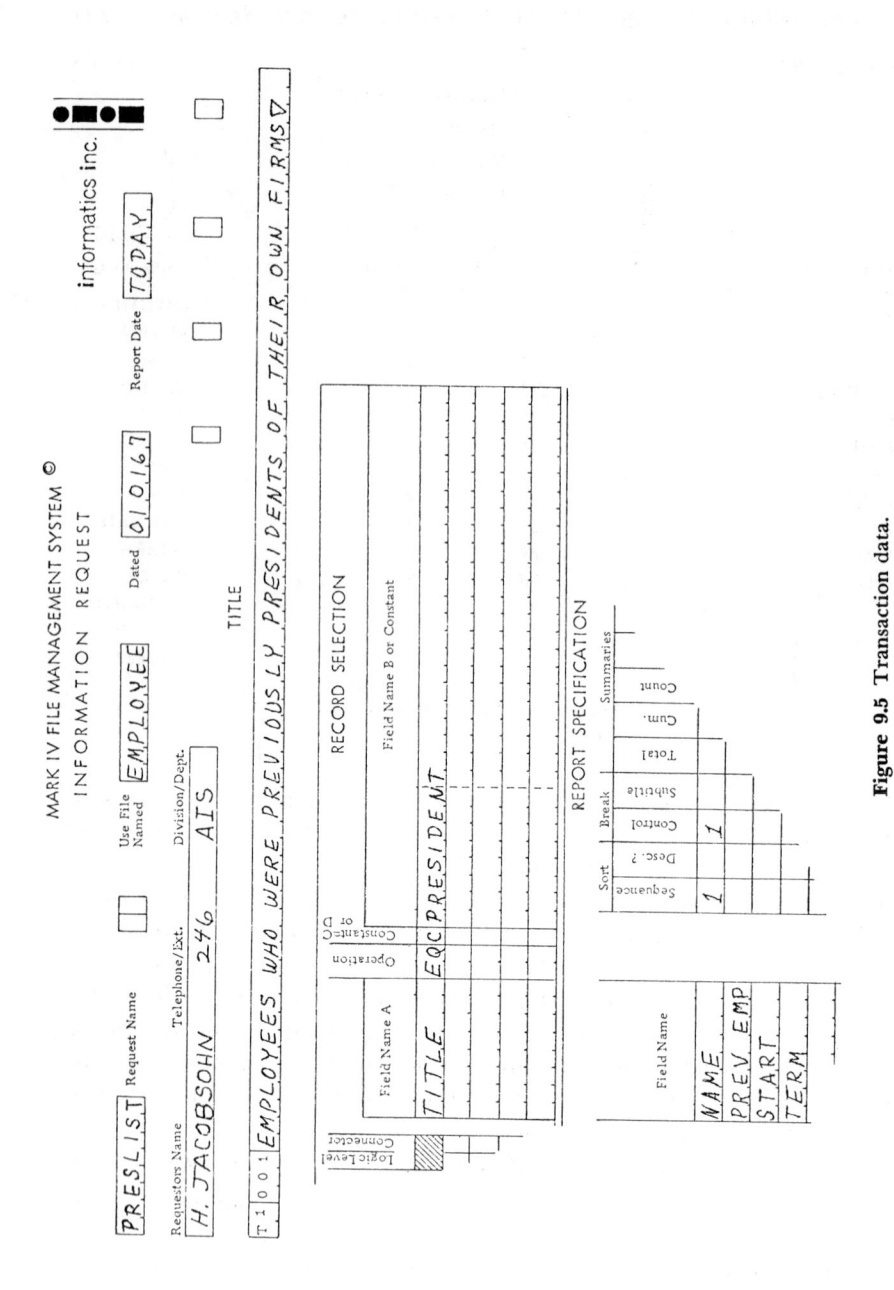

JUNE 15, 1967   PAGE 1
EMPLOYEES WHO WERE PREVIOUSLY PRESIDENT OF THEIR OWN FIRMS

NAME	PREVIOUS EMPLOYER	START DATE	TERMINATION DATE
ADAMS, J. Q.	ADAMS ELECTRONICS	JUNE 1, 1953	OCT. 1, 1956
BROWN, C. C.	ELECTRONUCLEAR, INC.	JAN. 1, 1949	JUNE 1, 1959
CHESTER, F. X.	WEST SIDE CLEANERS	AUG. 1, 1956	OCT. 1, 1956
DUGAN, J. J.	DUGAN MOTORS	JAN. 1, 1939	DEC. 31, 1966
	DUGAN, INC.	JAN. 1, 1967	MAR. 31, 1967

Figure 9.6 Report from specifications of Figure 9.5.

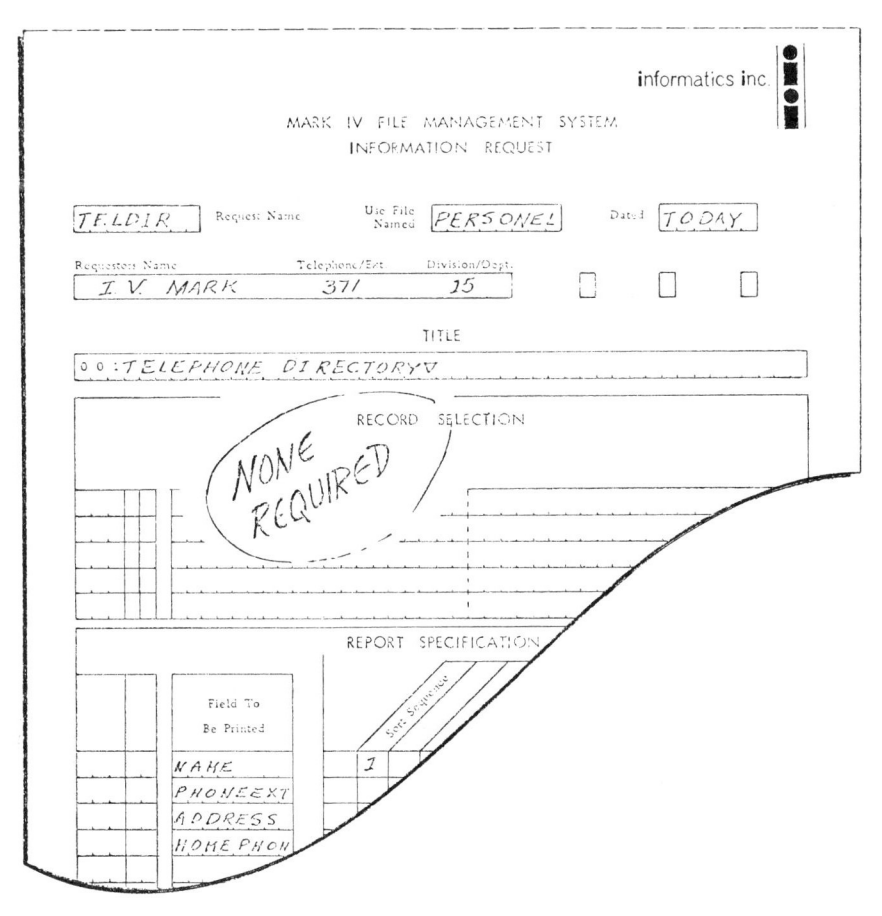

Figure 9.7 Simple selection and report specifications.

168 Systems for Managing Complex Data Structures

```
8/28/67                  TELEPHONE DIRECTORY                    PAGE 1

                     PHONE              HOME                 HOME
       NAME         EXTENSION          ADDRESS               PHONE

  ADAMS, SHIRLEY      345        134 RODDA AVE             781-2345
  BAUER, W.F.         321        1781 WEST BLVD            781-7783
  BLAUNER, D.         678        1214 HILL ST              345-7829
  BLIESNER, R.G       478        891 WESTLAKE AVE          347-7865
  BUETTELL, T.D.      471        812 N. ORANGE AVE         378-2121
  BRADDOCK, F.        128        121 NATIONAL BLVD         347-8876
  COOPER, W.R. JR     341        144 E. GROVE AVE          873-4211
  CORYELL, N.T.       321        782 S. BRAND AVE          781-9782
  COUCH, S.J.         217        817 W. ROSCOE ST          871-3131
  CUTLER, W.C.        117        1218 STANDARD AVE         781-9650
  DOWKONT, A.J.       228        1814 NATIONAL BLVD        781-9600
  FRANK, W.L.         229        161 E. MAIN ST            347-2011
  GATTO, O.T.         382        128 COMMERCE ST           781-2515
  GLENN, R.C.         340        130 AVIATION BLVD         347-
  HASKELL, E.L.       821        161 TRADE ST
  JACOBSOHN, H.       671        170 ALLEN BLVD
  KINN, C.J.          421        1117 MAPLE AVE
  KREINER, P.F.       487        444 IVY ST
  LAMIA, A.           507        411 LEAGUE
  MARK I.V.           875        1007 HIL
  MASON, R.J.         218        1025 T
  MULHAUPT, L.M.      788        784
  POSTLEY, J.A.       220        41
  REDEKOPP, J.A.      871
  STONE, R.D.         733
  SUNDERLAND, R.S.    225
  TAYLOR, J.R.        217
  UTT, G.G.           371
  WAGNER, F.V.
  WHITE, R.R.
  ZANICCHI, J.A.
```

Figure 9.8 Specifications for report with no special selection criteria.

A more complex request is made to MARK IV through the output-format-specification form. Though similar to the basic information request, it does, however, have greater power. The user has the ability to perform arithmetic computations and to specify features of the system, such as automatic line numbering or adjustment of page size. A sample of these features is illustrated in Figure 9.9.

Just as MARK IV can store master- and transaction-file definitons in its catalog, it can also store entire requests. Thus it is possible to call out a cataloged request. This is performed by using the "use cataloged request" form as illustrated in Figure 9.10. This form is so brief that it is printed directly on the input-data card to the computer.

MARK IV FILE MANAGEMENT SYSTEM ©
OUTPUT FORMAT SPECIFICATIONS

informatics inc.

Request Name

Summary report only?	Page title at bottom of page?
Vertical spacing	Column Headings Type
Print 8 lines per inch?	Column Headings Position
Width of page	Date position
Height of page	Page number position
Number of repeated images	Start page numbers at
Number of copies	Line numbers
Only one selection per record?	Labels on summary lines
Maximum number of lines per page	Report handling
Maximum number of pages	Select data/punch
Maximum items selected	Subfile name
	Subfile blocking factor

Figure 10. Typical Extended Request Specifications

Figure 9.9 Report generated from the specifications of Figure 9.8.

Note that it is necessary only to provide one field on this form—namely, the request name. All other fields are either ignored or MARK IV makes a suitable assumption. This is true of all MARK IV forms. MARK IV always assumes a standard set of parameters unless the user specifically overrides them.

This then is MARK IV, an easy method of obtaining results quickly. There is no debugging—the worst one can do is get the information on the wrong part of the page. However, we would be failing in our duty to the user if we did not make as much of the power of the computer avail-

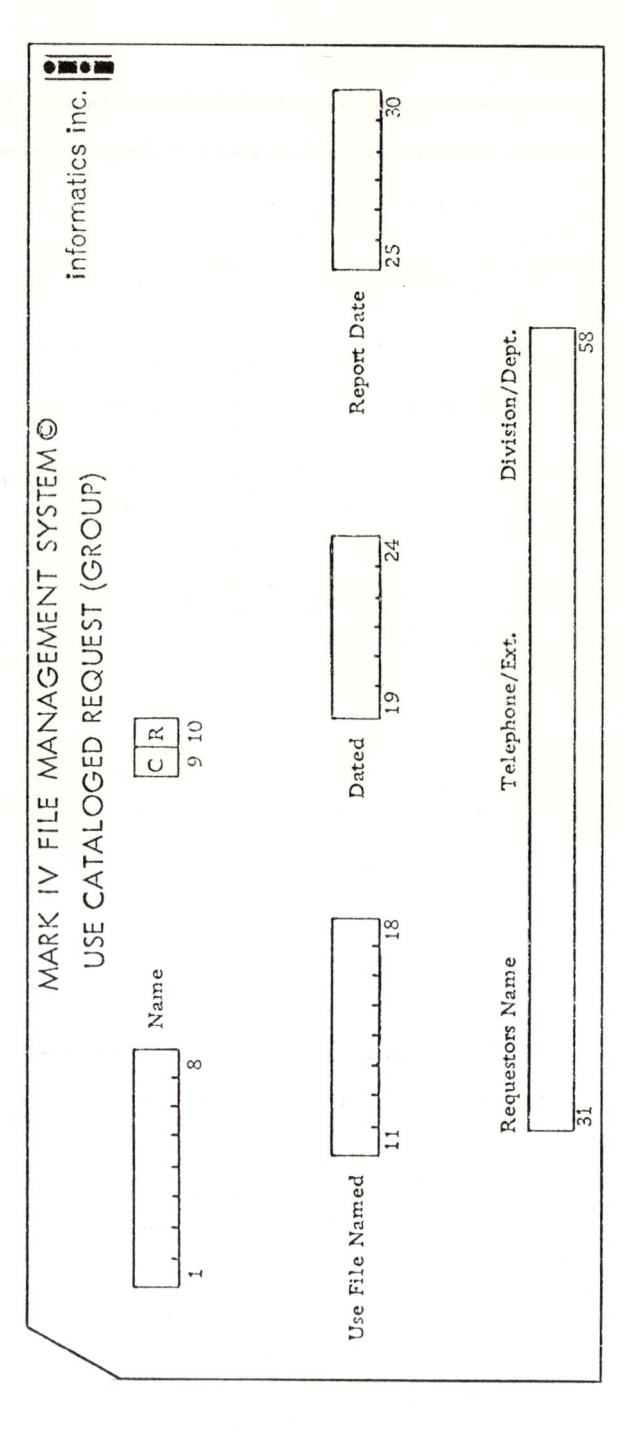

Figure 9.10 Typical extended request specifications.

The Informatics MARK IV File-Management System

able as possible. Thus MARK IV does have other features and attributes, such as the following:

1. The ability to manipulate and concatenate requests on the catalog.
2. The ability to have coordinated files—that is, to line up records on different files to make all the information readily available.
3. The ability to write a request to change all records of the master file—a "mass transaction."
4. A computational capability.
5. The ability to create temporary computational fields and pass information between requests.
6. The capability of processing many requests at the same time, thereby reading the master file only once.
7. The ability to have sequential or indexed sequential processing. Here we should mention that MARK IV runs as a job under IBM OS or DOS systems for system 360 and uses IBM-supplied access methods.

MARK IV is a system designed for the user who does not have the time or perhaps the need to learn complex programming. It is not a real-time system; hence the user does not have to sit in front of a computer. It is designed for the man or woman in the office, be he president or personnel clerk. MARK IV has been designed by the Advanced Information Systems Division of Informatics who have experienced the frustration of trying to get what the computer user wants promptly in a short time, trying to educate the user, understanding his data-processing needs, and dealing with computers in all shapes and sizes. Typical of the experience that has gone into MARK IV is the simple fact that the designers appreciate that keypunch operators will make errors such as punching zero for the alphabetic O. Thus, wherever the letter O is required (e.g., OR) the numeric zero (0) will be accepted as well. Trivial? Ask any computer user how many dollars that one has cost him in computer time.

The use of the MARK IV file-management system by non-computer-oriented research personnel makes available the power of third-generation computer equipment to process large amounts of data in a short period of time without the requirement to become educated in computer techniques. Thus with MARK IV social scientists can devote the majority of their efforts to data collection and analysis of the processed results through a system that automates most of the processes connected with "programming" a computer, and can make special requests for new processing with relative ease.

Part V Handling Missing-Data Problems

As long as I count the votes, what are you going to do about it?

"Boss" Tweed

The concept of missing data can be defined in various ways. The lay observer would probably understand the concept to mean simply information that is absent, but in the social sciences the phrase has a much more specific meaning—namely, observations or "facts" about given entities that can be or are observable but have not been recorded in a systematic data-collection process. Missing data in the social science usage causes special problems for social science research because the theory behind almost all social statistics assumes complete data about a sample or universe of entities. Complete data, however, are hardly ever possible in the social sciences: some survey respondents refuse to answer particular questions, and there is always some proportion of entities (individuals, political or geographical units, etc.) for which there is no data whatsoever.

The most prevalent method of handling missing-data problems in the social sciences is to ignore, in analyses, those entities for which data on a pair or set of variables are missing. Thus in a correlation matrix, for example, the number of cases varies from cell to cell: in one cell the correlation may be based on N cases, but in another it may be based on $\frac{1}{2}N$, $\frac{1}{4}N$, or even $\frac{1}{10}N$ cases. Similarly in a cross-tabulation analysis one table may be based on nearly the total number of cases for which data have been collected; another table may be based on only a fraction of the cases.

A number of statistical and other techniques exist or have been proposed to handle the problem of missing data. Maximum-likelihood calculations, various random-assignment methods, weigting methods, and certain multivariate techniques have been proposed, explored, and occasionally used. The chapter by the Elashoffs explores problems and prospects of regression methods, and the chapter by Miller demonstrates the utility of a form of maximum-likelihood approach.

A simple form of the maximum-likelihood approach is illustrated by so-called precision-matching methods. We begin with an assumption that people who are similar on measures of independent variables should be similar on measures of dependent variables. The method is particularly useful in a computer context where many comparisons can be made in seconds: we begin by comparing an individual case containing missing information with all cases containing complete information on a given set of variables; missing data are substituted by the observations of any entity that matches on the largest number of nonmissing independent variables. Any entity for which missing data have been substituted is not eligible in the comparison process if the set of matching variables includes the substituted missing-data variable. This requires that the computer routine be able to identify missing data substituted in a given entity record by the matching process. We recognize that for a given data set we cannot substitute all missing observations through matches with a maximum number of independent variables: consequently the program would continually relax the number of matching observations required before a substitution is made. Once the precision-matching process is completed, the revised data set is compared with other data sets to determine whether the matching process has produced valid results. However, some data may still remain missing.

The method described by Miller is much more complex than the more simple procedure described above. Miller's methods depend very much on the presence of multiple data sets that can be linked and compared; his approach represents a highly sophisticated approach to the solution of missing-data problems by maximum-likelihood methods. It is also important to stress that Miller's chapter also considers privacy problems.

The chapter by the Elashoffs considers the difficulties and promises of regression techniques, an important form of multivariate analysis. At the 1967 conference of the Council of Social Science Data Archives

Handling Missing-Data Problems 175

the Elashoff's contribution was criticized as not too relevant to the social sciences, because the social sciences have only small amounts of data that qualify as being at the interval level of measurement. This is true only if one takes a very limited view of the scope of the social sciences or limits his perspective to data collected by traditional survey methods. Public-health and economic data are often at the appropriate level of measurement, and many surveys yield data that justify handling missing-data problems by their approach.

Chapter Ten

Some Ways of Handling Missing Data—A Case Study*

Roger F. Miller†

The general investment and portfolio behavior of individuals is one of the most difficult and least well investigated aspects of their behavior. Yet it is also of potentially great significance, as is evidenced, for example, by continued controversy over the taxation of capital-gains

---

* This chapter is part of a series of projects that have received financial support in substantial amounts from the National Bureau of Economic Research, the Brookings Institution, the Social Security Administration, the National Science Foundation, and through the University of Wisconsin Graduate School Research Committee, from the State of Wisconsin and the Wisconsin Alumni Research Foundation. The author is grateful to Project Assistant Wynn V. Bussman, who assisted in the preparation of this chapter and would also like to acknowledge his personal and intellectual indebtedness to his colleagues Martin H. David, Guy H. Orcutt, and Harold W. Watts.
† Social Systems Research Institute, University of Wisconsin, Madison.

177

178 Handling Missing-Data Problems

income. Although people can certainly vary their consumption expenditures, they tend to follow fairly stable and consistent patterns of major expenditures for food, clothing, and housing. Their discretionary power over their portfolios and the compositions thereof is much greater. In the past the combined effects of all persons exercising this power has resulted in such critical phenomena as bank runs, stock-market breaks (or jumps), and balance of payments crises (via "capital flight"). Perhaps of longer run significance, such behavior affects the success or failure of new financing for both private and governmental sectors.

Successful investigation of the investment and portfolio behavior of individuals has been hampered by a lack of an adequate body of data with which to test hypotheses and estimate relationships. Perhaps because of this, the theoretical development of models appropriate for the understanding and analysis of such data has been rather fragmentary. In another paper Harold W. Watts and I have laid out the structure of a more comprehensive model.[1] The Wisconsin Assets and Incomes Studies (WAIS) data archives contain data appropriate for such portfolio analysis, being micro time series of individual income sources (see Chapter 7).

This chapter describes ways we have found to handle missing-data problems in the course of analyzing stock-portfolio information by using tax-return data. Before we give full attention to the problems and our approaches it is useful to see how the processing analysis would be handled if the data set were "ideal," to describe the data files actually available to us, and to indicate the kinds of missing-data problems with which we are confronted.

THE METHOD WITH IDEAL DATA

The listing below enumerates the variables relating to a particular common stock and a particular individual.

Ideal Set of Variables

A. Individual's Variables
  1. Dates of stock purchases (or receipts of gifts or requests).
  2. Amounts of stock purchased (received).
  3. Purchase prices of stock (market values).
  4. Dates of sales of stock (or donated or given away).
  5. Amounts of stock sold (or otherwise disposed of).

Some Ways of Handling Missing Data—A Case Study

6. Sale prices of stock (market values).
7. Dates of receipt of stock dividends and number or shares received.
8. Values (market prices) of stock dividends.
9. Dates of receipt of cash dividends.
10. Amounts of cash dividends received.

B. *Stock's Variables*
1. Dates of payment of cash and stock dividends.
2. Dividend rates per share (both cash and stock dividends).
3. Market prices per share (for each point in time).

Clearly from such information we can completely construct a time series of the amounts and values of the person's holding of the stock, the income he received from it, and the division of the value between basis and unrealized capital gains.* For example, the number of shares held at any one time is provided by full knowledge of items 1, 2, 4, 5, and 7 in part A of the listing above. On the other hand, some data are redundant. If we know the number of shares held on a cash date and the corresponding dividend rate per share (item B.2), we can easily compute the amount of cash dividends received on that date (item A.10). Similarly items A.1 and B.3 allow determination of A.3. These redundancies are the essence of the method we shall use to reconstruct the history of a person's holdings and their values when certain of the information is missing, as it will usually be.

Redundancies also serve another very important purpose when they are available in the data (i.e., the data that are redundant are *not* missing). They are useful in validity studies for checking on sources of error in the records such as taxpayer or interviewee misreporting or such as coding, keypunching, and matching errors made in the course of our handling this mass of detailed data. Here the multiyear aspects of our files introduce another form of redundancy. Suppose we have a time series of annual dividends for an individual identified as being derived from the ABC Company and we also have the time series of quarterly dividend payments made by this company (on a per-share basis). Aggregating the latter to arrive at the time series of annual per-share dividend rates for the company and dividing these into the individual's corresponding annual total dividends received, we derive a time series of the number of shares held by the individual.† Even

---

* For these purposes we consider such things as stock rights and warrants as essentially fractional stock dividends. Stock splits are simply treated as divisions of the unit of measurement. These are significant due to our use in some cases of a round-lot assumption, described in the section entitled "Overcoming Data Deficiencies."

if no other information is available, substantial and otherwise unexplained variation in the latter time series would lead us to suspect that the identification of the individual's dividend stream with holdings of ABC Company stock was incorrect. This can be checked by going back to the original files. Although the basic documents themselves may be in error, we will at least have had an important check on the coding and other file-handling procedures that we used. This type of use of redundancy is of considerable importance when handling large-scale data bodies of considerable complexity, although it may be possible to dispense with redundant information after its uses have been exhausted.

Our basic method then is to use *partial* information from the set of ideal data that contains redundancies to fill in the missing pieces of information needed to reconstruct a person's history of stockholdings for each stock he is known to have held. The collection of such records for an individual can then be considered his reconstructed stock portfolio and incorporated into models of portfolio analysis. Where some of the actually available data are also redundant they will be used for validity checks on the files. Finally, in some cases even the partial information will be insufficient to allow exact reconstruction of an individual's holdings, but is may be sufficient to allow estimation of such holdings based on analyses of all of the other data in the files, as described at various places in succeeding sections.

THE DATA SOURCES

The WAIS data are incorporated into a number of separate files (on magnetic tape unless otherwise reported below). Some of these files relate to individuals, and each person's records in each file carry his own identification number (distinguished from all other persons, but carrying a 0, 1 digit indicating sex and otherwise identical with the identification number of the person's spouse, allowing aggregation into husband-wife units rather than individual units where appropriate). Some files relate to specific income payors such as corporations, and here again each distinguishable payor carries a separate identification number for any record in any file that relates to that payor. These numbers also distinguish among reasons for payment by the same payor: ABC Company's different classes of common and preferred stocks each

---

† This is essentially the method used by Thomas R. Atkinson in his study using data similar to ours.[2]

Some Ways of Handling Missing Data—A Case Study 181

carry a distinct number. Two of the files contain data relating both to individuals and payors, and where this is the case both identifying numbers appear in each such record.

The order in which the files are discussed is primarily determined by the manner in which references from one file to another are introduced. Furthermore, only the WAIS files that are relevant to this chapter * will be discussed.

The Lorie-Fisher (Merrill) File

Rather than being a WAIS file per se, this is an important file of data for our study to which we have direct access. Financed by the Merrill Foundation, James Lorie and Lawrence Fisher developed these data at the University of Chicago. For 2020 companies listed on the New York Stock Exchange and for the years 1926–1960, the data include monthly stock prices (actual closing prices on the last trading day of the month—asked prices for stock not traded on that day); quarterly dividends per share; and information about stock dividends, rights, mergers, exchanges, reorganizations, and spinoffs. It is thus a basic source of data of the type listed as stock's variables on p. 000.

The Standard and Poor Compustat File

The Compustat file was also created elsewhere, by the Standard and Poor Corporation, and is available for our use at Wisconsin. For 1000 companies, for the years 1946–1965, a great deal of information is included. Of relevance to us are the dividends per share and for each year the high, low, and closing stock prices (bid prices for those stocks for which sale prices are unavailable).

The Lorie-Fisher and Compustat files have independent firm-identification numbers, but we have a special cross-index file associating the numbers in one file to the corresponding number of a given firm's stock in the other file. Because of the greater number of firms in the Lorie-Fisher file, our own firm (and issue) identification numbers use the Lorie-Fisher numbers where available.

The Supplementary Firm File

This is a WAIS-created file, containing at present only firm- and issue-identification numbers and names of corporations from which

---

* A discussion of the other WAIS files may be found in Chapter 7.

our individuals reported receiving property income but which are not listed in either the Lorie-Fisher or Compustat files.

The Property-Income File

This is one of the most important of the WAIS files for the purposes of this study. From Wisconsin individual income tax returns for a sample of persons filing at any time in the years 1947–1959 (and for some persons including data from 1946 and 1960) we have detailed information on all nonwage and salary or "other" income sources (dividends, capital gains, rental property, interest, etc.). Of particular import for creation of a common-stock portfolio are the annual dividends from each company, and if any stock were sold during the years for which we have returns for the individuals, we also have purchase date and price and sale date and price, as well as quantity sold. The prices are "net"; that is, brokers fees paid are included in purchase prices and deducted from selling prices. The amount of captial gain (or loss) resulting is also included.

The asset-identification codes are six-digit numbers. The first two identify the type of source (in this case corporate common stock); the last four identify the company and issue and correspond to the Lorie-Fisher and supplementary firm file codes described above.

We also have in our basic folder filing cabinets data for the same sample for the years 1960–1964. Unfortunately at present we have no financing for the rather expensive job of coding, punching, verifying, editing, and validating these very important supplementary data. Such financing is being sought.

The overall tax-return sample contains data on about 20,000 persons. The property-income file contains data on roughly 10,000 of these persons.

The Asset-Diary File

The asset-diary file resulted from an interview survey in 1964 of a stratified subsample of persons for whom we had tax returns plus a small high-income supplement. It contains detailed data on many aspects of the financial and real-asset holdings for about 1100 usable replies, a respondent in this case being the head of the household interviewed and including in his responses the assets of other household members. Asset-identification codes were assigned in the same manner as for the property-income file.

Some Ways of Handling Missing Data—A Case Study

The data relating to stockholdings in the asset-diary file include month and year of acquisition of any stock held at any time during the period December 31, 1958, to December 31, 1963; number of shares acquired; and total cost of the shares at acquisition (including broker's fees). If the stock was still held as of December 31, 1963, and was not quoted in a common source, its value was supplied by the respondent. For any stock during the period we also obtained the month and year of sale, number of shares sold, and net proceeds from the sale.

The Interview (Survey) File

The survey described in relation to the asset-diary above contained usable responses from about 1,300 individuals. The attrition of 200 persons from the interview-file sample to the asset-diary file sample is partly due to the fact that a person with substantial asset holdings was requested to fill out the asset-diary schedule himself, consulting his records as much as possible, and return it to us by mail in preaddressed and stamped envelopes supplied by us, after the interviewer had completed the basic interview schedule whose data appears in the interview file.

The interview file contains no detailed data on stockholdings, although it does have some data bearing directly on portfolio management and investor attitudes and does indicate whether or not the interviewee held assets of certain types such as stock. It thus has some value for a validation study used in connection with the other files. Its most important use, however, will be as a source of a great deal of demographic and other income data in any analysis of the portfolios held by the interviewees.

The Master File

The master file contains all relevant data from the tax returns, except that for all items for which the detailed data is in the property-income file only summary data are included, such as total dividends (from *all* stockholdings). These summary totals are useful in an interfile-consistency check now under way for the years for which the property-income data are available on tape. Beyond that the master file provides other data useful in analyses and in validity checks described below.

Master-file data for 1946–1960 are now on tape. We subsequently went back (with National Science Foundation financing) for later year records and obtained returns for the same sample for the years 1959–1964, the overlapping years proving invaluable as aids in matching the data from the earlier and later periods for each individual. These later year master-file data are now being processed.

One of the uses of the master-file extension to 1964 is to provide a link of sorts between the earlier data and data from the interview and asset-diary files. This link would of course be much more strongly and appropriately made by a similar extension of the property-income file. Even the master-file extension, however, allows some very rough interfile-validity checking with the two survey files.

The History-Selection File

This file exists essentially to provide a link between all the other WAIS files relating to individuals (including three not described herein). For each individual it includes certain basic demographic information and tells what types of data are available for what years in each of the other files. The history-selection thus provides us with the ability to choose subsamples of persons with particular characteristics and to select their relevant records from the other files for special studies.

SOME DEFICIENCIES IN THESE DATA

One obvious deficiency is the fact that some income derived from stockholdings is not reported on income-tax returns, either through taxpayer "error" or because the taxpayer's gross reportable income is so low that he is not required to file a return. These missing data may be intermittent if taxpayer error is due to forgetfulness, which is not systematic or consistent through time, and also if a person's gross reportable income fluctuates about the rather low Wisconsin filing limit.*

Missing data can also be a problem with respect to cases in which there is complete and accurate reporting. For example, an individual who purchased a stock prior to 1946 and made no further transactions in

---

* There are other reasons why our tax records may not represent a full time series for an individual over the period. Moving into the state after 1945 may account for a later starting date. A series may terminate for a variety of reasons where the taxpayer ceases to earn reportable gross income in Wisconsin (becoming a resident at some out of state location, retiring, or dying). Changing residence first out of and then back into the state can cause gaps similar to fluctuations of gross reportable income. For women these problems are more severe and are additionally complicated by the fact that the basic sample is based on name-group clusters so that women may marry into or out of the sample.

Some Ways of Handling Missing Data—A Case Study

that stock until after 1964, and who also was not an interviewee represented in the assets-diary file, will never have been required to report purchase date and price. If the stock is represented in the Lorie-Fisher file we will still be able to reconstruct the person's holding of the stock (number and total value of shares) from his reported dividends. However, without the purchase information we could do no better than estimate his basis, so that only an estimate of the amount of unrealized gain in his portfolio attributable to this stockholding could be made.

The deficiency just described is a little less severe if, *ceteris paribus*, the person purchased the stock after the beginning of our time series of information for him. In that case we at least have the year of purchase, the year in which he first reported dividends (not identical with a calendar reporting year, but extending from the last ex-dividend date in the prior year to the last ex-dividend date in the current reporting year). As is explained further in the next section, we may even be able to make a reasonable inference as to the quarter of purchase. This is confounded by another complication or deficiency in these cases where absence of sale or asset-diary data deprives us of purchase information—there may be subsequent purchases of stock already held, as evidenced by an otherwise unexplainable increase in dividends reported from this source.

The above deficiencies relate to those files containing data about individuals, the property-income receivers. In addition there may be missing information about corporations, the payors. The most extreme cases are those in the supplementary firm file, where only the identification data are available. Companies in the Lorie-Fisher file but not in the Compustat file have data only through 1960 recorded. For later years even companies in the Compustat file have less detailed price data than is contained in the Lorie-Fisher file.

Finally we note the case in which data are completely missing in both types of files. Stock in a corporation (probably closely held) that never pays a dividend and whose stock is never traded by our sample individuals (or at least for which no dividends or sales are reported by the individuals) may well be held (and involve substantial unrealized gain) by some of the persons in our sample, but we will be unaware of its existence (it will not even appear in the supplementary firm file). Hopefully, such cases are rare.

In all of the above we have referred to obtaining purchase information from the tax records if the person sold the stock. Before 1965, however, the person was also required to recognize the gain on "other disposition of intangible personal property such as stocks and bonds, regardless of their location." Thus the data are not deficient with respect to donated stocks: donations data prior to 1965 did not distinguish whether or not the donation was cash or other property but were only allowable for nonprofit and otherwise qualifying institutions in Wisconsin. On the other hand, Wisconsin did follow the federal rule on stock dividends, so that receipt of such dividends must usually be inferred from the conjunction of the individual and corporate data bodies.

The deficiencies noted above may occur in various combinations of course, which makes for an unfortunately rich variety of possibilities with respect to misreporting or missing information. Generally we may characterize the data listed on pp. 178–179 that might be available as individual acquisition, disposition, and total-cash-dividend data (with stock-dividend data available also from the asset-diary file) and as corporate-market-value and dividends-per-share data. We might summarize this section by saying that any combination of the individual and corporate data that *might* be available *might* also be *un*available for a given individual-payor combination in a given year. The next section contains our proposed procedures for handling these deficiencies.

OVERCOMING DATA DEFICIENCIES

The Corporate Payor Files*

The simplest but most time consuming and expensive way to overcome missing data problems is to seek out the missing information and enter it in the appropriate file. Indeed, we propose just this for some of the corporate data. For example, Chicago's Center for Research in Security Prices has more detailed price data on tape than that in even the Lorie-Fisher file for the years following 1960 and for the same firms. We hope to obtain at least some of these data from that source. Similarly we propose to obtain financing for extending the property-income file to the years 1960–1964; the desirability of doing so will be evident at various places in the discussion below.

With respect to other missing data our proposals are more complex. For at least some of the companies in the supplementary firm file we could obtain data on at least annual dividends and high, low, and closing prices for the year from Standard and Poor's *Security Owner's Stock Guide,* and we hope to obtain financing for this extension of the data. For closely held Wisconsin corporations we could obtain annual-dividend

---

* Lorie-Fisher, Compustat, and supplementary firm files.

Some Ways of Handling Missing Data—A Case Study

and net-worth data from the State Corporation Income Tax Archive and the Wisconsin Department of Securities, and we may seek financing for this if it would not be prohibitively expensive (we are investigating the cost of this procedure).

After all of the above had been accomplished, however, there would still be some companies in the supplementary firm file for which no data had been collected. Even here not all is lost, because at least *some* information on these companies appears in the individual files (property income and asset diary), otherwise we would not have the company listed in the supplementary firm file at all. If all that the individual files contain is the annual-dividend receipts of one person from the company in question, no improvement is possible in our knowledge. However, if *any person* in the file ever reports a disposition of stock for *any year* for which we have his records, we immediately obtain a great deal of additional data. For the disposition date and at least one acquisition date we obtain per-share-price information and some data on the number of shares, which allows dividend-per-share calculation. Each additional reported disposition will tend to add such information for other dates, since it is unlikely that all dispositions reported will be for exactly the same dates, the typical exception to this being the case when a group of original owners are being bought out. Obviously the longer our time series, the more likely we are to observe dispositions of stock of any one company and thus the better able we will be to reconstruct this partial information.

Given these partial price data, interpolation may be used for intermediate dates. A linear interpolation between two adjacent price-dates established a trend, and the actual price would be presumed to fluctuate about this linear interpolation in the same manner as an appropriate stock index fluctuates about its trend between the same dates. A general index such as Standard and Poor's index might be satisfactory enough, but, since we can get industry classification codes for the Wisconsin companies from the State Industrial Commission, we could perhaps construct indexes more closely identified with the company in question from the Lorie-Fisher and Compustat file data for similar companies.

Even if no dispositions are reported we may at least be able to derive some dividend-per-share data and determine acquisition of additional shares during our reporting period if we have dividends per year from a given company for several persons in the property-income file. To the extent that the year-to-year fluctuations in total dividends received from the company are perfectly correlated as amongst individuals they would be presumed to have not acquired additional shares. If one person ex-

188   Handling Missing-Data Problems

periences a jump at some time in his dividends greater than the percentage increase experienced by others, he will be presumed to have acquired additional shares during the year. Of course it could be that any person reporting a smaller percentage increase than the maximum reported over all persons was engaged in a disposition that he did not report. Indeed, if he were an extreme observation, the only one of, say, 10 persons when all the rest were reporting the same percentage change, this would be the presumption. Thus it is important to have as many persons and years data as can be obtained—an additional reason for extending the property-income file for the years 1960–1964.

Reported dividend streams from several individuals also may give us an approximate procedure for estimating number of shares and dividends per share, since the number of shares for which dividends are received can be presumed to be an integer unless the persons are a husband and wife with joint ownership of the shares. We can get around the latter problem by aggregating the dividends received from the same company by both partners of a marriage. We then have a sequence of dividends plus (perhaps) indications of changes in shares held as described in the preceding paragraph. Then we look for the smallest integer that divides all dividend receipts of a person (adjusted for changes in holdings) such that the resulting number is the same for all persons in any one year, this resulting number being the dividend per share for that year (which *may* be fractional). Here again additional years of data in the property-income file would immeasurably increase the precision of the procedures.

To clarify the procedures involved in the above two paragraphs an example will be helpful. Suppose we have dividends received from the XYZ Corporation by individuals A, B, and C for five successive years as reported in Table 10.1 below. These data imply, according to the first

Table 10.1
Dividends Received from XYZ Corporation

| | Individual Dividend Recipient | | |
Year, t	A	B	C
1	$10	$15	$20
2	12	18	24
3	12	18	30
4	9.6	18	30
5	9.6	18	30

of these paragraphs, that C increased his number of shares by 25 percent in year $t = 2$, whereas A is suspected of disposing of one-fifth of his shares in $t = 3$. The dividend rate per share appears to have risen 20 percent from $t = 1$ to $t = 2$ and remained constant thereafter. A's holdings in $t = 1$ must be an integral multiple of five shares; B's must be 50 percent greater and be an integer; C's must be twice A's and an integral multiple of 4. The resulting inferred shareholdings and dividends per share are exhibited in Table 10.2.

Table 10.2

Inferred XYZ Dividend Rate and Shareholdings of A, B, and C

Year, t	Dividend Rate	Shareholdings of Individuals (No.)		
		A	B	C
1	$1.00	10	15	20
2	1.20	10	15	20
3	1.20	10	15	25
4	1.20	8	15	25
5	1.20	8	15	25

For all the above we have primarily relied on the property-income file for supplementing the supplementary-firm-file data. But the asset-diary file also contains data on closely held corporations and other stockholdings. Here again the data in the individual file can give information about the company file. However, the asset-diary-file data are in some ways less reliable, if only because the individual was not subject to penalty due to misreporting or plain carelessness. Especially this is so in those cases where we asked the respondent to list dispositions of assets from 1958 through 1963—to the extent they relied on memory instead of records an underreporting bias exists. One of the important effects of extending the property-income file to 1964 is that it gives us a vital link between these two files and allows us to estimate various types of reporting biases.

In those cases in which we do not have price data for a company but do have dividends, earnings, and net worth per share we propose to use a procedure that adjusts net worth per share by a factor that reflects previous earnings and dividend history and the length of that history, as derived from a study of the similar data in the Compustat and Lorie-Fisher files for corporations in which these data plus prices are present. Naturally this will also take into account some general measure of the level of stock prices as well and may be done on subgroups of firms classified into broad industries.

For companies in which we only have an inferred dividend-per-share figure an overall average of price-dividend ratios for each time period will have to be used to approximate the price. Some measure of dispersion of price-dividend ratios for each time period should also be included in order that we could estimate "probable high or low" figures as well as a mean.

The above approximative procedures can be checked for their efficacy by applying them to instances in which the actual data available are extensive enough for approximations to be unnecessary. Comparing the approximations with the actual data then gives us a measure of the degree of reliability of the procedure. The results are of interest per se.

Individual Files*

The nonreporting of income sources by individuals is generally thought to be less of a problem for Wisconsin income tax returns than in other states, due to Wisconsin's long history of effective enforcement and cooperation with federal authorities in exchanging information. Still, there is no question but that some bias exists, particularly for rent and interest.[3] This bias is expected to be much less for the years 1962 and after, due to the reduction in the federal requirement to file information returns on business interest and dividends from $100 to $10 (or more). This gives us yet another reason for extending the data in the property-income file to 1964. Some aggregate data are available on the jump that occured in reporting these sources on tax returns, but we would like to investigate these jumps on the microlevel to see the characteristics of the persons who appeared to have a sudden accretion of wealth at that time. This will also give us a valuable check on the accuracy of earlier year data and permit some inferences of stockholdings that were "hidden" in those years. It also means that the approximating procedures described in the preceding section on the corporate payor file will be more complete. The marginal accretion of knowledge due to adding data for 1963 will exceed that of adding data for 1960 or 1961, for example.

Where the missing data are due to a missing return for a person, we are now already engaged in procedures using information in the master file to infer whether or not this omission is legitimate or due to our having missed a return that should be present. These procedures rely partly on the answers to questions such as, "Is your spouse filing a return for this

---

* Property-income and asset-diary files.

Some Ways of Handling Missing Data—A Case Study   191

year?"; and for both husband and wife, "Did you file a return in [last year]? If not, give reason." The property-income file itself can be helpful in this gap-plugging operation, because persistence of substantial dividend and interest income in the periods before and after a gap, with no indication that there had been capital-loss realizations or other possibly negative gross-income sources in the gap year(s) would be prima facie evidence that no gap should exist.

One possible difficulty in our methodology occurs when a company has had more than one class of common stock issued, or has had preferred stock issued, and the taxpayer never indicates which he is holding. If there is a disposition, the identity of the holding may be inferred from the detailed acquisition date and the acquisition- and disposition-price data. Failing this method of determination we have additional devices at hand. With dividend-per-share data available for each issue and year, we can divide the taxpayer's reported annual dividends by each dividend rate and choose the issue that yields the most suitable record of integral-shares holdings consistent with absence of acquisition and disposition data. This method might fail if, for example, all dividend-per-share rates of the company's issues always experienced the same percentage changes from year to year. In such cases we would invoke the further criterion of a "round lot assumption." If for any issue the above method gives a number of shares that is an integral multiple of 100, it would be assumed that that issue is the one held.

The round-lot assumption is also helpful in overcoming another deficiency. No acquisition data are available but otherwise unexplainable increases in dividends during the period in which we have a person's data occur, so that acquisitions within a given dividend year (between last ex-dividend and payment dates) may be inferred. The question arises in some cases whether such acquisitions occurred in two successive years for which dividends jumped or whether the successive dividend jumps are due to a single acquisition after the first ex-dividend date in the income year. The first test to be invoked here is of course the integral number of shares test, similar to that described in connection with Tables 10.1 and 10.2. This may be inconclusive when quarterly dividends per share are very stable over the period in question, and in that case the round-lot-assumption criterion may be invoked (if *any* allocation of purchase dates will yield round lots). Where neither criterion is conclusive we propose to include all viable alternatives in the person's record (separately coded) so that we can in analysis observe the individual's behavior under each hypothetical case in order to see what difference it makes to the analysis.

192 Handling Missing-Data Problems

For example, it might be critical in making a division of unrealized gain between short- and long-term gain, etc.

The purposes of trying to pin down the acquisition dates should be obvious: accurate determination of portfolio values in the shortrun; accurate division of value between basis (acquisition value) and unrealized gain in the longer run. Table 10.3 presents a hypothetical

Table 10.3
Hypothetical Patterns of Dividend Payment and Receipt

Year, t	Quarterly Dividend Payments by Company				Annual Dividend	Total Dividends Received by A
	1st	2nd	3rd	4th		
1	$0.25	$0.25	$0.25	$0.25	$1	$ 0
2	0.20	0.30	0.25	0.25	1	50
3	0.00	0.50	0.25	0.25	1	100
4	0.25	0.25	0.25	0.25	1	100

example of a combination of quarterly dividends per share paid by a particular company over a period of four years and the total dividends reported received by individual A in the four years.

Assuming complete and accurate reporting and no dispositions, a little figuring allows us to make the following statements with certainty:

1. Stockholder A held none of the stock prior to the last dividend-payment date in $t = 1$.

2. Stockholder A acquired 100 shares of the stock between the last dividend-payment date in $t = 1$ and the ex-dividend date for the third quarter dividend in $t = 3$ and acquired no further shares thereafter (through the fourth quarter ex-dividend date of $t = 4$.)

3. It is not possible to distinguish acquisitions in the first and second quarters of $t = 3$ from each other (any acquisitions are indeterminately distributed between the two quarters).

4. Acquisitions in the first quarter of $t = 2$ did not exceed 50 shares.

5. Acquisitions in the second quarter of $t = 2$ did not exceed 62½ shares.

6. Acquisitions in the third quarter of $t = 2$ did not exceed 100 shares.

Some Ways of Handling Missing Data—A Case Study

7. Acquisitions in the fourth quarter of $t=2$ did not exceed $66\frac{2}{3}$ shares.

8. Acquisitions in the first or second quarters of $t=3$ did not exceed 50 shares.

The fact is that there exists an infinite number of patterns of acquisition unless we invoke the integral number of shares test. Six of these patterns are illustrated in Table 10.4, and they reflect the statements made in the preceding paragraph. It can be seen that patterns 2 and 4 violate the integral-holding requirement, but that still leaves four possible patterns. The round-lot assumption allows us to select pattern 3. However, if A had reported dividends of 0, 40, 80, and 80 dollars, not even this assumption helps, because then fewer than 100 shares were purchased in all.

Table 10.4
Hypothetical Patterns of Acquisition by Stockholders A Consistent with Table 10.3 (Number of shares)

Year		t = 2			t = 3	
Quarter	1st	2nd	3rd	4th	1st or 2nd	3rd or 4th
Pattern:						
1	50	0	0	0	50	0
2	0	62½	0	0	37½	0
3	0	0	100	0	0	0
4	0	0	0	66⅔	33⅓	0
5	10	50	0	0	40	0
6	25	20	20	20	15	0

The above procedures are likely to yield good approximations of actual purchase prices and dates for most cases of purchases within the reporting period. Naturally we do not know these exactly and would record both high and low prices (where available) for the period of purchase chosen by our criteria (high and low monthly closing prices for the Lorie-Fisher file through 1960). Again we may check the efficacy of this procedure by using it on data where subsequent dispositions of stock acquired after the start of the reporting period give us actual acquisition dates and prices. Naturally, the greater the number of years, the more likely it is that we will find a representative sample of stocks for which we have both acquisi-

194 Handling Missing-Data Problems

tion and disposition within the period. Again we have strong reasons for extending the property-income file to 1964.

The only serious remaining problem concerns stock acquired before the individual's first reporting year, held continuously throughout the period and not reported in the asset-diary file. The basis having been established prior to the first reporting period, it would seem that we have virtually no reasonable means of assigning such a basis value. If the values are available for prior years, we do expect to record high and low values to allow alternative treatments in analysis. We believe we can do much better than this, however, because we know considerably more about our individuals than what is in the property-income file; for example, we have age available, and we do not consider it possible to acquire stock prior to birth (trust income is separately reported). Indeed, a major piece of work involved will be to look at all cases in which we do have basis values and estimate a relationship among our variables that would allow us to predict (backwards) acquisition dates for the person's given demographic, income, and other portfolio characteristics, as well as for the characteristics of the company and stock and their history.

ESTIMATION OF THE REST OF THE PORTFOLIO—A BRIEF SURVEY

The discussion so far has been concerned solely with the common-stock subsection of the portfolios of individuals. Data similar to that for common stocks but relating to other negotiable securities issued by corporations are also available in our various files except for the Lorie-Fisher file, and the above procedures should be even more simply applied to preferred stocks and to corporate bonds. Bond issues of state and local governments do not appear in either the Lorie-Fisher or the Compustat files, but we can get data regarding them for entry in the supplementary firm file, both directly from the property-income file and from the asset-diary file. Federal government bond issues appear only in the asset-diary file at this time and need similar supplementation.

Time series of average annual interest paid on bank savings accounts, credit-union shares, and savings and loan shares should be readily obtainable by state and can be used to capitalize reported interest receipts from these sources. No demand-deposit information is available except for December 31, 1963, in the asset-diary file, and it is unlikely that we can do anything to remedy this deficiency.

Real property is a substantial stumbling block at this time. Home ownership is indicated where it is clear that "nonbusiness interest paid" included in the master file is for a personal-residence mortgage, but it is often impossible to tell this, especially for the older and wealthier populations (where the relative sizes of interest payments to various sources may be misleading clues), and for the lowest income segments and others who do not itemize deductions. Even so, the longer the time series of such payments in a person's master file that steadily and smoothly decline, the greater the presumption that they are mortgage-interest payments. On the other hand, the interview and asset-diary files contain positive evidence of home ownership over a period of time and should be helpful for the interview and asset-diary respondent subsample. Sales of principal residences may give rise to gains and losses in the property-income file but are subject to the same type of rollover provision as in federal taxation and thus are not necessarily reportable.

In any event reported "nonbusiness interest paid" indicates a claim against the assets in the portfolio (as well as against those we do not include, such as durable goods). Some average capitalization rate should be applied to these payments to give at least the approximate magnitude of such claims, since their presence may greatly influence the person's desired portfolio composition.

Other sources of information about real property are similarly troublesome. If the property is located outside of Wisconsin, income from it is not even reportable. In this way it is similar to federal bond interest, and our only information is in the interview and asset-diary files. Rental property within Wisconsin appears in considerable detail in the property-income file, including original cost of the property, depreciated value, etc. However, actual market values need to be estimated. For cases in which persons sell rental property, of course, such market values are established at the end as well as the beginning of the period, at least approximately (the buyer may be a poor bargainer, but he is a part of the market). Pooling data from many such sales according to some sort of reasonable classification scheme reflecting the type, location, and quality of the property may yield sufficiently detailed time series to permit some average rough market values to be assigned to the rental properties.

Income from a business, profession, partnership, or farm tends to be a mixture of wage and salary income with return on invested capital, which is very difficult to unscramble, especially where rather loose accounting practices are followed. Straight underreporting is also a serious problem here. Detailed information additional to that in the property-income file is contained in the interview and asset-diary files, but it is doubtful that it is of significantly helpful quality. At this point it is difficult to know how these problems should even be approached.

Other items that might be considered part of a person's wealth, aside from his earning power, include present values of interests in trusts, estates, expected inheritances, retirement-income plans (including social security), life insurance, patents, unexercised stock or other options, deferred compensation schemes, and non-cash-income-producing property. On many of these items we have information only in the interview or asset-diary files; on a few we have data in the property-income file; on some we have no information at all.

It appears clear from the above that we will never be able to completely reconstruct the portfolios of our sampled persons. Many analyses can be performed with only partial portfolio data, however, and one of the purposes of going ahead with only the common-stock subsection of individual portfolios is precisely to take advantage of the portion where the most complete and reliable data are available. Successful analyses on this portion will hopefully be instructive in pointing out where more detailed data on the remainder of the portfolio will provide the greatest payoff.

SUMMARY AND SOME CONCLUDING OBSERVATIONS

The proposed treatment of the common-stock portion of individual asset portfolios provides great challenges and opportunities not only for missing-data problem solutions but also sophisticated data-manipulation and estimation techniques. It also has great interest from the standpoint of potential analyses of individual behavior. In the absence of complete estimation of the entire portfolio it is still possible to "control for" much of the non-common-stock portions of the portfolio by taking account of the property incomes reported from other sources (e.g., net rent or interest) as "predetermined" or "regressor" variables, estimating "conditional" relations.

The basic technique of capitalizing reported income streams to arrive at wealth estimates can be extended beyond the common-stock portion of the portfolio, but with somewhat less precision. Partly this is due to the less detailed or less reliable data available; partly it is inherent in the fact that other properties than common stocks have, to more or less degree, a uniqueness that at least the widely traded stocks cannot claim. Except with respect to other marketable securities, the relative degree of information present in our files for different types of property incomes and values reflects the real world relative availability of such information to individual decision makers. Perhaps rough and ready estimates and approximations will better capture the information base of decision makers than more sophisticated knowledge, such as direct appraisals of properties by the most knowledgeable experts. The difficulty with this argument is that individuals will probably know more about the properties they actually own than they know about the general classes of unowned properties. Also we must recognize the distinction between approximating data (average interest rates on savings deposits) and missing data (complete absence of knowledge of federal bond holdings for persons not in the asset-diary file).

Nevertheless, the belief is widespread that the portfolio behavior of investors, especially with respect to common stocks, exerts a considerable influence on the rate and direction of growth of our economy and may provide valuable clues to the way in which less developed nations might serve their needs by structuring their institutional framework using such control variables as the parameters of taxation functions.

To summarize, the proposal to estimate common-stock portfolios and the degree to which they embody unrealized capital gains has many potential payoffs—methodological studies of manipulation of, and checking consistency among, interrelated complex data files; substantive studies of the determinants of human behavior in important aspects; and substantive studies involving prediction of the collective responses of groups of persons to parameters subject to administrative control. The opportunities are unusual and significant.

REFERENCES

1. R. F. Miller and H. W. Watts, "A Model of Household Investment in Financial Assets," in *Determinants of Investment Behavior*, Universities–National Bureau Conference Series No. 18, National Bureau of Economic Research, 1967, pp. 357–380.
2. T. R. Atkinson, *The Pattern of Financial Asset Ownership: Wisconsin Individuals, 1949*. Princeton, N.J.: Princeton University Press (for the National Bureau of Economic Research), 1956.
3. See M. E. Moyer, *The Validity of Income Distributions from a Multi-Year Sample of Wisconsin Income Tax Returns*, WAIS Monograph 1, Madison, Wisc., 1966; and R. A. Bauman, M. H. David, and R. F. Miller, *Sources of Income Variability for Male Individuals in Wisconsin, 1947–1959*, presented at the Universities–National Bureau Conference on Income and Wealth, March 1967 (obtainable as Research on the Economic Behavior of Households Workshop Paper No. 6704, Social Systems Research Institute, University of Wisconsin, Madison).

Chapter Eleven

Regression Analysis with Missing Data

R. M. Elashoff and Janet D. Elashoff

The problem of incomplete or missing data is a major one for investigators, especially in clinical medicine and the social sciences. It occurs because of nonresponse, loss of subjects, transcription errors, and a variety of other reasons. What statistical techniques are available to deal with incomplete data? Can we simply ignore the missing observations? The answers depend on why the data are missing. We must know something about the kinds of observations that are missing and which variables influence the loss of certain observations before advice is possible.

In this chapter we present several specific probability models to describe which observations are missing and why, and discuss the statistical techniques appropriate for regression analysis under each of the models. An extensive bibliography is included.

Incomplete data problems may be categorized as nonresponse problems or as partial-information problems. In a nonresponse problem we have complete information for most individuals but no information at all on the rest. In a partial-information problem more than one variable or factor is under study and some variables have not been observed on every individual, so we have incomplete information for some individuals in the sample.

Partial-information problems may occur in many ways. For instance, in a followup panel study of treatment for a chronic disease all sampled individuals have initial measurements, but some individuals leave the cohort before the study ends. In an epidemiological survey or a study contrasting the relationship between standard and experimental measuring instruments some people may refuse to undergo all the tests or certain tests may be given only to a random subset of the individuals. Many more examples could be mentioned.

In this chapter we discuss some general probability models that have been proposed to account for the occurrence of missing observations in regression-analysis problems. To bring out the essentials of each model we assume that one independent variable x and one dependent variable y are under study for each individual. We further assume the following:

1. y has a linear regression on x—it might be necessary to use transformed y- and x-scales.

2. No hidden variables exist.

3. n individuals are sampled, with n_y individuals recorded on the y-variable, n_x individuals recorded on x, $m_y = n - n_y$, and $m_x = n - n_x$, and n_c observations are complete.

PROBABILITY MODELS FOR INCOMPLETE DATA—THE RANDOM MODEL

The first probability model for missing data that we shall study is model 1—the random model. We define the random model as follows:

1. Suppose that the x-variable is fixed so that at each point x we take one or more y-observations; for example, the x-variable may denote time or selected levels of a quantitative factor, and y is some response variable measured on individuals randomly assigned to the levels of x. We know the x-variable for each individual but some of the y-observations may be missing ($m_x = 0$).

It is commonly assumed that missing observations occur at random. The random model asserts that the probability that an individuals' y-value is observed is independent of both y and x. This random model seems appropriate where factors completely independent of y and x and

200   Handling Missing-Data Problems

their relationship are causing missing data. The random model of course is the basis of the missing plot technique in regression.

2. It frequently happens that both y and x are random variables. In this situation the random model has the same meaning as in the definition above, now extended to x also, and we drop the requirement that $m_x = 0$. Useful estimators of the linear-regression function may be obtained by exploiting the randomness of the x-variable instead of conditioning upon the values of x, at least insofar as Neyman-Pearson theory is concerned.

Regression Analysis with Randomly Missing Data

First let us suppose that the levels of x were fixed in advance of the experiment. Suppose that one y-observation was supposed to have been taken at each of the n-values of x; however, some y-observations were not obtained or not recorded. Thus n_y y-observations are available, $n_y < n$. Presumably n different x-values were used in order to check the linearity assumption.

The distributional assumptions are

$$y_i = \alpha + \beta x_i + \epsilon_i$$
or
$$y_i = \mu + \beta(x_i - x_c) + \epsilon_i \tag{11.1}$$

if y_i is observed, the ϵ_i are independent and identically distributed with $E(\epsilon_i) = 0$, $\text{var}(\epsilon_i) = \sigma^2$, where

$$\alpha = \mu - \beta \bar{x}_c, \quad \bar{x}_c = \sum_c x_i/n_c,$$

n_c is the number of complete (x, y) pairs (equal to n_y in this example) and $\sum_c$ is the sum over the index i such that both y_i and x_i are observed. (These definitions are motivated by future use.)

We want to obtain estimators of μ, β, and σ^2, test certain hypotheses about these parameters, and then establish confidence bounds for the regression line and the parameters.

If the ϵ_i are normally distributed, the maximum-likelihood estimators of μ and β are the minimum-variance linear unbiased estimators. Thus the least-squares estimators are identical to the maximum-likelihood estimators and are given by the familiar formulas

$$\hat{\mu} = \sum_c y_i/n_c = \bar{y}_c, \quad \hat{\beta} = \frac{\sum_c (x_i - \bar{x}_c)y_i}{\sum_c (x_i - \bar{x}_c)^2} = \frac{S_{x,y}}{S_{x,c}}. \tag{11.2}$$

Other estimators of μ and β are possible (see, for example Acton[1] when nonnormal ϵ_i's are probable). These estimators make no use of the missing y's—and quite properly so. Thus, when x is fixed, $m_x = 0$ and the random model obtains, statisticians should estimate μ and β as they usually do. Furthermore, the best quadratic unbiased estimator of σ^2 is then

$$s^2 = \sum_c [y_i - \hat{\mu} - \hat{\beta}(x_i - \bar{x}_c)]^2 / (n_c - 2). \qquad (11.3)$$

If the ϵ_i are normally distributed, the t- or F-distributions can be used to test hypotheses about μ, β, σ^2 and put confidence limits on the entire line. If the ϵ_i are not normally distributed, the t- or F-distributions might still be used in practice if the distribution of the error terms and the conditions on the x_i's satisfy those given by Box and Watson.[2] These conditions can be summarized by saying that sensitivity to nonnormality in the y's is determined by the extent of nonnormality in the x's. When nonnormality may make the t-test unattractive, a test of H_0: $\beta = 0$ can be made by methods given by Acton[1] Jogdeo;[3] confidence limits on the regression line are not given in the statistics literature.

Now let us take up the situation where both y and x are random variables. When the sample is complete we assume that

$$y_i = \mu_y + \beta(x_i - \mu_x) + \epsilon_i \quad (i = 1,2, \ldots, n),$$

$$E(\epsilon_i) = 0, \quad E(\epsilon_i \epsilon_i') = \begin{cases} \sigma^2 & i = i', \\ 0 & \text{otherwise.} \end{cases} \qquad (11.4)$$

However, the data consist of n_c independent bivariate observations $z = (y_i, x_i)'$ (not necessarily having a bivariate normal distribution) and $(n_y - n_c)$ observations recorded on y and $(n_x - n_c)$ observations recorded on x (in all n_x x-observations and n_y y-observations). The assumptions now are

$$E_{y|x}(y_i) = \mu_y|_x = \mu_y + \beta(x_i - \mu_i)$$
$$\text{var}_{y|x}(y_i) = \sigma^2 \qquad (11.5)$$

if x_i is observed, and

$$E(y_i) = \mu_y$$
$$\text{var}(y_i) = \sigma_y^2 \qquad (11.6)$$

if x_i is not observed, and furthermore x has a linear regression on y. We do not assume that (y, x) has a bivariate normal distribution.

202　Handling Missing-Data Problems

Our goals are to estimate the parameters μ_y, β, $\mu_y|_x$, and σ^2 and then to construct tests and confidence intervals for several problems in regression.

Let us consider the estimation problem first. The least-squares estimators for μ_y, β, $\mu_y|_x$, and σ^2 defined previously remain linear unbiased estimators of these parameters. Then why not use these estimators? It is possible to obtain estimators of these parameters that have smaller mean-square errors [variance + (bias)^2] than the least-squares estimators.

We have investigated several alternative estimation procedures and found that the following two-stage estimation procedure compared favorably with the others in large and small-sample efficiency.[4] First, estimate the regression of x on y from the n_c complete observations by ordinary least squares; second, estimate the m_x missing x-observations from the preceding linear-regression equation; third, estimate the regression of y on x from the n_y completed "observations." The estimated linear-regression equation is then

$$\hat{y}^{(2)} = \overline{y} + \hat{\beta}^{(2)} [x - \hat{\mu}_x^{(2)}],$$

where

$$\overline{y} = \underset{n_y}{\Sigma}\ y/n_y,$$

$$\hat{\mu}_x^{(2)} = \overline{x}_c + \hat{\delta}^{LS}\frac{m_x}{n_y}(\overline{y}_m - \overline{y}_c),$$

$$\hat{\beta}^{(2)} = \frac{\underset{n_y}{\Sigma}\ (y-\overline{y})(x)}{\underset{n_y}{\Sigma}\ [x - \hat{\mu}_i^{(2)}]^2}$$

and $x_i = \overline{x}_c + \hat{\delta}^{LS}(y_i - \overline{y}_c)$ when x_i is missing and

$$\overline{x}_c = \underset{n_c}{\Sigma}\ \frac{x}{n_c},$$

$$\overline{y}_m = \underset{m_x}{\Sigma}\ \frac{y}{m_x},$$

$$\overline{y}_c = \underset{n_c}{\Sigma}\ \frac{y}{n_c},$$

$$\hat{\delta}^{LS} = \underset{n_c}{\Sigma}\ (x - \overline{x}_c)y\ /\ \underset{n_c}{\Sigma}\ (y - \overline{y}_c).$$

Regression Analysis with Missing Data

The symbol Σ, for example, means the summation over those y-observations for which the corresponding x-observations are missing.

Several remarks about this two-stage method are in order. This method does not make use of the m_y x's corresponding to the missing y-observations. The estimator $\overline{y}$ is an unbiased estimator of μ_y; however, $\hat{y}^{(2)}$ and $\hat{\beta}^{(2)}$ are not unbiased estimators of $\mu_y|x$ and β, respectively. However we can modify these estimators so that they are nearly unbiased estimators. Thus we estimate β by

$$\hat{\beta}^{(2)}_u = [\frac{n_c}{n_y} + (1 - \frac{n_c}{n_y})\rho^2]\hat{\beta}^{(2)}$$

and estimate $\mu_y|x$ by

$$\hat{y}^{(2)}_u = \overline{y} + \hat{\beta}^{(2)}_u [x - \hat{\mu}^{(2)}_x],$$

where

$$\hat{\rho} = \hat{\delta}^{LS}\left[\underset{n_c}{\Sigma} (y - y_c)^2 / \underset{n_c}{\Sigma} (x - x_c)^2\right]^{1/2},$$

an unbiased estimator of σ^2 is

$$s^2_u = [1 - (1 - \frac{n_c}{n_y}\rho^2)]^{-1} \underset{n_y}{\Sigma} [y - \hat{y}^{(2)}_u]^2/(n^y - 2).$$

How do these estimators compare with the least-squares estimators? Afifi and Elashoff show that when m_x and m_y are each less than 30 percent of n and $n \geq 20$, these estimators are nearly unbiased and are almost always better than the least-squares estimators when ρ, the correlation coefficient, is less than 0.90 and (x, y) is bivariate normal.[5] In large samples these estimators are nearly as good as the maximum-likelihood estimators under the above assumptions. No tests or confidence limits are presently available for these estimators.

PROBABILITY MODELS FOR MISSING DATA IN WHICH THE *x* VARIABLE INFLUENCES WHETHER *y* IS MISSING OR NOT

The probability that an observation is missing may depend on the actual values of the variables. We define model 2—independent variable influences missing data—for two cases: (1) x is a fixed variable ($m_x = 0$) (2) x is a random variable and x's missing at random.

1. The variable x is a fixed, or mathematical, variable. (No x-observations are missing.) We assume that the probability that an

204 Handling Missing-Data Problems

individual's y-value is observed depends on the value of x but is independent of y. For example, suppose patients are observed on some variable y at several times x during the day. Due to visiting hours, etc., y-observations are much more likely to be missed at certain times of the day then at others.

2. The variable x is a random variable and x's are missing at random, and the probability that an individual's y-value is observed depends on his x-value but not on his y-value. This model is possibly most useful when individuals are selected on x first and then measured on y.

Regression Analysis with Missing Observations Governed by Model 2

It is important to note that the statistical properties of the least-squares estimators derived under the random model (model 1) are no longer correct under model 2; that is, under model 2 these estimators are not unbiased, do not have minimum variance, and the t-statistics computed by using these estimators do not follow a t-distribution.

Very little work has been done on estimating regression equations with missing data except when the random model obtains. We report the solutions available for certain special cases.

When both x and y are random variables and x is measured on all individuals and then y-measurements are taken only if x is in some interval (x_a, x_b), then work by A. C. Cohen [6] is applicable. This author shows how to compute estimators for μ_y, β, σ_y, and σ and makes some comments on hypothesis testing; he also gives a good bibliography.*

PROBABILITY MODELS WHEN THE DEPENDENT VARIABLE y INFLUENCES MISSING DATA

Model 3: Dependent Variable y Influences Missing Data

Here again we define model 3 for two particular situations:

1. x is a fixed variable. No x-observations are missing. The probability that an individual's y-value is observed depends on his y-value but not on his x-value. This model may occur when the y-observation is

---

* See also the Chapter by L. E. Moses in the *International Encyclopedia of Social Science*.[7]

discarded because of a seeming gross error and we suspect that the probability of a gross error depends on the true value of y.

2. Both y and x are random variables. We assume that x-observations are missing by the random model and y-observations are missing as above: x may, for example, denote the standard basal-metabolism test measured without error, and y may denote a new basal-metabolism test where gross errors can occur due to the unfamiliarity of the technician with the new test procedures, etc.

Regression Analysis with Model 3

As in the case of model 2, the usual properties of the ordinary least-square estimators do not obtain if model 3 holds. We report the solutions to estimation and testing problems that are available in the literature for two special cases of model 3.

We assume that y is known for some individuals and that for the remaining individuals we know only that their y-value, y_i, is greater than some constant c_{0i} ($y_i \geq c_{0i}$).

If the ϵ_i in Equation 11.1 are normal, estimators for μ_y, β, σ^2 have been found. For fixed x's ($m_x = 0$) Glasser gives estimators and shows how to construct large-sample tests and confidence intervals;[8] when the c_{0i} are all equal to some c_0, the simpler expressions in Cohen[9] may be used. For the x's random, the work of Cohen[10] may be modified to apply to this situation.

CONCLUSIONS

We have discussed estimation problems for simple linear regression with missing data. The ordinary least-squares procedures do not hold up well when data are missing. If observations are missing at random there exist satisfactory general estimation procedures. If the probability of a missing observation is dependent on an individual's x- or y-value, estimation procedures and tests have been worked out only for certain special cases.

REFERENCES

1. F. S. Acton, Analysis of Straight-Line Data. New York: Wiley, 1959.
2. G. E. P. Box, and G. S. Watson, "Robustness to Non-Normality of Regression Tests," *Biometrika*, 49 (1962), pp. 93–107.
3. K. Jogdeo, *Nonparametric Methods for Regression*. Amsterdam: Stichting Math Centrum, Report S–330, 1964.
4. A. A. Afifi and R. M. Elashoff, "Missing Observations in Multivariate Statistics III: Large-Sample Analysis of Simple Linear Regression." *Journal of the American Statistical Association;* and "Missing Observations in Multivariate Statistics IV: A Note on Some Small-Sample Results," *Journal of the American Statistical Association* 64 (1969)
5. See ref. 4.
6. A. C. Cohen, Jr., "Restriction and Selection in Samples from Bivariate Normal Distributions," *Journal of the American Statistical Association*, 50 (1955), pp. 884–893.
7. L. E. Moses, "Censoring," Chapter in the *International Encyclopedia of Social Science*, Statistics volume. Collier, 1968.
8. M. Glasser, "Regression Analysis with Dependent Variable Censored," *Biometrics*, 21 (1965), pp. 300–307.
9. A. C. Cohen, Jr., "Estimating the Mean and Variance of a Normal Distribution from Singly Truncated and Doubly Truncated Samples," *Annals of Mathematical Statistics*, 21 (1950).
10. See ref. 6.

BIBLIOGRAPHY

Afifi, A. A., and Elashoff, R. M., "Missing Observations in Multivariate Statistics I: Review of the Literature," *Journal of the American Statistical Association*, 61 (1966), pp. 595–604.

Afifi, A. A., and Elashoff, R. M., "Missing Observations in Multivariate Statistics II: Point Estimation in Simple Linear Regression," *Journal of the American Statistical Association*, 62 (1967), pp. 10–30.

Anderson, T. W., "Maximum Likelihood Estimates for a Multivariate Normal Distribution when Some Observations are missing," *Journal of the American Statistical Association*, 52 (1957), pp. 200–203.

Bartlett, M. S., "Some Examples of Statistical Methods of Research in Agriculture," *Journal of the Royal Statistical Society Supplement*, 4 (1937), 137–183.

Bhargava, R., *Multivariate Tests of Hypotheses with Incomplete Data*. Applied Mathematics and Statistics Laboratories, Technical Report 3, 1962.

Buck, S. F., "A Method of Estimation of Missing Values in Multivariate Data Suitable for use with an Electronic Computer," *Journal of the Royal Statistical Society*, Series B, 22 (1960), pp. 302–307.

Cochran, W. G., *Sampling Techniques*, 2nd ed. New York: Wiley, 1963, Chapter 13.

Dear, R. E., *A Principal-Component Missing-Data Method for Multiple Regression Models*. Santa Monica, Calif.: System Development Corporation, SP-86, 1959.

Edgett, G. L., "Multiple Regression with Missing Observations among the Independent Variables," *Journal of the American Statistical Association,* **51** (1956), pp. 122-132.

Eklund, G., *Studies of Selection Bias in Applied Statistics.* Uppsala, Almquist and Baktryckeri AB, 1959.

Fiering, M. B., "On the Use of Correlation To Augment Data," *Journal of the American Statistical Association,* **57** (1962), pp. 20-32.

Glasser, M., "Linear Regression Analysis with Missing Observations among the Independent Variables," *Journal of the American Statistical Association,* **59** (1964), pp. 834-844.

Hocking, R., and Smith, W. B., "Estimation of Parameters in the Multivariate Normal Distribution with Missing Observations," *Journal of the American Statistical Association* **63** (1968).

Lord, F. M., "Estimation of Parameters from Incomplete Data," *Journal of the American Statistical Association,* **50** (1955), pp. 870-876.

Matthai, A., "Estimation of Parameters from Incomplete Data with Application to Design of Sample Surveys," *Sankhya,* **2** (1951), pp. 145-152.

Nicholson, G. E., Jr., "Estimation of Parameters from Incomplete Multivariate Samples," *Journal of the American Statistical Association,* **52** (1957), pp. 523-526.

Rao, C. R., "Analysis of Dispersion with Incomplete Observations on One of the Characters," *Journal of the Royal Statistical Society,* Series B, **18** (1956), pp. 259-264.

Sampford, M. P., "The Estimation of Response-Time Distributions III: Truncation and Survival," *Biometrics,* **10** (1954), pp. 531-561.

Tocher, K. D., "The Design and Analysis of Block Experiments," *Journal of the Royal Statistical Society,* Series B, **14** (1952), pp. 45-100.

Trawinski, I. M., and Bargman, R. E., "Maximum Likelihood Estimation with Incomplete Multivariate Data," *Annals of Mathematical Statistics,* **35** (1964), pp. 647-657.

Walsh, J. E., *Computer-Feasible General Method for Fitting and Using Regression Functions when Data Incomplete.* Santa Monica, Calif.: System Development Corporation, SP-71, 1959.

Wilkinson, G. N., "Estimation of the Missing Values for the Analysis of Incomplete Data," *Biometrics,* **14** (1958), pp. 257-286.

Wilks, S. S., "Moments and Distributions of Estimates of Population Parameters from Fragmentary Samples," *Annals of Mathematical Statistics,* **3** (1932), pp. 163-195.

Yates, F., "The Analysis of Replicated Experiments When the Field Results Are Incomplete," *The Empire Journal of Experimental Agriculture,* **1** (1933), pp. 129-142.

Part VI Data-Linkage Problems and Solutions

With the advent of data-archive organizations come increased opportunities for combining data sets from several individual sources. Some research requirements do not necessitate an ability to link together information about individual entities (e.g., persons or businesses); others do. The research by Pool, Abelson, and Popkin requires only the ability to combine data sets that have common variables (by one definition or another). Other research requires that different kinds of data collections be linkable according to the characteristics of certain kinds of specific, more "personal," entities (e.g., individuals or corporations), and still other kinds of research necessitate the ability to combine information about areal units—such as geographic, demographic, and political entities.

This part contains two chapters on methods of identifying for linkage purposes, areal or geographic entities, and another chapter on the problems of linking information about individuals.

Linkage capabilities have consequences for the protection of privacy, and this problem is discussed in the final part. It has already been stressed that a system for data linkage is necessary if advantage is to be taken of complex data structures.

Chapter Twelve

Problems of Area Identification

William T. Fay*

Problems of area identification are being faced and solved in various ways, and differences in the resolutions of these problems by collectors of statistical information may seriously affect the validity of data summaries and the comparability of statistics from different sources.

In most of the work at the Bureau of the Census we try to identify accurately the location of each structure, whether housing unit or place of business, about which we are gathering data. To identify that location with respect to the actual boundaries of the geographic area for which we plan to tabulate the data is not an easy chore and not an inexpensive one. Other gatherers of data, lacking the funds that are required or lacking the need for precision that the Census Bureau feels it must attain, may use methods of identification that are less precise. Although such methods may be quite adequate for the purposes for which the data are being collected, nonetheless they do cause inaccuracies that can lead to serious

---
* Bureau of the Census, Washington, D.C.

212   Data-Linkage Problems and Solutions

misinterpretations if the data are not used with a firm understanding of the geographic concepts that underlay the tabulations.

There are four methods of area identification—methods which are not truly mutually exclusive but which provide a convenient framework for this discussion. These methods, for the sake of brevity, are called as follows:

1. Go look.
2. Look at a map.
3. Use an index
4. Rely on the address.

GO LOOK

The "go look" method has been used in census enumeration for more than 150 years and by others as well. Essentially this method requires the existence of maps that correctly portray the boundaries of all of the geographic areas of significance and an actual on-the-ground identification of the unit for which the statistics are being gathered. In this visit the observer, or enumerator, identifies the location of the structure on his or her map and then records, from the map, the appropriate area identifications. For example, in the 1960 census each enumerator was supplied with a map on which there was a colored line surrounding the area, or enumeration district, within which he or she was to make a complete enumeration. As each dwelling unit was enumerated the documents were marked with the geographic identifications appearing on the map.

Potentially this method can achieve virtual perfection, but it does require that the boundaries be correctly shown on the map; for example, it requires that the city limits, at the desired date, be recorded and that recent annexations not be overlooked. It requires that the enumerator fully understand the map and the method of marking the questionnaire *and* that he or she follow instructions. Enumerators can and do misinterpret their maps or forget their instructions; for example, by continuing to record the identification number of the previous block in which they enumerated, rather than the one within which they are actually counting families. Our experience has demonstrated a very low error rate in the enumerators' recording of enumeration district numbers. On the other hand, there have been unsatisfactorily high error rates in the recording of block numbers by enumerators whose districts included a group of city blocks that were to be identified separately by the census documents.

Problems of Area Identification 213

After the enumerator has finished his or her work, errors can still be introduced. The writing can be misinterpreted or the correct answers can be erroneously transcribed (e.g., in a card-punching process).

Among the methods that are being discussed today "go look" does have the advantage of potentially greater accuracies than the others, but it has the very important disadvantage that it is expensive to go out in the field each time you wish to record geographic identifications for statistical and for data-linkage purposes.

LOOK AT A MAP

The second method described is "look at a map." This method implies (1) that an address is given, (2) that a map exists and shows the boundaries of the unit or areas that are considered significant, and (3) that a clerk or technician can identify the location of the address on the map and pick off and record the appropriate area identifications. Since most maps do not include identification of house numbers, other reference materials are immediately required. Generally the most suitable of these are city directories, particularly the sections of the city directories that list addresses in house-number sequence along each street. Among indexes of this type the most useful are those that insert into the list of addresses the identifications of the interesecting streets. For example, in one section of a city directory you may find that Fourth Street starts at Adams Road and runs south. Let us suppose that the first address on Fourth Street is 27 and following that there are a series of addresses ending with, let us say, 98. Then, after 98, the listing shows that Brown Lane intersects Fourth. Thereafter the directory identifies addresses and intersections throughout the length of the street. Suppose the observation we wish to match to the map is 39 Fourth Street. Presumably we can locate Fourth Street on the map and find the section of that street that lies between Adams Street and Brown Lane. That brings us close to pinpointing the location of house number 39 on the map.

If Fourth Street is not the boundary between two significant units of geography, then we need only record the appropriate codes. On the other hand, if Fourth Street is the boundary of a city, of a census tract, or of any similar area, we must go a step further and discover on which *side* of Fourth Street number 39 is located. We may find that the city directory indicates the house-numbering system; showing, for example, odd numbers on the east, even numbers on the west. Alternatively, information of this type can be assembled from other sources.

214   Data-Linkage Problems and Solutions

The "look at a map" method is a valid one and can lead to a high degree of accuracy if adequate reference materials are available and if quality safeguards are applied to identify and correct processing errors. Nonetheless it is not an inexpensive method. The cost of assembling the materials needed to do the search work for allocation tends to be a significant part of the total cost. If a large number of addresses within a single area are involved, the unit cost of material assembly drops to a low point when spread across all cases, but there is a significant amount of investigation required for each address, and the cost may exceed what the project sponsor is willing to spend for this activity.

USE AN INDEX

The third method described is "use an index." Obviously the first requirement for the use of an index is the availability of an index that identifies the geographic unit or units that are applicable for each address, or at least a high portion of all addresses, within the given study area.

One type of index is the census tract-street index: such indexes have been prepared for one-third of the tracted areas throughout the United States. Given an observation at 39 Fourth Street and the availability of an index it is relatively an easy job to pick the appropriate volume off the shelf, go through it (first to locate the street and then the range of addresses that includes 39), and, finally, to transcribe the area identifications that are appropriate for that address.

The use of indexes of this kind is generally considerably less expensive than the use of maps. Furthermore, a lower order of skill, or training, is required before an inexperienced person can begin to produce an adequate volume of work. The objections are twofold. First, the creation of an index is a fairly expensive operation and can be justified only by an anticipated substantial work load, so that the cost of preparation may be spread over, or amortized against, a large number of cases. Second, there is a specific amount of clerical work to be done for each address: whether the amount be 1, 5, or 10 minutes, the total usually involves thousands of addresses, and thus the cost can be very large.

RELY ON ADDRESS

The fourth method described is "rely on address"; this method is applicable only to relatively large areas, not to units such as tract and block. If I were to ask a group of people to write their complete home

Problems of Area Identification   215

addresses on a piece of paper, I could do a fair job of identifying how many of them come from each zip-code area, each state, and each city throughout the United States. It is this kind of identification that I have in mind in describing the "rely on address" method. However, almost certainly the interpretations that I would make from their addresses would be faulty, to some degree, and if I can add my address to the pile I can guarantee at least one misleading bit of information. My mailing address reads Washington, D.C., but actually I live in the State of Maryland. Similar situations are relatively infrequent, but they do occur often enough for statistics that might be gathered by this method to be necessarily used with caution by those who understand the limitations. If I were to attempt to apply this method to the Los Angeles area, my results would be even more faulty at the city level. Postal service within the city of Los Angeles is supplied by a number of post offices. One of these is called Los Angeles, but others, whose service areas are entirely within the city, have other names; furthermore, there is an added group of post offices whose service areas lie partly within and partly outside Los Angeles.

Now, if we were to tabulate data from the address identifications in the Los Angeles area, we would have tallies for postal areas, not for cities. Assuming that we knew what we had done, the resulting data could be quite useful. Trouble arises, however, when we or others start to match these data with information that is truly tallied for cities. Our counts would be substantially low for the city of Los Angeles, and very serious misinterpretations could result.

The point then is that postal identifications are geared to postal delivery requirements, not to needs for area identifications for statistical purposes. Postal delivery areas do cross city limits, county lines, and even state lines. Postal names for an area may be a variant of, or completely different from, the legal names.

The use of address, then, could be described as "good," at the state level, "reasonably good" at the county level, but only "fair" for cities. "Rely on address" certainly does have the advantage of being a rapid and an inexpensive method of assigning information to areas, providing, as it does, a sort of self-coding supplied by the respondent. Differences between data collected or tabulated in this fashion and those that are tabulated by the other methods previously mentioned often are insignificant but in some instances may lead to very serious error. Accordingly this is a method to be used with discretion, with an understanding of the problems that may result, and with an eye open to detect problems that may arise when comparisons are made to data from different sources.

Zip-Code Areas

A number of business firms at the regional and national level are suggesting a different approach to "rely on address." Their arguments, in my own terminology, echo what I have said and then continue by saying that they have a great deal of information identified by address; information that can be coded and assembled by zip-code area. What is needed, they say, is census-type data by zip-code area.

Although there are 35,000 or more bits of geography identified by the full five-digit zip-code number, the large majority of those who have written us would be pleased to secure census information only for the 600 or so postal sectional centers identified by the first three digits of the zip code.

Although no decision has been reached concerning 1970 tabulations on this basis, we have developed tentative procedures that seem within reason from a cost viewpoint. These procedures could develop fairly close estimates of census information for zip-code areas containing 50,000 or more inhabitants.

THE 1970 CENSUS

At this point let us progress from generalized methods of geographic identifications to discuss what the Census Bureau is planning to do for the 1970 census in many areas throughout the United States. The Bureau expects to be enumerating something on the order of 60 percent of the population of the United States through what is called a mailout/mailback technique. The methods for this system are being extensively tested and offer substantial promise for improving the quality and the accuracy of the 1970 census.

In essence the mailout/mailback technique requires the preparation of a master mailing list of all residential addresses within the scope of this procedure. Census questionnaires will be mailed to each address, and the occupants will be asked to complete their questionnaires and return them to the local census office by mail. Those who do this in a satisfactory manner will not be contacted by a census enumerator. However, census enumerators will follow up all cases of nonresponse, or of faulty response, in order to secure acceptable returns.

In urban areas where street addresses are available we will not have enumerators visiting every household and, consequently the "go look" methods of earlier censuses will no longer be used. The solution to the problems involved in this approach is the preparation of indexes, or

Problems of Area Identification 217

address-coding guides, as we call them. The completed address-coding guides will be on computer tape and will be organized initially by postal-zip-code numbers. Each record within a zip-code area will identify a street, a range of numbers along the street, either odd or even, and a series of geographic codes that are applicable to all addresses that fall within this specified range. These codes will usually include numeric representations of block number, census tract, municipality, township or equivalent, county, state, congressional district, plus standard metropolitan statistical areas, and other area identifications.

In use the mailing list for the city delivery portions of the census-by-mail areas will be matched to the address-coding guide by computers: the appropriate area identifications will be extracted from the guide and recorded with each house number.

This method is not applicable to postal rural delivery areas principally because these areas lack a structure of address systems that are comparable to those of the cities. In rural delivery areas included in the census by mail the area identifications will be added for each housing unit by a "go look" method during the course of the preparation of the address list for these areas.

A large part of the list for city delivery areas will be purchased: on-the-premises identification of areas for these addresses would be extremely expensive.

It should be made clear that the preparation of address-coding guides is not an endeavor of the Bureau of the Census alone. Similar devices have been prepared by others for other purposes, and in its own efforts the Bureau of the Census is trying, reasonably successfully, to secure local assistance and cooperation in the preparation of the coding guides. People who live and work within Los Angeles or Seattle or Jacksonville, for example, are far better able than we in Wasington are to place their hands on reference materials that adequtely describe the location of specific house numbers with respect to local streets and other boundaries, and if necessary to go out in the field and look as specific problem cases are encountered.

It is not expected that local officials will cooperate out of the goodness of their hearts but rather in anticipation of the advantages that will accrue to them through cooperation with the Bureau in a joint effort. Obviously their assistance in preparing coding guides can lead to significant quality improvements in the guides and thereby to substantial improvements in the accuracy and usability of the data collected in 1970. No less important is the fact that once a coding guide has been prepared, by cooperation between the Bureau of the Census and local agencies, it

218 Data-Linkage Problems and Solutions

can be duplicated and can be used within the local area for work similar to what we have in mind.

Information collected locally from police departments, health authorities, school agencies, welfare departments, and others, and that linked to street address, can be matched to the coding guides previously described, and thereby each observation can be assigned to political, administrative, or other areal units according to analysis requirements. The set of areas that were noted earlier are those that are significant for the work of the Census Bureau, but there is no reason why a coding guide for city X cannot be locally modified to include additional codes—such as those for police precincts, school districts, health areas, and any other appropriate areas. Then at one pass a computer can assign data collected by, let us say, the health authorities to police precincts, to all of the census-tabulation areas, to health areas, to school districts, and to every other kind of area for which codes are provided in the coding guide.

If information from multiple sources within a metropolitan area is coded in this fashion, then significant improvements can be achieved; for example, if school authorities have a problem, they can secure tabulations, by school-attendance areas, not only of information collected through the school system but also of such data as juvenile-delinquency rates, incidence of diseases, numbers of residential building permits, distributions of age and income at the time of the last census, or disbursements of welfare. There would have to be restrictions to protect the confidentiality of census information about persons or families, but the available data would definitely offer a breakthrough from the present situation where statistical data of one department can infrequently be satisfactorily used by another because of the differences in the geographic areas to which data are identified.

It will require considerable cooperation between agencies within a metropolitan area before something even approaching the ideal situation is achieved, but, given the necessary cooperation, it would be possible for a local group, facing a problem, to identify the areas that are most significant for the analysis they must perform and then to secure tabulations of census information in combination with locally collected data, fitted within the specific network of areas for which analytic information is required.

One other point that should be made about the census address-coding guides is the inclusion in the worksheet to be used as guides for an operational field. This is a six-digit field, reserved entirely for local use, that will be carried in Census copies of the coding guide. The key purpose of the field is to permit those within an area to add area identifications to

Problems of Area Identification 219

our copy of the coding guides. Then, once the census data have been tabulated, we shall be able, at modest cost, to recast the statistics to match areas identified in the optional field, such as school-attendance areas, health areas, and other units.

The address-coding-guide approach in area identification is an attractive one. The use of computers for this purpose is not essential, but it is helpful to have indexes prepared that can be used by clerks or by computers to assign addresses to small areas. One of the significant stumbling blocks in the widespread use of this method is the fact that city-type address systems break down at the interface between city and rural delivery areas. A number of cities and states throughout the nation are beginning to establish city-type address systems in rural areas. Where such local efforts are successful *and* the resulting addresses can be used for mail-delivery purposes, address-coding guides will be applicable for entire counties. In other words, in such cases a uniform method of processing statistical information can be developed.

It is hoped that eventually the address system will be extensively used in rural areas. This is not a job that is going to be accomplished in the short run; however, perhaps in 10 or 20 years a substantial portion of the task will be completed. Then the Bureau of the Census and all who use our data will have one method for data linkage in an area, and much of the money that is now being expended in resolving area identifications can be put to other purposes.

BIBLIOGRAPHY

Fay, W. T., *The Geography of the 1970 Census—A Cooperative Effort*, presented at the Annual Meeting of the American Society of Planning Officials, Philadelphia, April 18, 1966. Bureau of the Census, U.S. Dept. of Commerce.

Fay, W. T., and Hagan, R. L., *Computer-Based Geographic Coding for the 1970 Census*, presented at the annual meetings of American Institute of Planners, Portland, Ore., August 14, 1966, and American Statistical Association, Los Angeles, August 15, 1966. Bureau of the Census, U.S. Dept. of Commerce.

Hansen, M. H., and Fay, W. T., *Outlook for Census Information by Zip-Code Areas*, presented at the meeting of the Direct Mail Advertising Association, Inc., Washington, D.C., March 8, 1967 revised July 12, 1967. Bureau of the Census, U.S. Dept. of Commerce.

Chapter Thirteen

Grid Coordinate Geographic Identification Systems*

Edgar M. Horwood†

The principal objective of this chapter is to present the concept of a universal spatial information system of specific importance to urban economic and ecological analysis that is at the same time a completely general system satisfying the needs of almost all urban and regional analysts. To keep within reasonable space allocations the limited amount of text and graphics presented here constitutes a primer only.

At the outset a distinction is made in this presentation between an information system designed to operate on a given data base and the data base itself, which can be extensive to varying degrees and include

---

* This chapter is also part of a document now under preparation by the author and his associates for the Dominion Bureau of Statistics, which has tests of the system under way in Ottawa and London, Ontario, and anticipates the possibility of widespread use of the system for the 1971 Canadian general census.
† University of Washington, Seattle.

Grid Coordinate Geographic Identification Systems

various subjects. These two elements have not been sufficiently clarified in a philosophic, economic, and management concept in the general literature on data banks, and a considerable amount of confusion and disappointment have arisen thereby. The information system itself must be considered as autonomous from the data base as an assembly line is from the product manufactured by its use. Obviously there is a relationship between the design of the assembly line and the product produced, just as there must be between the design of an information system and the information product produced by it. Separation of the information system from the data base should result in an information-retrieval capability that is entirely independent of preconceived notions of areal aggregation units, which delimit various spatial zones or ground areas. The separation concept presented here is generally thought of as the basis for a geocoded information system.

REFERENCING LOCATION BY CARTESIAN COORDINATES

Figure 13.1 illustrates the fundamental concept of referencing a datum observation in two-dimensional space. Geographers have traditionally used latitude and longitude to reference points on the ground as illustrated in the upper part of Figure 13.1, which shows a town A on a regional map referenced in two-dimensional space by latitude and longitude at 45°25′ north of the equator along the north-south axis and 75°43′ west of a standard meridian along the east-west axis.

The lower part of Figure 13.1, showing a portion of town A on a street map at a large scale, illustrates how a datum observation (e.g., a survey, monument, traffic accident, or residence) may be referenced within a city area. A standard distance unit for large-scale maps, the foot, is substituted for longitude and latitude. Thus the point circled in the lower example is $X = 1150$ feet, and $Y = 3765$ feet from some point of origin defined by the intersection of the X and Y reference axes.

The process of geocoding involves the same principles of referencing points or areas in space based on Euclidean geometry as have been applied in the fields of geography and surveying for many years. Any number of standard measure units (e.g., feet, meters, miles, kilometers) may be used as reference measures, as well as any number of axis origins and orthogonal directions for the reference axes.

Thus to geocode the location of a datum observation in a geocoding

222 Data-Linkage Problems and Solutions

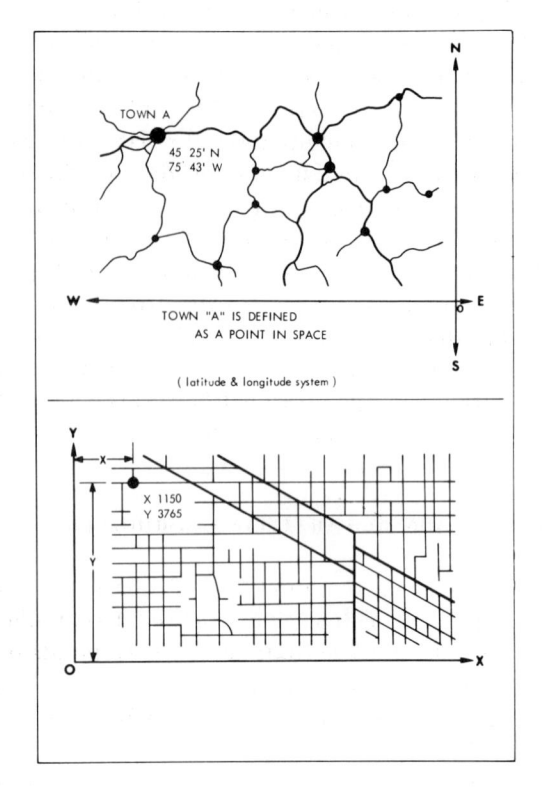

Figure 13.1 A point within a city defined as a point in space.

system a set of X- and Y-coordinates in a Cartesian coordinate system is assigned. These X- and Y-coordinates are referred to as grid coordinates.

COORDINATE TRANSFORMATION BETWEEN SYSTEMS

Figure 13.2 shows how a given point in two-dimensional space can be referenced by two sets of axes. By following standard geometric rules it is possible to transfer from one set of axes (coordinate system) to another—for example, from a latitude and longitude system to a land-survey system. Given the displacement between the two origins and the angular difference between their axes, the transformation may be performed by trigonometry. The importance of this flexibility to

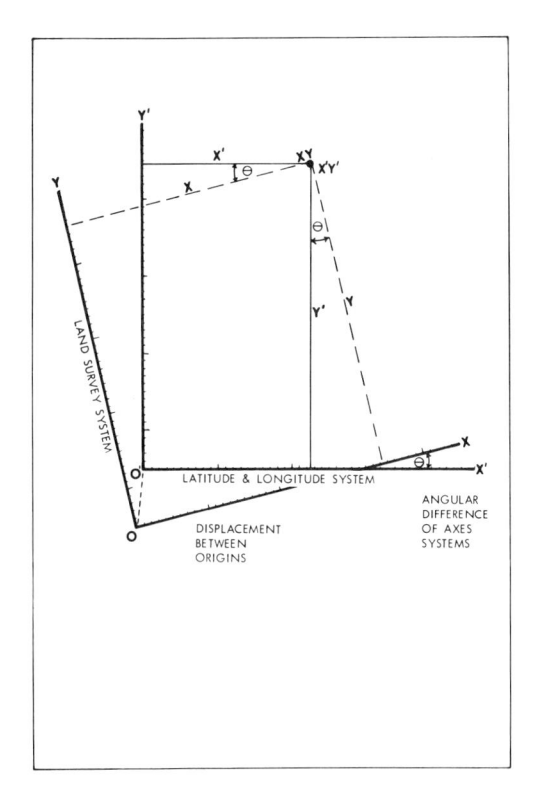

Grid Coordinate Geographic Identification Systems

Figure 13.2 Coordinate transformation.

the user of a geocoding system is that he is not bound to the use of a single grid system or point of origin but is able to convert from one system to another as dictated by special problems through time.

CONCEPT OF THE GRID BLOCK

Figure 13.3 illustrates a grid block, which is a concept fundamental to the use of geocoding. In such a system a block, the areal unit formed by the intersection of four perpendicular grid lines and identified by the X and Y grid coordinates of its lower left corner, is technically referred to as a grid block, which is a particularly useful proxy for ground observations with finite size, such as parcels of land or buildings. A grid block has a uniform area in a given grid-coordinate system, sized

224 Data-Linkage Problems and Solutions

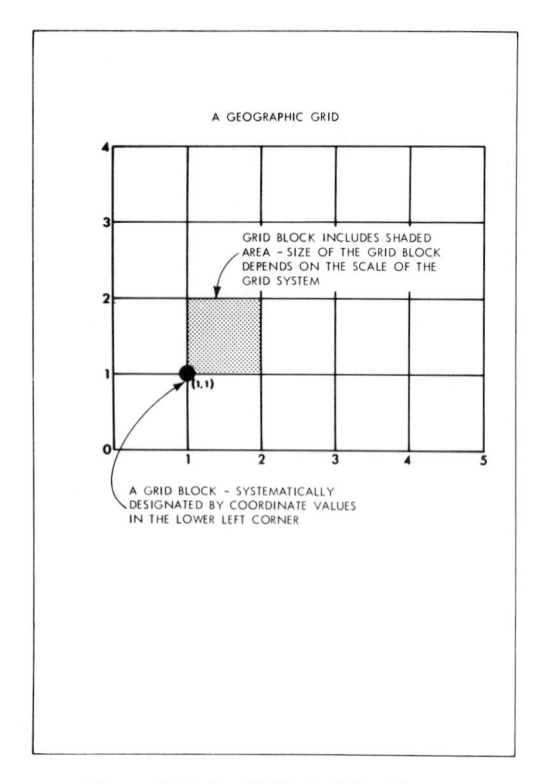

Figure 13.3 A grid block defined in space.

by the spacing of the grid scale. In designing a geocoding system it is important to consider the implications of the spacing of the grid lines and the consequent size of grid blocks for the use application. This spacing should be based on the degree of detail desired in referencing observations. The importance of thinking in terms of grid blocks as referencing units, rather than specific grid-coordinate values, stems from practical and economic considerations. If one considered referencing by coordinate values only, there would be no concept of scale inferred (see Figure 13.4).

GRID-BLOCK SCALE CONSIDERATIONS

Figure 13.4 illustrates the effect of scale, or the spacing of grid lines in a grid-coordinate system, on the ability of a grid block to uniquely

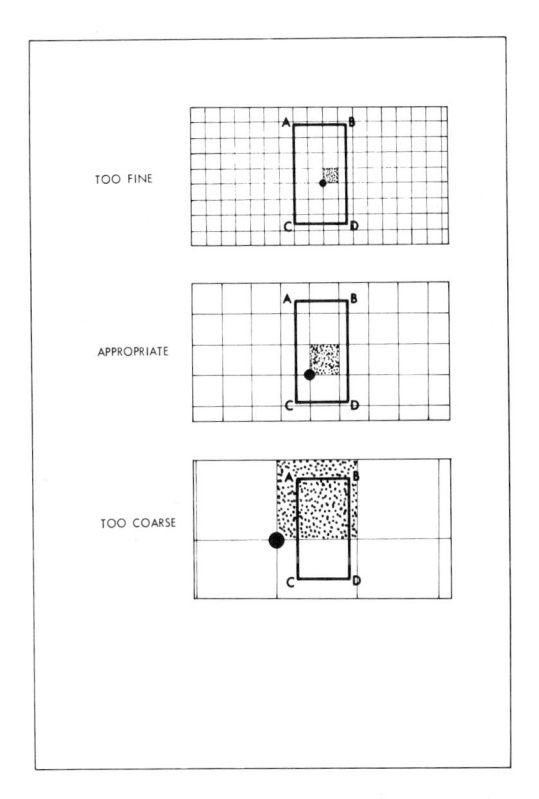

Grid Coordinate Geographic Identification Systems 225

Figure 13.4 Examples of grid block referencing at various scales to reference ground space A, B, C, and D.

reference ground space (*A, B, C, D*). The top example illustrates too fine a grid; that is, many grid blocks fall within the ground-space perimeter and all are able to reference the given space as a generalized proxy area. The middle example shows that one of two grid blocks (only one shaded) is a better proxy of the given ground space by virtue of the enlarged scale. The lower example illustrates that the grid size is too coarse because all grid blocks lie substantially outside the ground space (*A, B, C, D*) and any one grid block is a poor proxy of the ground observation. In practice the attempt is made to approximate the location of the ground-space units under study by a grid block rather than to code specific coordinate values that connote a point without any size. This concept permits a grid scale that can be applied with the greatest economy for the particular use. For example, most residential buildings cover at least 1000 square feet of ground space and can be

226 Data-Linkage Problems and Solutions

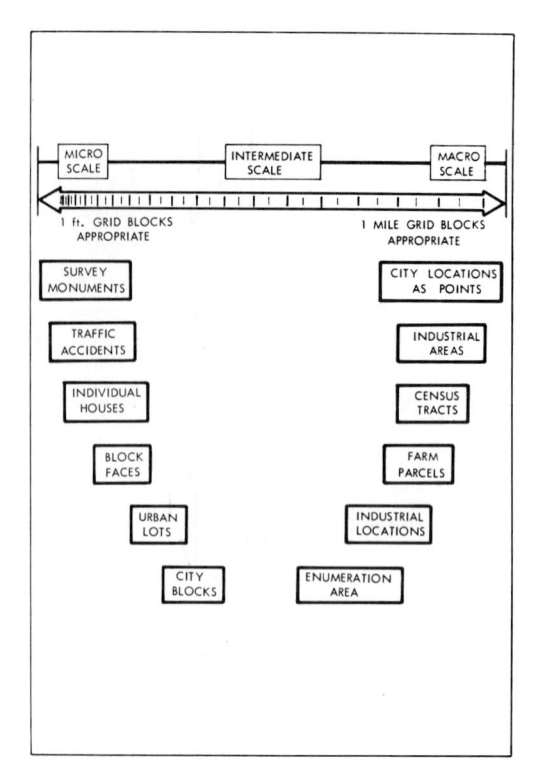

Figure 13.5 Range of scales in geocoding applications.

well described by grid blocks of 10 × 10-foot dimensions. Thus a grid spacing scale of 10 feet would be ample. The point here is that without reference to grid blocks that are appropriately scaled to the given application an inappropriate and costly grid scale could be selected, resulting in the following:

1. Measurements could be made to an unnecessary detail.
2. Computational work would be costly because of excess digits.
3. Locations could not be easily replicated by the same measurements.
4. Coordinate values for each observation would not be unique.
5. Problems would be introduced by the use of mechanical digitizers with fixed minimum scale of readings.
6. The human eye could not differentiate between observations.

Figure 13.5 lists some examples of the scale range of mapped

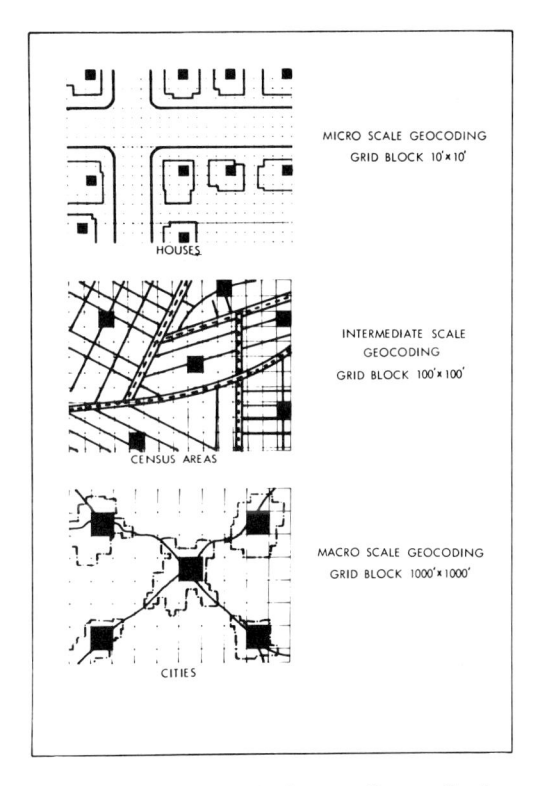

Grid Coordinate Geographic Identification Systems

Figure 13.6 Examples of scales in geocoding applisations.

observations in geocoding. The microscale, the most detailed map scale, requires the smallest grid blocks. The macroscale, or most general map scale, permits referencing by relatively large grid blocks. Geocoding grid scales should be selected according to the use objective.

Figure 13.6 shows selected examples of micro, intermediate, and macro geocoding scales. The upper example (microscale) shows individual houses referenced by 10 $\times$ 10-foot grid-block proxies. In the middle example (intermediate scale) indicates 100 $\times$ 100-foot grid blocks referencing census tracts. The lower example (macroscale) portrays 1000 $\times$ 1000-foot grid blocks referencing individual towns within a region.

228 Data-Linkage Problems and Solutions

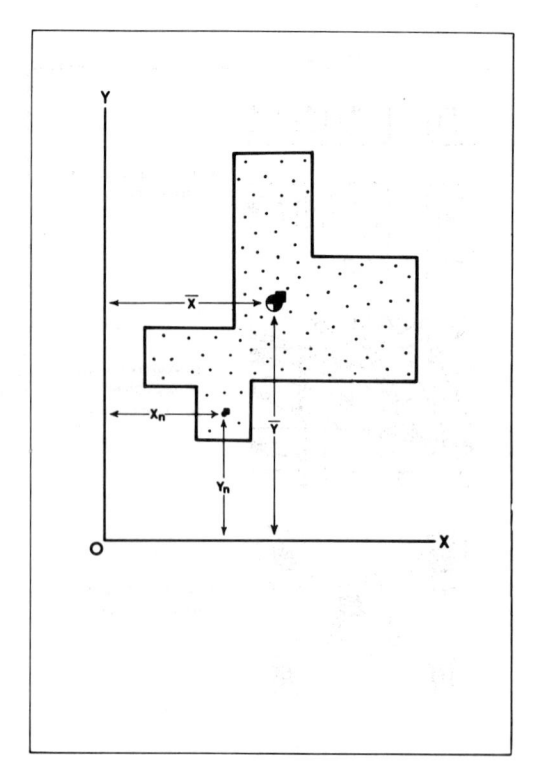

Figure 13.7 Single grid block representation for multiple observations.

THE GENERALIZED GRID-BLOCK PROXY

Figure 13.7 shows how a grid block may be a proxy position for the location of data observations. The grid block X_n, Y_n shows the specific location for an individual data observation. For some applications, rather than viewing or retrieving the fine detail of a number of individual observations, a generalized central location may be selected as a proxy for a given area of ground space on which the set of observations is located. The grid block X, Y shows the proxy for all the observations located on the given ground-space area. For example, in urban areas it may serve no analytical purpose to view the location of individual buildings within a block or block face, although their unique positions may be recorded. It is not mandatory that a geocoding system retain *unique* spatial referencing for the entire universe of

Grid Coordinate Geographic Identification Systems 229

data. Different levels of spatial retrieval may be effective, depending on user requirements and available resources. Generalized grid-block positions may be used under two distinct circumstances:

1. To report or retrieve summarized data for the generalized area.
2. To serve as a common spatial identifier for individual observations within the generalized area.

In both circumstances the unique locational identity of each observation may be retained in the system for cross-referencing data with regard to the same entity (e.g., the household), although the display of individual identity or aggregation at that level of fineness is not required.

GRID BLOCKS REFERENCING MAPPED IMAGERY

Figures 13.8, 13.9, and 13.10 all relate to the generation of reference lines on maps through the use of grid blocks to identify straight-line segments of streets, political boundaries, water courses, and other physical line configurations by means of which data may be interpreted. In conventional information systems a manual link must be made to reference data to ground-landmark representations that relate the data observations to reality. As an example, it serves no purpose to summarize data by census tracts unless a map can be viewed showing where the census tract is in relationship to some easily identifiable ground objects, such as streets. Automated geocoding systems, on the other hand, give a common referencing system for both the data and the map imagery by which the data are interpreted. This permits a recall of both the data and the imagery of the physical objects that permit the data to be linked to reality. The use of automated plotters and cathode-ray-tube retrieval devices make the integration of data and map imagery feasible in the same system. This automation technology marks a significant departure from past technologies.

The grid scale needed to identify mapped imagery may be greater than that needed to identify datum observations, although this is not invariably so. In automated digitizing of coordinate values extremely fine scales can be used to serve both purposes. Furthermore, in automated systems it is easy to vary the scale used in the development of the map imagery from that used in the representation of data locations. In general, however, the scale of the grid block used for representing

230 *Data-Linkage Problems and Solutions*

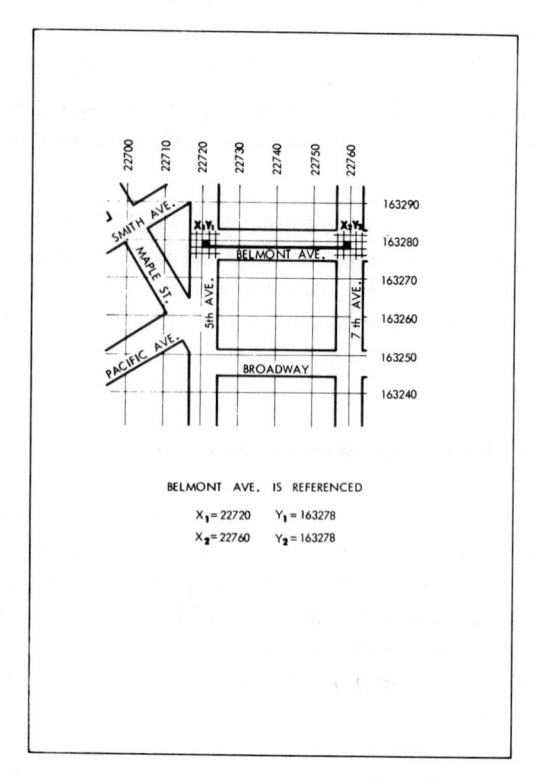

Figure 13.8 Referencing of a street segment by grid blocks.

mapped imagery is the same as that used for the representation of the data-entity location.

Figure 13.8 illustrates the concept of two grid blocks referencing a line. The terminal ends of this line defining a street segment are ref-

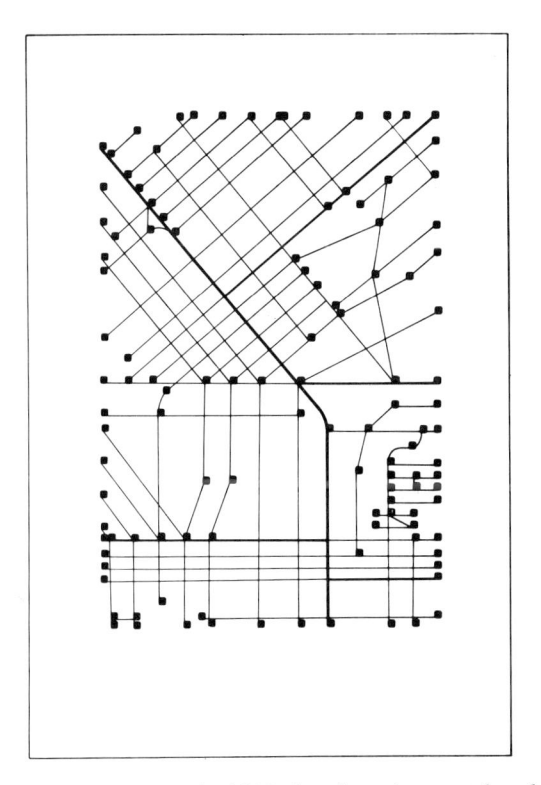

Grid Coordinate Geographic Identification Systems 231

Figure 13.9 Examples of grid blocks referencing street legnths.

erenced by the grid blocks. The capability of referencing a line, in this case a street segment, provides the opportunity for constructing map imagery to serve as a reference for information retrieval.

Figure 13.9 shows how it is possible to reference a network of streets within a city with a composite of grid-block sets. This network

232　Data-Linkage Problems and Solutions

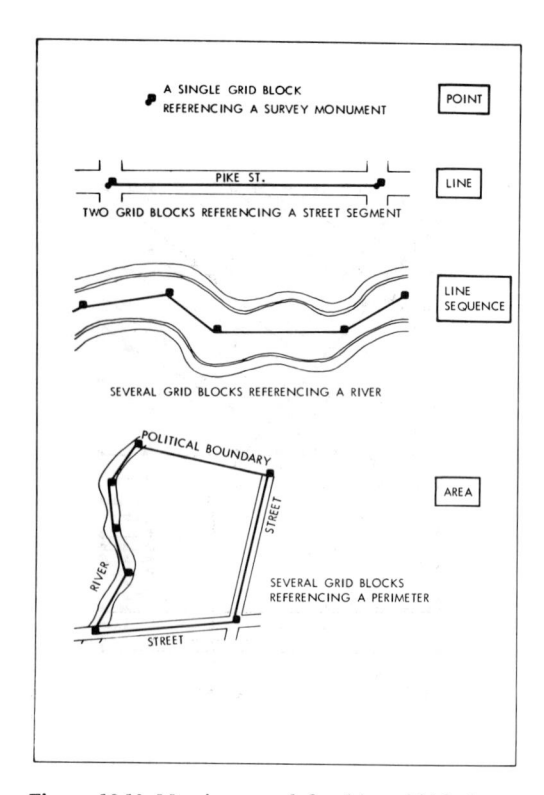

Figure 13.10 Map imagery defined by grid blocks.

can be machine plotted at different scales using the grid-block referencing as digital input. The street pattern may be useful as a product itself or as a background for interpreting other geocoded data.

Figure 13.10 illustrates the development of the map-imagery capabilities provided by grid-block referencing. Building on the capability of referencing a single point by a grid block, two grid blocks can be used

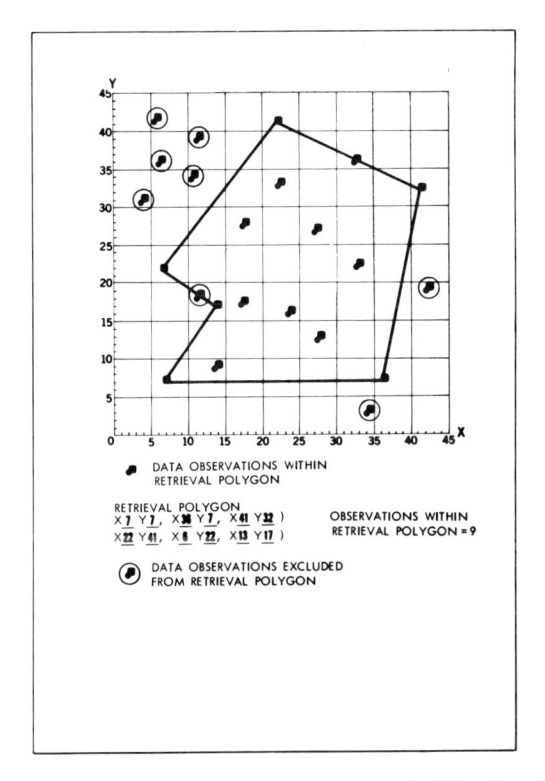

Grid Coordinate Geographic Identification Systems 233

Figure 13.11 Example of point-in-polygon retrieval of data by grid block defined retrieval polygon.

to reference a line, and in turn multiple grid block sets can be used to reference implied linear configurations abstractly (e.g., a river center line). The lower example shows how the capabilities of grid-block referencing are combined to define an areal unit bounded by line sets. Given the referencing by grid-block sets, it is also possible to retrieve areal configurations, such as political jurisdiction boundaries, as graphic map imagery via automatized plotting techniques.

POINT-IN-POLYGON DATA RETRIEVAL

Figure 13.11 illustrates that, given a distribution of data observations referenced by grid blocks, it is possible to retrieve only those individual observations of the total spatial distribution that fall within

234 Data-Linkage Problems and Solutions

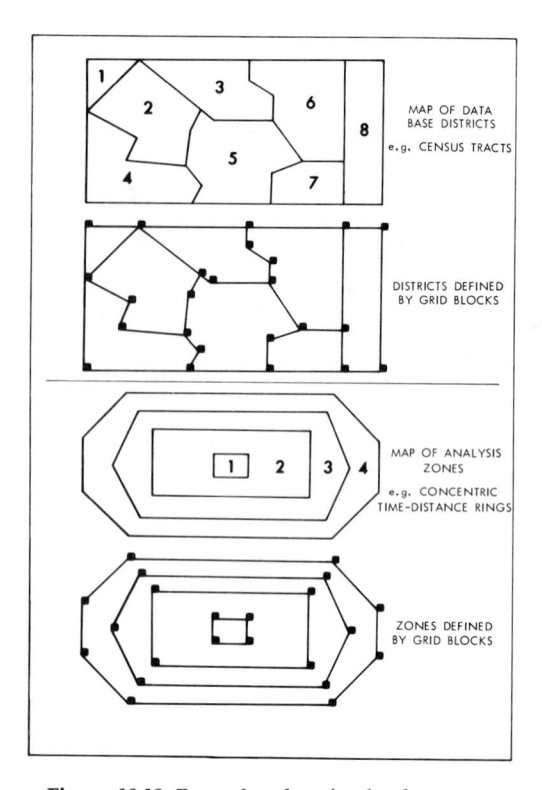

Figure 13.12 Examples of retrieval polygon sets.

a query perimeter referenced also by grid blocks. This query areal unit is referred to as a retrieval polygon (e.g., a spatial analysis zone, census tract, jurisdiction area). In automated applications the geocoded data observations that fall within the perimeter of the retrieval polygon may be programmed for summarization. This retrieval technique is referenced to as point-in-polygon retrieval.

Figure 13.12 illustrates two different sets of retrieval polygons defined by grid blocks. In a geocoding system it is possible to construct any number of randomly defined retrieval polygon sets. These sets, such as the exemplified districts and zones, are defined spatially by grid-block records in which values may be stored and altered independently of the substantive data.

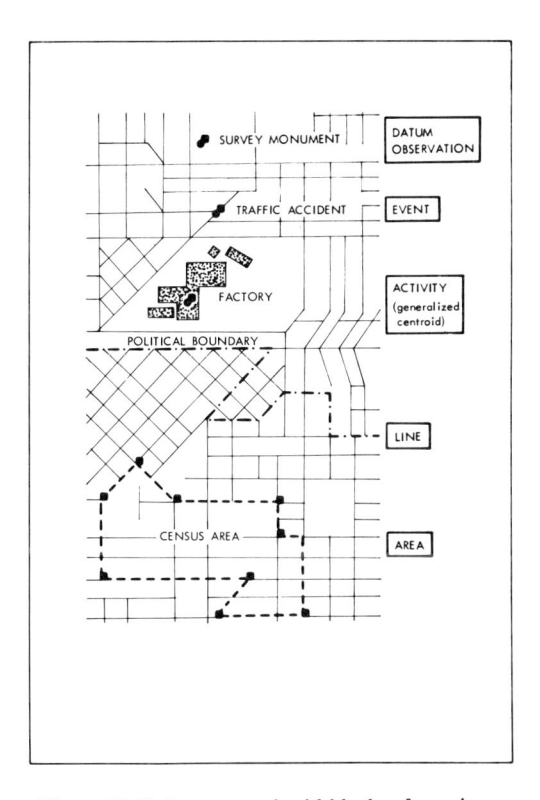

Grid Coordinate Geographic Identification Systems

Figure 13.13 Summary of grid block referencing.

SUMMARY OF GRID-BLOCK REFERENCING

Figure 13.13 illustrates by simplified examples a review of the fundamental referencing capabilities of the grid block. Referring to the upper example, we are able to see that a grid block may be used as follows:

1. As a proxy reference for the specific location of a data observation (e.g., a survey monument).
2. To reference an event (e.g., a traffic accident) that is not directly related to a physical structure but whose location can be derived from some surrogate identifier, such as a street address.
3. To reference the proxy location of a physical object (e.g., a factory) occupying a small area of ground space.

4. To reference lines (e.g., a political boundary).
5. To reference an areal unit of ground space.

GEOCODING BENEFITS

Geocoding offers numerous advantages in data-base development, data processing, information retrieval, analysis, and by-products. These may be summarized as follows:

Data-base-development benefits
1. Simplification of data development through separation of data-variable values and location codes into unique files repetition of information.
2. Ease of automatic conversion from street-address records to grid-coordinate values, simplifying the use of data spatially identified by street-address code.
3. The opportunity to use and develop data coded by street-address identifiers through subsequent coded automatic conversion of addresses to grid-coordinate values.

Data-processing benefits
1. Ease and efficiency of editing and updating information through division of the data-variable values and spatial-location codes in separate files.
2. Spatial editing via machine plotting.

Retrieval benefits
1. Ad hoc query via random areal aggregation units.
2. Linking data with reference to the same entity by matching unique grid-coordinate identifiers.
3. Plotting and display of discreet observations and small summary area data via map imagery at random scales.

Analysis benefits
1. Opportunity for the determination of areal query units ex post facto to the development of the data base.
2. Facility for the spatial interpretation of data value change over time with respect to discreet coordinate locations and areal aggregation polygons.
3. Refinements of model calibration by use of data value relationshipes (parameters) of the basic entity rather than average values for areal aggregation units.

Grid Coordinate Geographic Identification Systems 237

4. Refinement of model calibration through testing by selection of sets of areal aggregation units of varying size or internal homogenity.

By-product benefits
1. Map construction at varying scales.
2. Efficiency in the management of spatially oriented data.

BIBLIOGRAPHY

Calkins, H. W., *Operations Manual for Street Address Conversion System*, Research Report No. 2. Seattle: Urban Data Center, University of Washington, 1965.

Clark, W. L., *Urban Geocoding Systems and U.S. Census Implications*, presented at the Fourth Annual Conference on Urban Planning Information Systems and Programs, Berkeley, Calif., August 21, 1966.

Crawford, R. J., Jr., *Utility of an Automated Geocoding System for Urban Land Use Analysis*, Research Report No. 3. Seattle: Urban Data Center, University of Washington, 1967.

Dial, R. B., "Street Address Conversion System," *Planning 1965*, pp. 319–330.

Dial, R. B., *Street Address Conversion System*, Research Report No. 1. Seattle: Urban Data Center, University of Washington, 1964.

Horwood, E. M., *A Fundamental Look at Urban Information Systems*, presented at the Second Annual Conference on Urban Information Systems and Programs, University of Pittsburgh, 1964.

Horwood, E. M., *The Use of Electronic Data Processing in Town Planning*, a summary of information presented to the Symposium on Employment of Electronic Data Processing in Public Planning, sponsored by the Danish Society of Civil Engineers, September 3 and 4, 1965.

Chapter Fourteen

Some Aspects of Statistical Data Linkage for Individuals

*Joseph Steinberg**

Proposals for statistical data linkage for individuals long preceded the advent of the computer. About 100 years ago William Farr had proposed the idea of linkage of health records,[1] and perhaps there were others before him. Since that time many other proposals have been made, and many have been implemented with existing facilities.[2] Recently the availability of machine-read information and the desire to do secondary analysis has stimulated some implementation at several social-research centers that have access to computers.[3]

Many matching studies have been carried out, using full-name and other available identifiers (e.g., address, date of birth, names of other family members). Varying rates of matching have resulted. Matching studies were part of the evaluation programs of the 1950 and 1960 population censuses. Some of the results, as reported, pointed to vary-

---
* Social Security Administration, Washington, D.C.

Some Aspects of Statistical Data Linkage for Individuals

ing degrees of success.[4] Genetic studies involving record-linked data in which birth certificates are matched to marriage records have been carried out by the Canadian Atomic Energy Board.[5] This approach to linkage has used the identifying information currently recorded on Canadian vital certificates for computer linkage into family groups (but with no common identifying number). Some feel that reasonable success can be achieved without a common numeric identifier. Several efforts are under way to develop models for optimal approaches to record linkage.[6]

The initiation of the social security system in the United States in 1936* ushered in a substantially universally used nine-digit numeric identifier—the social security account number. At the Social Security Administration (SSA) this number, either in manual or in computer use, has served as a necessary, but not always sufficient, identifier for administrative and statistical data linkage for individuals. From time to time studies have been undertaken by groups interested in linking vital records to consider whether an alternative number, assigned at birth, might be more useful and acceptable also for Social Security Administration and Internal Revenue Service use.[7]

The need for confidentiality of information and preservation of privacy of the individual played a role in resolving policy issues on the structure of the social security account number when it was first established and in the statutory base and regulations involving data available from the social security program.[8]

The Social Security Administration has created a number of mechanisms to serve the interests of social scientists who need access to some social security data for research. These mechanisms have been created with built-in safeguards of confidentiality.

SOCIAL SECURITY ADMINISTRATION DATA AND POLICIES ON AVAILABILITY

There are several sources of social security statistical data for individuals. The first comes from the information given for the establishment of an individual's account number. The primary demographic variables available are date of birth, sex, and race. Other information obtained are place of birth, mother's maiden name, and father's name. Then the Administration gets earnings data (up to the taxable maximum). Data are reported quarterly by employers (annually by agricul-

---
* The first number was issied on November 24, 1936.

tural employers). Self-employment reports are sent together with federal income tax returns. The machine-readable information summarizes earnings for each year since 1951, together with information on quarters of coverage by type of earnings. The 1965 amendments to the Social Security Act provided coverage of virtually all persons 65 and over for hospital insurance benefits and on a voluntary basis for medical benefits. This program will provide a source of data on characteristics of persons 65 and over as well as some data on the use of health benefits.

Another source of data is the cash-benefits programs for retirement, survivors, and disability. For the universe of persons in these programs additional information becomes available at the time of application for benefits, as well as data on the amounts of the periodic benefits. These data are computer linked and provide a further source of research data.

Samples of individuals selected with the account numbers as a frame are the basis for statistical tabulations; for example, the continuous-work-history sample (CWHS) is a 1 percent sample. Specified combinations of the last four positions of the nine-digit social security account number are used to identify account numbers as sample elements. The same combinations have been used continually since the start of CWHS in 1940. This sampling scheme thus makes provision for the new entrants into the account-number system. The continuity of sample identification makes possible over-the-quarter and over-the-year linkages of detailed quarterly earnings information. One tape file shows a state-county code of place of employment and a four-digit industry code of employer.

By statute and administrative regulation data for individuals are treated confidentially.[9] However, from time to time questions may need to be raised with an employer when efficient and proper administration requires, such as when there is a question concerning the correctness of the earnings information or to whom it should be credited. Specific provisions for administrative use of SSA data by others are carefully restricted and spelled out in Regulation 1.

There are substantial amounts of data that are made available through statistical tabulations. As described more completely later in this chapter, some means have been developed for making microdata available from CWHS. Another technique, described more completely later, that of standard tabulation, makes possible cross-tabulations of data from other sources with SSA earnings data. In no event are data that might be of detriment to an individual made available.

NUMERICAL IDENTIFIERS

In the United States the social security number has been and continues to be the primary numerical identifier for individuals for many records. It has been adopted as an individual's identification number by the Internal Revenue Service and facilitates linkage among records of dividends, interest, and tax reports. Many other organizations have begun to use this number as a means of identification and for record linkage. Within the federal government other agencies are using or have just begun to use the social security account number for personal identification. This is possible under the provisions of an Executive Order.[10] There are, however, appropriate safeguards of confidentiality of the SSA information for the individual, while permitting use of the account number for other than the SSA programs.

When the social security number was being devised in the mid-1930s some proponents advocated introduction of two digits for year of birth. This suggestion was not adopted. The basic policy adopted was that is was important to preserve, in every way possible, the privacy of information concerning the individual. It was decided that availability of birth year might lead to limitations on older persons' employability, with consequent economic detriment to the individuals concerned. The form of the nine-digit social security number, as adopted, has remained the same since the beginning. The first three digits are an identification of the service area within which the person was resident at the time of issuance. The second set of two digits provides for serial identification within the area and is a chronological index of account-number issuance within the service area. The last four digits of the account number are simply systematically used serial digits within the initial five digits of the account number. This nine-digit number does not contain a check digit.[11] Usually wives and minor children of social security beneficiaries do not have an account number in their own right but are assigned a letter suffix in addition to the wage earner's number as a means of identification for the SSA master benefit record.

Some people have advocated the issuance of a standard number at birth. The proponents feel that this should then be called the social security account number. In the 1940s, many states started using a birth number. Many hoped this numbering scheme would be adopted in all states on a uniform basis and be used as a common identifier for linkage of vital records. One basic difference between the proposed birth number and the social security number is the use of the last two digits for year of birth. (The problem in the use of this scheme by the

242   Data-Linkage Problems and Solutions

Social Security Administration has already been mentioned.) The other essential difference is the use of a fresh start for the serial number portion each year.

Many persons who are covered by the Railroad Retirement Act have for that program a six-digit numerical identifier, and a one-, two-, or three-letter prefix. The letter prefix identifies the individual beneficiary in his relationship to the primary Railroad Retirement Board beneficiary in the same way that a suffix does in the SSA system. Those among them, 65 and over, covered under the 1965 SSA amendments for health insurance benefits have had this basic alphanumeric identifier used as their identification in the SSA central health-insurance-benefits records system. For a number of years now, the Railroad Retirement Board has begun to make use of the standardly issued social security number for new persons while retaining the previous system for persons already issued numbers under the old system. These SSA account numbers are issued as part of the basic SSA system of numbering and are not separately identifiable.

On July 1, 1967, the Defense Department began to use the social security number as a personal identifier rather than issuing service serial numbers as heretofore. So, as time goes on, in many ways and for many reasons the population with a social security account number will increase.

In any of these agency uses of SSA account numbers the responsibility of the Social Security Administration is limited to issuance of the number. (There are of course provisions for reimbursement of the cost involved.) Cooperation in providing information to any other agency is restricted to making available to the participating agency only the information provided originally through that agency.[12] Because of administrative advantages, the Social Security Administration has begun to cooperate in some instances in issuing account numbers to ninth-grade students. However, the costs of issuance and maintenance of numbers from birth as well as other policy questions not yet resolved have been deemed to be significant enough to inhibit the Social Security Administration from undertaking too broad an administrative task.

In data linkage of administrative records the Social Security Administration uses not only the nine-digit account number but also the first six letters of the surname in order to identify possible mismatches. In a similar fashion the Internal Revenue Service uses the account number and the first four letters of the surname.

Obviously the quality of matching or linkage is a function of the kinds of identifiers available. To the extent that the social security

Some Aspects of Statistical Data Linkage for Individuals 243

account number is supplemented by surname, sex, and date of birth, this provides a basis for even greater assurance of match.

In any system there exists the possibility that some identifying numbers are shown improperly on newly created data records. For its own needs for efficient administration the Social Security Administration has created a microfilm registry of all account-number holders, called the National Employee Index. This index uses the soundex system for coding the individual's surname. The soundex system uses the first initial of a surname and a three-digit numeric code of the first three (succeeding) consonants of the surname. The National Employee Index also lists the last name, first name, middle name and initials, exact (alleged) date of birth, and the social security account number. A high probability of identification of the correct account number for most persons is then available when full name and date of birth are made available. The index uses a highly automated microfilm system for determining either the unique account number or the several potential account numbers where all given identifiers turn out to be the same. Paper records of the account-number application can then be used for narrowing down the specific number if the added information on mother's maiden name, father's name, place of birth, and color or race are subsequently or at the same time made available. With all of these items the correct account number can be located for virtually all persons who have social security numbers.

SOME LINKAGE SYSTEMS FOR ACCESS TO SSA

Recognition of the research value of its substantial data files has led the Social Security Administration to evolve several linkage systems for facilitating access to data for statistical purposes. The first system involves a random encoding of the individual, in a consistent manner, on existing SSA statistical data files. Thus there is available for research use the basic quarterly data of the continuous-work-history sample. The sole identifier of the individual records is a nine-digit encoded number. The file, when available, has been resequenced on the encoded number. The consistency of encoding, over time, provides the basis for the researcher's linkage of microdata over the quarter or over the year to suit his purposes. This makes possible a variety of studies of industry and individual mobility for the population of persons with social security coverage. It has been proposed by some that the Social Security Administration (or someone else) consider the possibility of providing a similar

244 Data-Linkage Problems and Solutions

encoding service under appropriate administrative restrictions so that other data files, which also contain SSA number as an identifier, might be encoded for possible linkage among themselves or with CWHS data. To avoid violation of confidentiality of the SSA data through the obvious decoding possibilities a different matrix than the present one would be used.

Another system has been developed by the Social Security Administration for linkage with its data from the overall-earnings-record system. This is a special standard tabulation program. In this approach the researcher makes available to the Social Security Administration his own data in a specified format (up to 35 columns of information) and then receives standard cross-tabulations. The standard program provides for cross-classification of the researcher's data with that of the SSA summary earning record, which shows data up to the maximum earnings base. The standard program can also produce sums of squares and sums of cross-products for the researcher.[13]

Social security numbers have been collected on the Census Bureau's Current Population Survey since October 1963. A three-way data-linkage project has been initiated linking SSA data with data from the Census Bureau's Current Population Survey and that of the Internal Revenue Service.[14] In order to set up this project appropriate interagency procedures had to be developed for ensuring confidentiality and avoidance of detrimental effect to any individual. At no time are any microdata from either of the two other agencies available to the Internal Revenue Service. The tape to be run for research tabulations contains only a case identifier. The sole joint identification among all identifiers and the case number is held only by the Census Bureau. Any access to this identifier tape requires a joint double-key approach of the Census Bureau and the Social Security Administration.

OTHER ASPECTS OF DATA LINKAGE AND CONFIDENTIALITY

Some of the most difficult elements in systems development regarding statistical data linkage for individuals arise because of the moral and legal needs to protect confidentiality. Conformance to the statutory provisions of a variety of agencies requires exceedingly careful and sensitive analysis of the many potentials for legal and ethical error that lie in the path of the unwitting researcher. A cardinal need with respect to confidentiality in data linkage of a variety of sources would seem to be full joint discussions. There also seems to be a need for determination,

Some Aspects of Statistical Data Linkage for Individuals 245

through preliminary analytic tabulations, that possible identifying characteristics have sufficient frequency and dispersion when cross-classified by the other variables.

There are of course many difficult elements of systems development inherent in the variety of concepts used in each of the linked sources. For example, in the three-way link mentioned above there are the differences between the coverage of the Internal Revenue Service and the Social Security Administration for dependency criteria and that of the Current Population Survey on family composition. There are differences in substantive concepts—transfer payments, sick-leave deductions treatment of capital gains, benefits for a year versus benefits received in a year, etc. There are differences in time references for coverage of the units involved.

That electronic computers can be used for data storage and retrieval is of course the basic unifying theme of this book. But this notion has stirred up a significant amount of controversy centering on the role of the federal government in the development of data banks and data centers.[15] The concerns that have been voiced relate both to the implied as well as the possible real threat to the right of privacy of individuals. Some people have tended to classify the data banks as equivalent in their threat to the right of privacy as electronic and laser eavesdropping.[16] It seems useful to note briefly that the interaction of these issues with long-term previous commitments to individuals creates a strong need to consider the appropriateness of various systems and procedures that might be used for ensuring that there be no breach of confidence. Some tentative proposals have been advanced for discussion.[17] These include the need for cost-benefit analysis of linkage versus original data collection, consideration of giving the individual the chance to correct or delete information, and the development of decision-making mechanisms and controls. While looking toward the maximum potential from the availability of cross-classified data from several sources to enhance our stock of knowledge, adequate legal and statistical controls seem necessary. The Social Security Administration has, both through statute and administrative regulation, a firm commitment to the principle that information available as a result of administrative processes shall not be used to the detriment of the individual. The SSA Regulation 1 identifies the specific uses that are permitted by other agencies for purposes of administration of programs promulgated under the Social Security Act or in situations in which the security of the Nation is involved.[18] This is a matter of public record. Thus all individuals making data available to the Social Security Administration can have full knowledge of the possible ways in which these data may be used administratively. Furthermore the use of such

246   Data-Linkage Problems and Solutions

data for statistical purposes is covered under an appropriate section of Regulation 1, which provides that "Statistical data or other similar information not relating to any particular person which may be compiled from records regularly maintained by the Department may be disclosed when efficient administration permits."[19] The critical question with respect to the use of SSA data for statistical purposes under this section of the Regulation is whether the identity of any individual is disclosed in any way to the recipient of the data. Thus the primary test relating to this issue of identifiability is whether any statistical tabulation or other data made available my in any way be used to the detriment of the person to whom these data relate.

The use of the social security account number as an indentifier by other organizations does not in itself appear to raise an issue of confidentiality. The individual presumably can decide for himself whether a particular use may raise for him a threat of a detrimental effect. He can decide whether or not to give his number (or an erroneous one) to that organization. For efficient administration the Social Security Administration attempts to ensure that there be but one account number issued for an individual. As a matter of policy, tying back to the original discussions even prior to the Social Security Act's enactment, there has been a policy that permits issuance of an additional account number to an individual when this is deemed by the individual to be to his interest. This general policy evolved because of a strong feeling that the social security number not be used as a means for tracing individuals or identifying individuals who have been blacklisted. The notion that a person has a right to a fresh start was considered very important. Administratively, when additional account numbers are requested and issued, appropriate notations for cross-referencing purposes are made in a confidential social security records system. Thus for purposes of administration the earnings records of all separate account numbers for a given individual are brought together when a claim is filed for benefits. In addition, because of the retirement test provisions and others for beneficiaries receiving cash benefits, it is necessary for proper administration that the Social Security Administration have knowledge of the amount and extent of all current earnings by wage earners as well as of other events that may cause suspension or termination of benefits. It is undoubtedly true that some people who change identities, for whatever reason, fail to be identified as multiple-account-number holders. Administrative practices of the Social Security Administration at the time of taking claims applications and in dealing with such matters after benefits have been approved are designed to provide appropriate safeguards of the use of social security

Some Aspects of Statistical Data Linkage for Individuals 247

trust funds. However, for purposes of statistical linkage it is necessary to recognize that some of the working population may have more than one number. Because of the confidentiality provisions under Regulation 1 and because of the problems of administration (owing to probable interference with its basic mission) the Social Security Administration has adopted the policy that there will be no provision made for identifying to an individual or organization, other than the person himself, whether a given account number is the correct one for that person. Of course, for purposes of correct handling of earnings records the Social Security Administration, by mail and, when necessary, through a field representative from one of its district offices, may need to contact an employer. Such efforts are of course designed solely to check whether a given account number has been properly ascertained by the employer and, if not, to determine the correct account number for the individual so that the correct account can be credited with the earnings being reported for a given quarter.

QUALITY OF LINKAGE IN A SURVEY PROGRAM

Some experience suggests that an additional source of potential problems in the use of the social security account numbers lies in the lack of recollection by the individual of his correct number or failure to report by a proxy respondent, for whatever reason, of the existence of an account number for the individual. In the three-way-linkage project previously mentioned an attempt was made to ascertain whether account numbers identified through a survey process were correct, given the other identifying information of the individual for whom that account number was reported. In addition, through the National Employee Index and other related record information an attempt was made to ascertain account numbers where there seemed to be some question or where no account number was reported. Table 14.1 shows some available results of the pilot project. There seems to have been but little difference among age groups, except for the youngest—14 to 19 years old—in the degree of failure to provide account numbers. Relatively few transpositions seem to have been made.

Table 14.2 provides some collateral information showing, for reported class intervals of income, the degree of respondent information concerning account numbers. It is true that for purposes of crediting earnings certain types of employment (federal employment and some state and local employment as well as miscellaneous farm and self-

Table 14.1
Proportion of Persons with Social Security Numbers, in Survey and after Initial Processing, by Age and Sex

Age	Total Survey	Total After Processing	Male Survey	Male After Processing	Female Survey	Female After Processing
Total, 14 and over	73.7*	82.1	78.9	87.8	68.9	77.0
14–19	39.3	56.2	42.4	59.9	36.2	52.6
20–24	80.7	89.8	81.0	91.9	80.4	87.9
25–29	83.0	90.7	84.2	93.2	82.0	88.5
30–34	82.2	90.1	84.4	93.3	80.1	87.2
35–39	83.2	90.0	85.1	92.1	81.5	88.1
40–44	83.6	90.4	85.7	93.1	81.6	87.8
45–49	83.0	89.8	86.5	93.6	79.8	86.3
50–54	80.5	87.6	86.7	93.9	74.8	81.6
55–59	79.7	86.7	86.9	93.6	73.0	80.3
60–64	77.5	83.2	88.1	93.5	67.9	73.9
65–69	76.0	81.0	90.3	93.9	63.9	70.1
70–71	72.7	77.9	90.2	94.1	57.5	63.9
72–74	66.0	72.2	86.7	92.7	49.1	55.5
75 and over	55.8	62.9	78.3	84.8	39.7	47.1

* Of this, 2.1 percentage points had to be corrected for inaccuracies.

employment activities) are not covered by the Social Security Law.[20] Nevertheless, virtually all people in such employment are likely to have account numbers. Most will have numbers for use on tax forms and others because of various record-keeping mechanisms instituted (notably for Federal Civil Service Commission use). The preliminary results seem to indicate some 5 to 10 percent additional persons for whom the survey process (and subsequent edits) failed to identify an account number.

LINKAGE AND ERROR CORRECTION

The last 10-year period has seen the issuance of personal identifiers by diverse groups as use of machines for record keeping has spread. Various numbers have been issued for credit-card purposes. Usually

Some Aspects of Statistical Data Linkage for Individuals

Table 14.2
Proportion of Persons with Social Security Account Numbers, in Survey and after Initial Processing, by Survey Income Class

Income Class	Proportion with Account Number	
	Survey	After Processing
Total, with income	74.2	82.7
$1– $499*	64.6	74.5
500– 999	70.3	77.7
1,000– 1,499	80.5	86.9
1,500– 1,999	84.3	90.5
2,000– 2,499	85.5	91.7
2,500– 2,999	86.4	92.4
3,000– 3,499	87.4	93.5
3,500– 3,999	88.9	95.2
4,000– 4,499	86.2	94.5
4,500– 4,999	88.2	93.8
5,000– 5,999	88.1	95.8
6,000– 6,999	89.1	95.9
7,000– 7,999	88.7	95.0
8,000– 9,999	88.3	96.1
10,000–14,999	85.7	94.9
15,000–24,999	84.1	96.5
25,000 and over	78.4	93.1
Without income	53.3	65.0

* Or loss.

separate numbers are used in identifying our bank account (s). We have, in most cases, in addition to our social security account numbers a driver's license number and health-insurance account number. For statistical purposes many government agencies have begun to maximize the possibility for coordination of information through use of the social security account number.* In every instance the individual is the one called on to make a number available. To the extent he deems it undesirable he has control over the decision as to whether he will make the number available and whether he will make it known correctly. In some instances, through desire not to make it available, forgetfulness, or lack of knowledge that a

---

* Effective January 1, 1966, the Veterans Administration began using the social security number as a hospital admission number and for other record-keeping purposes.

250   Data-Linkage Problems and Solutions

number had ever been issued, a number may not be made available. Then there are the occasions where through errors of memory or recording some juxtaposition of digits or other error may creep in when numbers are volunteered. As noted, the present SSA policy is not to provide any service for informing other agencies of proper numbers when numbers are lacking or when they are scrambled in some way. The evidence in Tables 14.1 and 14.2 suggests that on a national cross section, for many purposes, this may not constitute a significant handicap. The availability of an account number may represent but one of a whole series of identifiers (most others being non numeric). Such other identifiers, jointly used, are likely to create significant opportunities for useful statistical linkages. Beyond errors in or missing identifiers, records systems quite often contain some gaps in information. Usual methods for dealing with noninterviews or nonresponses in surveys merit consideration in data linkages as well.[21] Data in any of the sources may be used to supply "imputed" data not only for missing values but also for those elements that are not available because of failure to match.

This chapter has presented some aspects of the current situation affecting the use of the social security account number as an entity identifier for individuals. Useful results lie ahead for enhancing our store of knowledge while maintaining the necessary measures to ensure that the privacy of the individual will be respected in statistical data linkages.

REFERENCES

1. As cited by E. D. Acheson, "Oxford Record Linkage Study: A Central File of Morbidity and Mortality Records for a Pilot Population," *British Journal Prev. Soc. Med.*, 18 (1964), pp. 8–13.
2. U.S. Bureau of the Census, *List of References on Results and Methodology of Matching Studies*, (unpublished), 1966.
3. R. L. Bisco, "Social Science Data Archives. Progress and Prospects," *Social Science Information*, VI (1 Feb., 1967), pp. 39–74.
4. Joseph Steinberg and Leon Pritzker, *Some Experiences with and Reflections on Data Linkage in the United States*, presented at the 36th Session of the International Statistical Institute, Sydney, Australia, 1967.
5. H. B. Newcombe, A. P. James, and S. J. Axford, *Family Linkage of Vital and Health Records*. Chalk River Ontario: Atomic Energy of Canada, Ltd., No. 470, July 1957.
6. I. P. Fellegi and A. B. Sunter, *An Optimal Approach to Record Linkage*, presented at the 36th Session of the International Statistical Institute, Sydney, Australia, 1967.
7. Public Health Conference on Records and Statistics, *Progress Report of the Study Group on Record Linkage*. Washington, D.C.: Public Health Service, Document No. 603.5, pp. 17–26.

8. Joseph Steinberg and H. C. Cooper, "Social Security Statistical Data, Social Science Research, and Confidentiality," *Social Security Bulletin*, October 1967.
9. Section 1106, Social Security Act, as amended; Regulation No. 1 (as amended), "Disclosure of Official Records and Information" (Part 401, Chapter III, Title 20, Code of Federal Regulations).
10. Executive Order 9397, November 30, 1943, *Federal Register*, pp. 16035–16097.
11. International Business Machines Corp., *Reference Manual, IBM 29 Card Punch*, A24–3332–2 (March 1966), pp. 22–27.
12. Executive Order 9397, op cit.
13. Social Security Administration, Office of Research and Statistics, *Some Statistical Research Resources Available at the Social Security Administration*, 1967.
14. Steinberg, Joseph, *Interacting Data Systems and the Measurement of Income Size Distributions*, presented at the Conference on Research in Income and Wealth, The Size Distribution of Income and Wealth, University of Pennsylvania, 1967.
15. E. S. Dunn, *Review of Proposal for a National Data Center*. Washington, D.C.: U.S. Bureau of the Budget, Statistical Evaluation Report No. 6, November 1965; U.S. House of Representatives Committee on Government Operations, Special Subcommittee on Invasion of Privacy, *The Computer and Invasion of Privacy*. 89th Congress, 2nd Session, July 1966. (The Gallagher Hearings.)
16. *The Washington Post*, "Industrial Spies Turn to Laser Beam, Computer Snooping," March 16, 1967, p. D21.
17. Steinberg and Pritzker, ref. 4.
18. Regulation No. 1, ref. 9, Section 401.3.
19. Regulation No. 1, ref. 9, Section 401.3 (k).
20. *Social Security Bulletin, Annual Statistical Supplement*, 1965, p. 111.
21. See ref. 13.
22. U.S. Bureau of the Census, *1960 Censuses of Population and Housing: Procedural History*, Washington, D.C., 1966; see sections on Allocation.

Part VII   The Protection of Privacy*

The concern of this part is the appropriate balance between providing data needed for social research and policy making, and protecting individuals and organizations from invasions of privacy. Prior to the Gallagher hearings in 1966 the majority of attention to privacy-protection problems emphasized data-collection processes. Since midsummer 1966 the main concern has been data-delivery systems and data banks, particularly a proposed federal statistical data center. Now it is becoming to be recognized that the protection of privacy rights is a system problem, involving interrelations among data-collection processes, coding (particularly identification information), storage and maintenance, and computer systems for processing, analysis, and maintenance, among others. It is only in minor ways a technical problem: the major resources for reasonable protection will be educational, legal, administrative, economic, political, and moral.

Rothman wonders if the extent of current debate about privacy protection is at too high a level considering how poorly accessible and usable the available data are. He then describes the points in a system in which privacy protection must be given highest priority. Feige and Watts explain some advantages and disadvantages of aggregating microdata to improve protection.

---

* An excellent bibliography and analysis of the privacy problem can be found In Arthur R. Miller, "Personal Privacy in the Computer Age: The Challenge of a New Technology in an Information-Oriented Society", *Michigan Law Review*, **67**, No. 6, April 1969.

254 The Protection of Privacy

One final note needs to be made. People want their right to privacy protected, but there must be balance so that the system does not keep us from learning about neglected and disadvantaged groups. Perhaps if the black and poor in the United States were asked, they would express a desire that any new system not be so inefficient as the current one.

Chapter Fifteen

Protecting Privacy: Pros and Cons

*Stanley Rothman**

There is a strong, irrational element involved in the question of protection of privacy. As objective as people may try to be about the problem, there are a number of irrelevant, contaminating, and none-the-less compelling issues that tend to muddy the waters. First of all the computer, per se, although it is not the most important part of the problem, has become the object of the paranoid delusions of the twentieth century. For the New Left the computer has replaced Wall Street, and for the Right the computer has become synonymous with "big government." The adverse effects of toxic technology, sonic booms, and smog have begun to become altogether too apparent. Technology has monopolized national attention and federal budgets, and there are some elements of the intellectual community that are decidedly antitechnology per se. The word "dossier" has been used in connection with the proposed federal statistical data center, for example, and it is a loaded word. In a very real sense your driver's license, your tax form, your census question-

---
* TRW Systems, Inc., Redondo Beach, California.

256 The Protection of Privacy

naire are all dossiers, and no one is really proposing the elimination of these records. Yet the specters of Beria, Torquemada, and Heinrich Himmler all rise up with the word "dossier." Wiretapping, bugs, peepholes, and one-way glass have all been used in lurid, dishonest, venal ways; and there has been an extensive investigation of them in Congress. Lastly, the terrible prophecy of George Orwell's *1984* is sufficiently vivid now for the whole oppressive image to be evoked by only saying the numbers.

None of these issues is really relevant to such a proposal as a federal statistical data center, and yet they make it extremely difficult to get the real issues considered on their merits. It is relevant here when talking about technical protection to bring up these irrational elements because the acceptability of technical protections in the real world depends on how frightened people are. For example, is the aggregation of microdata a good method for keeping data statistically usable and yet still protecting the individual sample so no individual data are disclosed? However, if the original data still have to be there, this aggregation technique may not be sufficiently reassuring. Similarly the kinds of mechanical software and hardware protections that are discussed here may not be acceptable or really relevant to the concerns of a Congressman. Nonetheless there do exist fairly reliable methods of protecting privacy.

Any computer system (including data available to it) is accessible to machine operators, maintenance men, programmers who are improving programs, and possibly physically remote users. (The federal statistical data center was not proposed as a remotely accessible time-shared system, but that kind of a concern naturally arises because remote time-shared systems are currently so much discussed that the possibility is raised by the antagonists anyway.)

Machine operators, first of all, would have to handle and often duplicate the magnetic tapes containing the sensitive information, and thus strict control over their tapes and their mounting would be in order. The ability of operators to watch printers can of course be limited. The destruction of carbon paper and tapes, and the clearing of memory have to be, and can be, handled carefully. It will be difficult for maintenance men to be kept from operating system software because some forms of machine failure can be analyzed only in terms of the operating system; that is, the failure does not show up under any routine testing procedures. However, there could be an arrangement whereby no maintenance man ever worked on a machine by himself. The other threat to the system is the possibility that, like an occasional dishonest telephone repairman, a computer-maintenance man will illegally facilitate wiretapping of the

Protecting Privacy: Pros and Cons 257

computer. A dishonest computer-maintenance man could, say, covertly connect an operational tape unit through a buffer to one that he was "testing" or "fixing" and transcribe a tape. Conceivably he could, through suitably modified "test equipment," transmit the tape over an ordinary telephone line. Thus the telephone system for such a sensitive computer system would have to be isolated, and radio environment would have to be monitored and screened to ensure that electromagnetic emissions were not propagated. Similarly antitampering circuitry could be devised for the computer.

It is possible to distinguish between debugging access that programmers must have to the system and the access that the users have to the system. The programmers could always work with dummy files, whereas the users cannot. The user, on the other hand, need never have access to the programs. The programmer must have access to a copy of the functioning programs but not to the programs themselves as they operate with sensitive information.

The protection programs themselves *must* be protected. These separations can be maintained by hardware, memory-protection, and software techniques. It is quite possible to maintain absolute control over the programs that are in the system by checks against controlled duplicates maintained, again, by a separate, single authority. Changes to the programs can be rigorously checked for purpose and impact before being entered into the operational programs. Then there is the protection of the user console. Lock and key, safe combination, and identification-number systems can be used along with a system that specifies which class of access each person has. Some very involved software systems have been developed to control different classes of access (retrieval, in-filing, culling, and changing). Furthermore, the data-access code system can be put under separate security control and changed frequently. The ability to delete information from the system requires the ability to delete information wherever it occurs in the file. The system itself could keep track of who has had access to what information, and this is a capability that is difficult to achieve in manual systems. This supplies another kind of protection. A monitor system *could* inspect all queries or sequence of queries made by a single user to search for errors or tricks. Communication lines that carry personal information to users could be protected by encoding devices. However, even if these can be bought for nonmilitary purposes, and I understand that they can, these devices are so expensive that they could be used only between computers or major facilities containing a number of user consoles and a remote computer.

Specifically the Bureau of the Census experience indicates that careful protection is a very involved matter and raises a legitimate question as to whether public discussion of the protection technique can compromise the security of the system. Conversely, if the security measures cannot be discussed, can they be trusted? This may just argue for the same kind of restricted access to the protection systems that Congress has to the Central Intelligence Agency.

Presently security systems exist, of course, for running computer centers with classified military information. There are techniques for dealing with magnetic tapes by degaussing and with disks by overwriting. Printing, janitorial maintenance, keypunching, listings, visitors, and the disposition of waste are all to be handled with care.

What remains an unsolved problem is the operation of computer programs and data of differing security levels in the same computer simultaneously. This is the kind of operation that would be required if remote users with different requirements were to use the same time-shared, sensitive-type data base or if a computer were to be used in a multi-processing mode.

I think it is clear that a computer system containing sensitive information could be loaded down with all kinds of protective devices. It will certainly be both imperfect and expensive. The questions to be further pursued are how much cost will this protection add to the total, and what will be the probability of penetration? Roughly, the cost of running a secure computer installation is higher than the cost of running open and seems to be in the 10–30 percent region.

There are a number of other technically interesting problems having to do with the construction of such a system. Correlating files gathered, for example, in different places for different purposes is not simple. It is difficult to determine if two given records are really concerned with the same person. The only certain identification technique that law enforcement has for correlation is the fingerprint. As yet automatic processing of the fingerprint is not technically feasible. There are a number of different techniques for handling spelling problems having to do with names in general and names that are homonyms. Present solutions to the handling of name files are far from perfect. In the long run the social security number as a common identifier may facilitate the solving of these problems (and of course raise others).

So far we have really had rather little experience in protecting large-scale information-sharing networks. Willis Ware, of the Rand Corporation, points out that fewer than three dozen such systems have been built. He further points out that, as the rules and laws on privacy stand today, it is harder to protect private information in a computer system than it is to keep military information secure. Interestingly enough, Ware also notes that, since the system programmers who write the executive program must know all about the protection of privacy, they constitute a particularly high probability target for subversion.

Another control mechanism in our society for the protection of privacy is the institution of government itself. The question is, where in the federal government could personal information be safe from political misuse? The Federal Reserve Board and its antiinflation interest-rate decision, for example, has demonstrated that no power in the federal government could change its judgment and thus has shown that there are institutional arrangements that can be free of all pressure. So an institutution could be established to protect the information. Also, the relationship between the Bureau of the Census and Congress has shown for years now that the appropriations process is an adequate control for limiting even the nature of questions that are asked on Bureau of the Census questionnaires. Thus Congress could limit the content of any data base in government. It would seem then that with new disclosure laws, research in the technology of protection, and new government institutions, a redesigned federal statistical system could be protected better than the existing one.

Finally, an unresolved problem has to do with how well we must protect private information. We have experience in protecting the highly sensitive military-intelligence information systems. If such a system is penetrated, a man may lose his life because the leak exposes his location and his activity. And thus we understand why that kind of a system has to be protected. It hardly seems likely that anyone would lose his life if the connection between his social security number and home address were made or even if his entire census and internal-revenue record became public knowledge. However, what if the 40 percent of the American males who the Crime Commission predicts will accumulate a nontraffic police record get the feeling that their lives are an open book and that there is no longer any reason for them to try to regenerate their life pattern. This kind of motivation and incentive is certainly well worth preventing.

BIBLIOGRAPHY

Anon., "In Defense of Privacy," *Time Magazine,* July 15, 1966, pp. 38–39.
Brenton, M., *The Privacy Invaders,* 1964. Coward-McCann (Pub.) New York, New York.
Conine, E., "A Clear and Future Peril," *Los Angeles Times,* July 17, 1966.
Industrial Security Manual, Paragraph 19H.
Lockheed Missiles and Space Company, *California Statewide Information System Study,* July 30, 1965, pp. G-1–G-4, Appendix G, "Legal Considerations."

260 The Protection of Privacy

Michael, D. N., "Speculations on the Relation of the Computer to Individual Freedom and the Right to Privacy," *The George Washington University Law Review,* 33, No. 270, pp. 270–286.

Packard, V. O., *The Naked Society,* 1964. David McKay (Pub.) New York, New York.

U.S. House of Representatives Committee on Government Operations, Special Subcommittee on Invasion of Privacy, *The Computer and Invasion of Privacy.* 89th Congress, 2nd Session, July 1966.

Witt, E. G., *Security Equipment and Procedures Study.* Santa Monica, Calif.: System Development Corporation, TM-(L)-LO-1000/710/00, August 24, 1964.

Chapter Sixteen

Protection of Privacy through Microaggregation*

Edgar L. Feige and Harold W. Watts†

The enormous expansion of behavioral research coupled with what has been referred to as the information explosion has raised serious questions concerning the establishment, integration, and use of large-scale data collections, and the concomitant issue of the protection of privacy. The vast and rich data resources in the custody of governmental agencies, particularly at the federal level, present one of the most attractive fields of exploration for researchers. Without minimizing the problems associated with prospecting, assaying, and exploiting those data deposits, one must first find a permissible right-of-way through the no-trespassing signs which were erected to honor nondisclosure pledges made when the data

---

* The research underlying this paper was financed by a grant from the Board of Governors of the Federal Reserve System. The authors wish to express their thanks to Arthur S. Goldberger for his many helpful suggestions, comments, and criticisms.
† Social Systems Research Institute, University of Wisconsin, Madison.

261

were obtained and which must continue to be honored in order to defend the broad principle of protection of privacy.

We begin with the assumption that there does indeed exist a conflict between the principle of privacy and the need to discover new knowledge. Neither principle is regarded as absolute, and thus we can investigate the technical tradeoffs between the two. We specifically wish to investigate the costs associated with a particular scheme designed to protect privacy—namely, partial aggregation. Identities of individual reporting units and corresponding confidential information can be effectively obscured by combining the reports of several (or many) units into a single aggregated record. Partial aggregation replaces microunit observations, which are typically regarded as confidential, by nonconfidential observations on "statistical stereotypes." The observations on statistical stereotypes are constructed by combining microunits into groups and calculating the mean values for the grouped observations. If partial aggregation can be carried out without seriously impairing the usefulness of the data for legitimate research purposes, it can make a substantial contribution to our data base. Partial aggregation is not exactly a novelty; we have encountered it often in cross-tabulations, in parallel series on geographic subdivisions, and the like. Moreover, it has by these precedents been established as an acceptable means of preserving the confidential nature of the underlying data.

However, these familiar uses of partial aggregation may not adequately preserve the usefulness of the data. In particular they may be severely limited as primary inputs to regression analysis—probably the most widely used statistical procedure in social science studies. Although partial aggregation has been used in a variety of forms, there have been only a few studies that have explored the explicit costs of using partially aggregated data.* This paper is concerned first with establishing the properties of partially aggregated data as an input to regression analysis and secondly providing some preliminary results from an illustrative case study in which conjectures and procedures derived from an analytic investigation are given a trial on a major body of microdata.*

PARTIAL AGGREGATION IN THE CONTEXT OF A SPECIFIC REGRESSION MODEL

In an earlier paper we considered the effects of partial aggregation on a specific regression model.[8] Instead of going into the technical details

---

* See Orcutt and Watts,[1] Bauman, David, Miller,[2] Miller,[3] Feige,[4] and Feige and Watts.[5]
* The analytical sections are indebted to previous work by Prais and Aitchison[6] and Cramer,[7] who have considered a similar problem from the point of view of reducing the magnitude of computations.

of that paper we shall simply outline the approach and summarize some of the conclusions reached.

After reviewing the classical multiple linear regression model and summarizing the conditions for obtaining best linear unbiased estimates of the regression coefficients, we proceed to show how disclosure can be avoided by the use of a *G* grouping matrix that transforms the original microdata matrix into a matrix of group means. When the original data have been transformed by the use of the grouping matrix, the "generalized linear regression model" becomes appropriate, and the best linear unbiased estimator is the generalized least-squares estimator. Since it is typically very convenient from a computational point of view to utilize ordinary least-squares regression, we note that the generalized least-squares estimators can be obtained from an ordinary least-squares regression procedure when the microdata matrix is transformed by means of an *H* grouping matrix that is related to the *G* grouping matrix mentioned above. We then proceed to demonstrate that, given a grouping matrix, the least-squares estimator based on the partially aggregated data will be unbiased, providing that the grouping matrix is chosen independently and remains fixed over repeated sample realizations of the regression error term. This condition suggests that the choice of the grouping matrix is treated quite symmetrically with the choice of the independent variables in the regression model. It must be regarded as fixed in the same sense as the independent variables of the analysis. We can therefore ensure that estimators derived from partially aggregated data will be unbiased as long as the grouping matrix is chosen on the basis of the independent variables in the analysis, since the model assumes that the disturbance terms are identically distributed for all values of the independent variables.

If the grouping matrix is chosen on the basis of variables that have a systematic relationship to the disturbance terms, the resulting estimators will be biased. This means that if the grouping criterion is related to a variable that is omitted from the regression but systematically related to the disturbances, the estimator based on partially aggregated data will be biased.

The analysis goes on to show that partial aggregation does result in a loss of efficiency (increased sampling variability) for estimates of the regression coefficients and the residual error variance. The loss for the error variance is inevitable and proportional to the reduction in degrees of freedom. In the case of regression coefficients the loss depends on the nature of the grouping schemes. A trace-correlation index is defined that measures the relative efficiency of the grouped estimators as compared with the ungrouped estimators. In general it is shown that the loss of efficiency

264 The Protection of Privacy

from aggregation can be minimized by generating groups that are homogenous with respect to the independent variables of the analysis—that is, minimizing the within-group variation and maximizing the between-group variation. The relative efficiency index that we have constructed does not, however, provide an easy means of minimizing the loss of efficiency. The problem of classifying the microdata into groups so as to maximize the efficiency index is essentially an assignment problem and as such is not amenable to maximization via the familiar calculus methods. Nevertheless the efficiency index does provide a useful criterion for evaluating specific grouping schemes in the content of a specific regression model.

PARTIAL AGGREGATION IN THE CONTEXT OF MULTIPURPOSE DATA

When one considers current data usage as well as the proposals for a federal data center one must focus particular attention on the use of partial aggregation of *multipurpose data*. It now becomes necessary to investigate the consequences of aggregating a body of data without reference to a particular regression model.

At the present time a large number of government agencies have collected highly useful data that have not been made generally available for research purposes. The major stumbling block to the wider dissemination of such data has been their confidential nature, insofar as they relate to individual microunits such as firms and individuals. In special instances agencies have used a variety of methods to obliterate identification characteristics of confidential data and have made some of the data available for special research projects; however, this procedure is both cumbersome and costly since each project requires special data tailoring. More generally government agencies have drastically aggregated microdata and have published these aggregated data for large geographic regions or for the country as a whole. The statistical limitations of such highly aggregated data have been widely discussed in the literature, and there appears to be a growing consensus concerning the greater usefulness of microdata or "slightly" aggregated data. In order to make existing confidential microdata accessible to the research community at substantially lower costs it is necessary to investigate the feasibility of designing multipurpose partial aggregation schemes that avoid the disclosure problem and yet have desirable statistical properties. Since the primary purpose of this chapter is to investigate the feasibility of constructing multipurpose aggregation schemes, it is necessary to analyze the consequences of aggregating a body of data without reference to a particular regression model.

The aggregated data must avoid disclosure of confidential microdata and yet be amenable to the same range of uses as the unaggregated data. Ideally the aggregated data should have the following properties:

1. The relative loss of efficiency due to aggregation should be small for a wide range of regression models.
2. The estimators of the relevant population parameters applied to the grouped data should be unbiased.
3. The grouping scheme should be sufficiently flexible to permit the use of ancillary data that may or may not be subject to the disclosure problem.

The preceding analysis has considered the effects of data aggression on the estimators of a *specific linear regression* model. When the regression model is known in advance it is possible to devise grouping schemes that avoid disclosure of individual microdata and still maintain the property that the grouped estimators are unbiased. Moreover, given knowledge of the specific regression model and the microdata, it is possible to design a grouping scheme that results in relatively efficient grouped estimators. This latter objective can be accomplished by utilizing the independent variables of the analysis as grouping criteria and aggregating relatively homogeneous observations together in such a way as to minimize within-group variation and thereby maximizing between-group variation. The unbiased properties of the grouped estimators are ensured so long as the grouping scheme is chosen independently of the disturbance terms of the known regression model. For a specific regression model this condition rules out the selection of grouping schemes on the basis of the dependent variable of the model or any other variable that might be left out of the regression model, which is correlated with the disturbances. Operationally the above condition for unbiasedness is not difficult to fulfill. The variables to be used for the grouping criterion are the independent variables of the analysis, and, if the model is correctly specified, grouped estimators will be unbiased. However, when microdata are aggregated without reference to a *specific* regression model it is no longer possible to evaluate the effects of such aggregation on a priori grounds, nor is there any simple rule of thumb for "optimal aggregation." This is due to the fact that both efficiency and unbiased properties depend on the relationship between the grouping matrix and the disturbances in various regression models, which are not specified in advance.

If partial aggregation is to be used as a means of avoiding disclosure in the setting of the proposed federal statistical data center, then the problem raised by multipurpose aggregation are indeed significant. However, it may well be possible to design the operations of the federal statistical data center as to allow for *flexible aggregation* procedures. Such an approach would utilize a basic computer program that could be used for all analyses; however, the inputs to the computer would include prespecified preference priorities of the individual research worker requesting partially aggregated data.

An obvious case of prespecified preferences would arise where a researcher wished to avoid the assumption that behavioral parameters were the same for all groups of individuals in the population; for example, some investigators might wish to test the hypothesis that consumption coefficients differ between whites and nonwhites. If the data-organization scheme were perfectly rigid, partially aggregated groups would probably include both whites and nonwhites, and—although the average racial composition variable would vary from group to group, thus allowing some basis for discriminating different behavioral patterns —one might still prefer to treat the groups differently. Under a flexible aggregation scheme the computer could be instructed to segregate the population statistically into white and nonwhite groups and then to form partial clusters within each subgroup. Any prespecified preference that could be expressed in terms of a sorting operation could be included in this framework.

A similar problem arises when different researchers have widely different preferences concerning the relevant variables to be used for purposes of aggregation. It may well be possible to design a computer program that would utilize directly as inputs the specific preferences of the individual researcher. Included in the input would then be a listing of the variables that are to be used as the basis for clustering micro-observations.

As long as the variables to be used for clustering purposes are discrete in nature (i.e., income interval rather than income) the researcher can supply the computer with an *ordinal* set of grouping preferences that specify the priorities for consecutive sorts. The computer would of course reject any set of preferences that would result in less than a minimum number of individuals falling into any particular group.

More generally it is possible to inform the computer of the researcher's *cardinal* preference function with respect to the grouping criterion. The researcher in this case would have to regard the reduction of within-group variance of a particular variable as a scarce resource and would have to indicate to the computer the price that he would be willing to pay—namely, an increase in the within-group variance with respect to some other variable. If the individual researcher would specify a tradeoff function, the computer could proceed to minimize within-group variances with respect to several variables, given the constraints imposed by the researcher's cardinal tradeoff function. Thus, if the researcher specifies that he is willing to increase the within-group variance of income by $100 in order to get a reduction of within-group variance of IQ level of 10 points, the computer would take account of this tradeoff and proceed to choose "optimal" groups in light of the prespecified quantitive preferences.

Such a flexible aggregation approach might possibly lead to some combination of sorting procedures that together could reveal some information about an individual. Although we suspect that this would be mathematically possible, it is not clear how such a scheme could be devised without some prior knowledge concerning individual units. If some information about a microunit is available through nonconfidential sources, it would be possible to gain added confidential information by use of successive sorting instructions. This possibility is much more likely to occur with firm data then with data on individuals. Since partial aggregation is not viewed as a unique panacea for all such problems, it may be quite possible to avoid such suggested violations of disclosure by raising the costs of such violations by other means, such as strict legislation.[9]

The more complex the data base becomes, the more important it may be to move in the direction of flexible aggregation schemes. Current procedures among government agencies typically involve rigid and drastic aggregation schemes. One might therefore wish to inquire how a rigid aggregation scheme would fare when the outputs of such a scheme become inputs to a variety of regression models. Moreover, we would hope to know more about the relative efficiency of estimators based on "slightly" aggregated data as opposed to "drastically" aggregated data. Finally, for a given degree of aggregation we would like to know the effects of different grouping criteria on the relative efficiency of resulting estimators.

In order to investigate these issues we undertook to examine a large body of micro analytical data that included call report and income-and-dividend information on over 5000 commercial banks that are members of the Federal Reserve System. The two groups of data came from separate sources and were linked by means of a bank identification code. These data were in turn linked with relevant ancillary data from the

268 The Protection of Privacy

city and county census tapes by means of geographic location codes, which were common to the two sets of data.

In order to evaluate the effects of aggregation schemes on a variety of regression models we formulated 20 experimental regression equations. Each one of these experimental equations was estimated by using the underlying microdata and then reestimated by using aggregated data that had been generated by a variety of aggregation schemes. For each regression model and for alternative aggregation schemes we computed an ex post facto index of relative efficiency that described the average loss of efficiency due to aggregation relative to the unaggregated ideal.

An aggregation scheme is defined both by the degree of aggregation (i.e., the size of the subgroups) and by an array rule that indicates which variables are to be used as the sorting criterion. One current Federal Reserve practice is to publish data on member banks that are aggregated to the state level. Such an aggregation procedure is drastic in the sense that it groups together as many as several hundred banks in some states and uses geographic location as the sole array rule. The index of efficiency for each of the experimental regression equations under this Federal Reserve aggregation scheme is displayed in Table 16.1. An efficiency index of unity indicates no loss of efficiency due to aggregation.

Table 16.1

Relative Efficiency Index for State Aggregated Data

Regression number	1	2	3	4	5	6	7	8	9
Efficiency index	0.199	0.081	0.160	0.153	0.220	0.211	0.195	0.112	0.230
Regression number	10	11	12	13	14	15	16	17	18
Efficiency index	0.185	0.177	0.134	0.136	0.285	0.123	0.170	0.143	0.204
Regression number	19	20							
Efficiency index	0.038	0.037							

Average efficiency index over all regressions: 0.160

The results of Table 16.1 serve two purposes. First they indicate that the loss of efficiency from such drastic aggregation is substantial (its average efficiency index over all regressions is 0.160), and the loss of efficiency will, as expected, vary from equation to equation. In order to evaluate the effect of the degree of aggregation on loss of efficiency we used the same array rule (i.e., state and random within state) but computed the average efficiency index for different degrees of aggregation. In particular we considered groups consisting of 3, 30, and 100 banks. The resulting average efficiency indices were 0.446, 0.176, and 0.163, respectively. These results indicate that substantial gains in relative efficiency can be brought about by simply reducing the degree of aggregation.

Finally we experimented with using different array rules as criteria for aggregation. We found that some additional gains in efficiency could be brought about by using additional variables as grouping criteria. For example, when geographic location (state) was combined with a bank-size variable as an array rule the average relative efficiency index was raised to approximately 0.575 for "slight" degrees of aggregation.

The analysis strongly suggests that slight aggregation procedures, while still satisfying confidentiality requirements, can greatly improve our data base when compared to the current procedures of drastic aggregation. Looked at the other way, the results suggest that one cannot beat individual data when one's sole concern is with the highest statistical precision; but such precision might be well worth sacrificing to the principle of privacy. Moreover, aggregated data can be further improved by a judicious choice of array rules. On the basis of our analysis of bank data one is tempted to speculate that substantial gains in efficiency can be achieved by substantially reducing the degree of aggregation. Indeed, since the degree of aggregation appears to be more critical than the particular array rule chosen, one might argue that the gains to be achieved from flexible aggregation rules might not justify the marginal costs of such innovations. Although the rigid aggregation scheme does involve losses of efficiency in the multipurpose setting, it may be regarded as a useful starting point in the establishment of a federal statistical data center. A rigid aggregation scheme would not necessarily preclude using specially tailored aggregation schemes for particular high-priority projects that can demonstrate that the conventional mode of aggregation is simply inconsistent with the conceptual or statistical necessities of the project. Such special tailoring could be provided by means of the preference-function technique previously alluded to, as long as the data center maintained files on individual units.

The usefulness of a rigid aggregation scheme could be greatly enhanced if the data center also computed some of the common nonlinear transformations on the micro-observations before grouping those observations. In many research situations nonlinear models are specified but ultimately cast into the framework of linear regression models by utilizing transformations (squares, logs, reciprocals, products, etc.) on the microdata. If the microdata have been linearly aggregated, transformations on the partially aggregated data can lead to serious problems of misspecification, due to the difference between the mean square (or product) and the square (or product) of the means or between the mean of the logs and the log of means. Heuristically it is clear that it is the within-group variation of the variables that enter into nonlinear transformations which causes difficulty. Linear aggregation as a means of avoiding disclosure can be utilized in the context of nonlinear models if all the transformations that may be needed are carried out before aggregation. Short of a complete solution to this problem, it might be useful to extend the basic set of variables to include commonly encountered transformations.

As a final speculative step we might ask what type of multipurpose aggregation scheme would be least offensive. We shall assume that actual data-linkage problems are solved by collating all data from different sources that relate to a particular microunit. Given a set of linked files of individual microunits we might select spatial location as the fundamental arary criterion. Geographic location has the advantage of being a universal characteristic since every microunit can be uniquely located spatially. It may well be possible to develop a numerical micro zip-code system which would have the property that aggregation of subdivisions would yield the numerical-code equivalent of larger subdivisions, and so on.

From the conceptual point of view geographic location may provide a useful aggregation criterion insofar as many behavioral models would wish to combine actors in a homogeneous environment, and spatial homogeneity is likely to serve this function quite well.

Finally, spatial location is likely to be associated with the independent variables in most behavioral studies and thus would satisfy one of the conditions required of aggregated data if biased estimators are to be avoided and efficiency losses kept to a minimum. The obvious exception to the foregoing would be migration studies, in which spatial location might be the dependent variable of the analysis and thus the worst criterion for aggregation. It would be possible to deal with such an exception by recourse to a specially tailored aggregation scheme of the type described above. In general we would expect that the geographic location criterion is best suited for the aggregation of firms, whereas a closely related scheme of constructing cohorts on the basis of birth year and sex may provide an excellent scheme for individuals. Under such an arrangement migration studies of individuals could use

Protection of Privacy through Microaggregation

cohorts as the inputs to the analysis since birth year and sex are not likely to show much variability.

SUMMARY AND CONCLUSIONS

The great interest that has been aroused by the proposal of a federal statistical data center holds great promise and great problems. At the heart of the issue is the juxtaposition of conflicting values—the protection of privacy as opposed to the need to discover new knowledge. We have considered one possible means of partially reconciling these conflicting values—namely, the use of partial aggregation that obscures individual identification. Partial aggregation has the great advantage of satisfying all but the most severe of requirements for the protection of privacy and still offering great improvement over the data that are currently available to the research community.

The cost of adopting partial aggregation as a means of avoiding disclosure must clearly be measured in terms of the usefulness of partially aggregated data for research purposes. We have examined some of the consequences of using such data as an input to regression analysis and find that there are a variety of ways to reduce the potential loss of information due to aggregation. The most important gains may come from the adoption of "slight" as opposed to "drastic" aggregation schemes, and there do exist guidelines for the judicious choice of array rules that can further enhance the usefulness of partially aggregated data.

Partial aggregation cannot be regarded as a costless panacea for the many problems that have been raised concerning the proposed federal statistical data center, but it does provide a useful beginning toward reconciling some of the conflicting goals of such an establishment. It is surely possible to find some combination of statistical gimmicks and substantive legislative protections that can lead to both a maintenance of the privacy principle and an extension of our current data base and the concomitant expansion of our knowledge horizon. Although knowledge and privacy may be ultimately conflicting goals, it seems quite likely that, given the present state of both knowledge and privacy, a federal statistical data center, appropriately conceived and judiciously supervised, could indeed further both ends simultaneously.

REFERENCES

1. G. H. Orcutt and Harold Watts, *Consequences of Data Aggregation over Components for Prediction of the Effect of Policy on Economic Aggregates,* Systems Formulation, Methodology, and Policy Workshop Paper No. 6511. Madison, Wisc.: University of Wisconsin, September 1965.
2. R. A. Bauman, M. H. David, and R. F. Miller, *Sources of Income Variability for Wisconsin Male Taxpayers,* 1947–1959, Economic Behavior of Households Workshop Paper No. 6705. Madison, Wisc.: Social Systems Research Institute, University of Wisconsin, 1967.
3. R. F. Miller, *Confidentiality of Usability of Complex Data Bases,* Systems Formulation and Methodology Workshop Paper No. 6702. (Submitted to *The American Statistician,* May 1967.)
4. E. L. Feige, *The Organization of Financial Data for Research Purposes,* Financial and Fiscal Research Workshop Paper No. 6302. Madison, Wisc.: University of Wisconsin, October 1963.
5. E. L., Feige, and Harold W. Watts, *Partial Aggregation of Micro Economic Data,* Financial and Fiscal Research Workshop Paper No. 6601. Madison, Wisc.: University of Wisconsin, October 1963.
6. Prais and Aitchison, "The Grouping of Observations in Regression Analysis," *Review of the Internationl Statistical Institute,* 1954, pp. 1–22.
7. J. S. Cramer, "Efficient Grouping, Regression, and Correlation in Engel Curve Analysis," *Journal of the American Statistical Association,* 59 (March 1964).
8. See ref. 5.
9. For an excellent discussion of these issues see ref. 3.

Part VIII   Summing Up

Ralph L. Bisco

Man—the man of today—is wise . . . But the past eats away his soul like a cancer. It imprisons him within the ion circle of things already accomplished.

Leonid Andreyev

The phrases "archive," "data base," and "data set" are virtually static concepts, at least in connotation, and are inappropriate for many of the organizations concerned with the collection, updating, preservation, and diffusion of social and behavioral science data. A main objective of this book is to point out the directions we must move in if archives are to become something better and to service better the needs of decision makers, social and behavioral scientists, and other possible users of the data about the past that are becoming increasingly important for decision-making, research, and teaching. But an archive can be useful over the long run only if it can effectively meet the dynamic needs of users. Archive development is doomed from the beginning if the emphasis is solely on the collection, maintenance, and diffusion of individual data sets. There has to be more.

This should not be construed as an absolute criticism of the majority of archives that limit themselves to acquisition, processing, and diffusion of individual data sets. Before archives came into being most students found that the introduction of data-analysis courses involved survey work in the field and the conversion of data to a machine-usable form, etc., but left little time for actual analysis. The development of archives

273

is correlated with decreasing time spent on data collection and increasing time spent on various strategies for analysis. This is, to say the least, a profound change in the structuring of values regarding methodology courses and an equally profound change in the way that other courses are conducted. Suffice it to say that Pool, Abelson, and Popkin would not have been able to do a simulation of the American electorate without simultaneous access to many studies from the Roper Public Opinion Research Center at Williams College, Williamstown, Massachusetts.

However, more needs to be done if social and behavioral scientists are to have a more meaningful role in the solution of pressing social problems. To put it bluntly, a single data collection is useless for understanding better the minority-group social problems that dominate the news today. More and more social and behavioral scientists must be able to link a diverse array of data collections if they want to do more than give a general analysis of the American polity, etc. Unfortunately, however, most data collections do not have the information necessary for interdata set linkage. Most researchers accept as necessary a group form of research. But we are not yet at a point where multidata set linkage is an important value: that requires too much interaction between the funding agency, the individual principal investgator, and the many others who would be interested in using the data collection if they had some opportunity to, say, insert their own questions in a survey. In short, we are only beginning to look upon the present information-transfer network as a relatively expensive and inefficient system.

INFORMATION-TRANSFER NETWORKS OF THE FUTURE

In the next paragraphs we offer some descriptions of information-transfer networks of the future, but first we must offer some caveats. First, it should be stressed that these networks will not develop overnight: there are still technical problems to be resolved, political issues to be decided, and certain questions to be researched. Second, the future networks are not intended completely to supplant present physical and informal means of information transfer: we shall continue to mail data, to write and read books, and to attend conferences, seminars, and workshops. Finally, social scientists cannot simply sit back and wait for these networks to develop: natural scientists and engineers are now designing and constructing such networks, and they welcome the contributions of social scientists. But, just as computing facilities are now

Summing Up 275

oriented primarily to the needs of natural scientists, so will the new information-transfer networks if social scientists—by choice or default —do not join in the task of building them.

Let us now share some visions of information-transfer networks of the future. It should be noted that data banks, their accessibility, and their processability are important components. In Licklider's views the future electronic network will:

"1. Be available when and where needed.

2. Handle both documents and facts.

3. Permit several different categories of input, ranging from authority-approved formal contributions (e.g., papers accepted by recognized journals) to informal notes and comments.

4. Make available a body of knowledge that is organized both broadly and deeply—and foster the improvement of such organization through use.

5. Facilitate its own further development by providing tool-building languages and techniques to users and preserving the tools they devise, and by recording measures of its own performance and adapting in such a way as to maximize the measures.

6. Provide access to the body of knowledge through convenient procedure-oriented and field-oriented languages.

7. Converse or negotiate with the user while he formulates his requests and while responding to them.

8. Adjust itself to the level of sophistication of the individual user, providing terse, streamlined modes for experienced users working in their expertness and functioning as a teaching machine to guide and improve the efforts of neophytes.

9. Permit users to deal either with metainformation (through which they can work "at arm's length" with substantive information), or with substantive information (directly), or with both at once.

10. Provide the flexibility, legibility, and convenience of the printed page at input and output and at the same time the dynamic quality and immediate responsiveness of the oscilloscope screen and light pen.

11. Facilitate joint contribution to and use knowledge by several or many co-workers.

12. Present flexible, wide-band interfaces to other systems, such as research systems in laboratories, information-acquisition systems in government, and application systems in business and industry.

13. Reduce markedly the difficulties now caused by the diversity of publication languages, terminoligies, and 'symbologies.'

276 Summing Up

14. Essentially eliminate publication lag.

15. Tend toward consolidation and purification of knowledge instead of, or as well as, toward progressive growth and unresolved equivocation.

16. Evidence neither the ponderousness now associated with over-centralization nor the confusing diversity and provinciality now associated with highly distributed system (our emphasis).

17. Display desired degree of initiative, together with good selectivity, in dissemination of recently acquired and 'newly needed' knowledge".[1]

Overhage calls the information-transfer network of the future the "on-line intellectual community:"

"The list of services . . . begins with access to stored information. Whenever a user needs to employ a fact or refer to a document that is 'in the network,' he has only to specify the fact or the document uniquely . . . retrieval of stored information is the basic service upon which all the facilities of the on-line system must depend. The second fundamental service is processing of retrieved information with the aid of computer programs. It is essential to the concept . . . that there exist, within the on-line system, an extensive library of computer programs that can be called upon by any user, specialized (through commands given in a convenient language) to meet his immediate purposes, and directed upon any body or bodies of information he cares to name. If he knows how to write computer programs, the user can add to the publicly available armamentarium and process information in ways of his own particular choosing.

"A third fundamental service deals with display of information to the user. This service, also, is controlled by a language, designed to be natural enough for the user and formal enough for the computer, that deals with entities to be displayed, with the selection of display devices, and with the specification of formats. Through this language (which) can be embedded in other languages he can have alphanumeric text presented to him as soft (ephemeral) copy on a special alphanumeric display or typed out for him on a printer, and he can call for graphs, diagrams, sketches, and the like, mixed with alphanumeric text, on various display screens, and have the information captured photographically or xerographically for later reference.

"The fourth and final basic service is control. The user controls the system or addresses requests to it, through a few familiar devices: a keyboard, a penlike stylus, a microphone, and a small assortment of buttons and switches. Through those devices, he can communicate in strings of alphanumeric characters, by pointing, by writing clearly, by sketching or drawing, and by speaking distinctly in a limited vocabulary.

Built upon the basis of the four services just described are many derivative services. . . . There are arrangements . . . that facilitate the design of structures and devices. There are programs to facilitate the preparation and editing of text. There are programs to facilitate the preparation, editing, testing, modification, and documentation of computer programs. There are special-purpose languages, together with facilities for carrying out instructions given in the languages, for modeling or simulating complex processes. . . . There are arrangements to facilitate communication among members of the on-line community—for authorizing access to otherwise private files, for merging texts and pooling data, and the like. There are many courses and many techniques for computer-assisted instruction, including some that instruct the user in the operation of the on-line system and in the preparation of computer programs in various procedure-oriented and problem-oriented languages. . . .

"There are many other services, such as programs for statistical analysis of data, programs to facilitate conducting experiments through the system, and programs that conduct tests of all kinds. . . .

"The system is augmented not only through the contributions of its users, of course, but also through the contributions of full-time organizers, programmers, and maintainers of the system." [2]

In the "on-line intellectual community" many of the processes of data collection, data access, communication, and publication would change, some in revolutionary ways. Sitting at a combination television-and-typewriter console, a user could first retrieve relevant literature and data, then analyze the data by using software scattered about the network, and then prepare a report by using the text-processing capabilities of the system. During his research he might use the computer-assisted instruction capabilities of the network either to learn a new method or to refresh his understanding of a basic statistic or procedure.

The following are some of the advantages:

1. Manuscript drafts could easily be updated as the research progresses.

2. Editing functions—such as spelling corrections, punctuation, pagination, and hyphenation—would be automated features of the system.

3. Informal and preliminary reports could easily be directed through telecommunications to selected colleagues.

278   Summing Up

4. New data collections could easily be routed to the appropriate service-oriented data banks in the network.

Using the electronic transfer network to "keypunch" data or to prepare and edit successive drafts of a report would not mean that the resulting machine-processable information would automatically be available to all other persons connected to the network. Rather, the producer would make his machine-processable information available to the on-line information base, either to the public as a whole or selected colleagues, at his own choosing.

We recognize that we are many years away from any kind of *ideal* information transfer and processing network, but important steps in the development of such networks are being made. The potentialities seem worth considerable experimentation: modern technology has relatively untapped capabilities to extend the number of alternatives available to teachers and researchers, and to society as a whole. In the words of John McCarthy,

"The speed, capacity, and universality of computers make them machines that can be used to foster diversity and individuality in our industrial civilization, as opposed to the uniformity and conformity that have hitherto been the order of the day. Decisions that now have to be made in the mass can in the future be made separately, case by case. To take a practical example, it can be decided whether or not it is safe for an automobile to go through an intersection each time the matter comes up, instead of subjecting the flow of automobiles to regulation by traffic lights.... The decision whether to go on to the next topic or review the last one can be made in accordance with the interests of the child rather than for the class as a whole. In other words, computers can make it possible for people to be treated as individuals in many situations where they are now lumped in the aggregate." [3]

SOME OF THE PROBLEMS

Now we turn to the major problems that must be solved if the social and behavioral science community must face and solve if we want to be able to help guide the development of and to make use of these information-transfer systems of the future.

At present archives are underutilized for a variety of reasons, most of which relate either directly or indirectly to the ability of the archive

network to match present and possible data sources with user needs. Our basic theme is that many of the problem archives face are systemic and will diminish as more attention is given to make the various components of the social science information system work more in concert. In this respect we should be able to benefit from the experiences of the traditional library network, which has uniform systems for cataloging, indexing, abstracting, and the like.

Let us now turn to a description of the foremost problems of archives and their users. *The first problem is that the majority of users no longer know the best or even most likely sources of needed machine-processable information.*

Today many users are severely frustrated by the inability quickly to determine what specific information is available from a given data bank or other information-service organization, and they often give up their search at an early time. Also, with increasing frequency a user needs to query more than one archive or other information service to obtain data useful for a particular project; for example, he may need to combine data sets uniquely available in several different data banks. *Increasingly, therefore, the user is confronted with a diversity of manual, semiautomated, and low-level automated retrieval systems (such as KWIC indexes).* The proliferation of special information services within the social science information-transfer network, justfied from a number of standpoints,[4] requires that attention be given to the development of minimal standards about queries to, and outputs from, the individual archives, and necessitates better user and other documentation of the information stores.

Once a user ascertains that one or more archives *probably* are collecting the kinds or categories of data he needs, he is typically confronted with a two-step process for determining where a needed data collection can be obtained. He must determine which of the many archive organizations are likely to have the kind of data collection he wants, and then he must interrogate each of these about their ability to match his data needs with their data holdings.

The first step in resolving the user's dilemma is better information about the overall services of the various data-bank organizations. But the user does not want, and should not need, to go through a two-step process to determine where the data he needs might be obtained. The archive user would prefer to determine first which data collection(s) meets his teaching or research needs, and then to find out which archive or archives maintain, and will disseminate to him, the needed data collection(s). Consequently for the past three years the Council of

280 Summing Up

Social Science Data Archives and the Standing Committee on Data Archives have undertaken an inventory project in order to develop standardized descriptions of the individual data holdings of the various member archives.

Now we are preparing to establish a retrieval service for individuals and archives so that a request from a user can be matched with individual data-collection descriptions, and the user can be referred to the archive(s) maintaining the specific data collection that meets his needs. Many archives find their ability to provide referral services insufficient because of the present inadequacies for matching user needs with available data.

The next level of concern for the user is the utility of the product he gets from a successful request to an information service. Can the computer tape be processed on local facilities? In the area of machine-processable data services our experience is that the usability of information obtained is often the most critical factor regarding satisfaction of the user. From a negative standpoint the user may find that he has a data tape with a blocking factor too large for the input (or buffer) area of his local computer or that the header-label or end-of-file indicators do not conform to local requirements; or he may find, on close insepction, that there are some serious discrepancies between the data set and its documentation. These discrepancies may be so serious that valuable time will have to be spent determining the reasons and possibly correcting the errors—if the data set is to be used at all.

Taking a positive stance, a user may find the duplicate data set from an archive is readily usable. More specifically, he may be presented a data set that has been subsetted to include only the variables or information needed for his particular analysis, in which the data items have been recoded or transformed to meet the requirements of local software and for which the data are on a medium (card, disk, tape) and in a form such that they can directly be "read" by the local computing equipment. In other words, the user receives the requested data set in a form such that he can move *immediately* to his analysis interests: he does not have to spend days, weeks, or months manipulating or transforming the data so that they can be "inputted" to local analysis software.

Normatively, users should be able directly to apply information to project objectives. We desire to decrease the time and effort required between the time a user receives machine-readable information and the time he can apply it to a specific research or teaching activity.

Another problem is that the archive user may find that relevant data he knows have been collected are not available from any known archive or other information service. He may have determined from an examination of the literature or a query to a funding agency or other source that a particular data collection has been completed, but he may later learn that the data have been destroyed, that they cannot be released to him at the present time, or that the data-collecting organization does not have the means to make a duplicate of the data and documentation available to him.

Many problems of data utilities stem from the fact that nearly all data collections are undertaken for the specific needs of a local research staff. Present values give high priority to public distribution of research results or reports but low priority to preparing a data collection, from the beginning, for more widespread use. Consequently the task of preparing data for more public use has been shifted from the local data-collection specialists who know most about the data and their documentation, and who typically are in a better position than archive staffs to do the necessary cleaning and other processing to archival organizations. Therefore a fundamental concern is to develop guidelines and procedures for data preparation in concert with the data-supplying organizations and hardware and software manufacturers, so that the most important preparations of archivable data sets for public use can be done by the data suppliers themselves.

Often fairly rich data collections are reduced to more limited data sets in the coding process; for example, the information gathered by an open-ended question in a survey may be reduced in the manual coding process to a highly conceptual and project-limited representation. However, we expect that the more empirical the coding, the more generally and historically useful will be the data set. Moving in this direction requires close cooperation with, and special work by, data suppliers.

By empirical coding we mean capturing as much original information as possible by, for example, "punching" date of birth or actual age and income rather than bracket codes, and by capturing as much as possible of the specific detail in, for example, open-ended questions. Indeed, continuing progress in content analysis indicates that in the near future it will be preferable to preserve in machine-readable form the actual text of answers to such survey questions.[5]

Regarding other kinds of data collections—such as census, demographic, and economic information—"empirical" means the ability to aggregate or "disaggregate" the data set or specific data items within the data set. For example, one user may need county-level data, whereas another must have tract data; one user may need to distinguish numbers of persons under 21, whereas another needs to distinguish numbers of persons over 65 in given areal or other units. These various problems will have to be given more attention than has been the case heretofore if the data collections coming into archives are to have increasing public utility as time goes on. Perhaps needless to say, empirical coding can benefit the primary as well as the secondary analyst: often the primary analyst finds his analysis restricted by the original coding.

Another source of difficulty is that a user may require a highly interconnected data base for an analysis project. Preparing an interconnected data base requires the linking of a set of data sets, but the necessary linkage information is often lacking. It will become increasingly important to link, for example, survey data with census-tract or other contextual data. The crucial linkage often is not the name or address of an individual respondent but a geographic identifier to determine whether he resides within or outside a given ecological, geographic, or political entity. It is of course highly desirable that this kind of linkage information be included at the earliest possible point in the data-generation process. Consequently it is indispensable that some standards for data-linkage systems be developed as soon as possible.

Furthermore, there are notable gaps in the collections of archives. Some publicly useful kinds of data that have been collected and are already in machine-readable form have not been transferred to an archive or otherwise made widely accessible. Other kinds of data that are deemed important by a substantial number of possible users have not been converted to a machine-processable form. There are still other kinds of gaps.

The reasons are many. Not infrequently potential users find that apparently important data collections have been destroyed by intent or by neglect. Sometimes this is because the researchers concluded that the research report was sufficient and other times because storage conditions were such that data collections were rendered inaccessible by circumstances beyond the control of the data-gathering organization. In some cases certain kinds of useful information are legally proscribed; in other cases, such as civil violence, "early warning systems" such as social indicators [6,7] do not exist to indicate the need for new information. Concerted efforts among funding agencies, data suppliers, information services, and professional associations are necessary to resolve this critical problem.

Some data collections are not useful for some secondary analyses because they lack certain critical variables. Over time we can reduce the probability of events of this kind by developing lists of basic variables and tested question wordings in cooperation with the data suppliers

Summing Up 283

and the professional associations. We believe that most gaps of this kind are not due to unwillingness on the part of research design staffs but rather because the necessary guidelines and standards have not been developed. We expect that machine-readable codebooks (the computer-readable text of survey questions and codes) will be an important resource for the research that must be done.

Some archives are in many ways uniquely qualified to undertake the conversion to computer-usable form and the subsequent processing and maintenance of certain kinds of public printed information. The Inter-University Consortium's recovery of election, roll call, and census data from the 1800s to the present [8] is the major example of this capability. Several archives are undertaking to convert to machine-readable form certain important data collections that heretofore were not machine analyzible. We expect that archives will more and more be asked to take special responsibility for the collection and conversion to machine-readable form of certain public records useful for social research. Also, as state and local governments and other organizations automate their information-processing activities, more kinds of public-sector data useful for social research are becoming available in machine-processable form.

A basic concern of the Council is to improve the ability of archives to obtain and rediffuse relevant, publicity and historically useful data collections. We find that there is considerable waste in duplicative data-gathering efforts and in the current difficulties of relating present to past research results. Steps necessary to resolve these problems involve changes in the attitudes of researchers about the historical utility of certain data collections and changes in the availability of certain data collections to archival organizations. All of the above described problems involve greater or lesser attention to ethical issues. There must be standards that protect the data supplier, the archive itself, the entities involved in a data-collection process, and the user. It must be stressed that these problems cannot be attacked individually: sometimes the solution of one problem may exacerbate another and make the latter even harder to resolve.

For example, the need for data-set linkage is in opposition in some ways with the need for protection of privacy. The editor has a "threshold" theory about the apparent contradiction between the two values for data-set acquisition and dissemination. Simply put, there is a boundary in the minds of many below which the need for privacy (or threat of revelation of damaging information) controls and above which the citizenry have confidence that information about them will be used for constructive social purposes. Support for this hypothesis comes from the fact that to date there is no privacy problem in Scandinavia, but there is one in the United States.

In short, those countries whose government and social science community are distrusted have a privacy problem, and those where the two components have confidence from the populace do not. I find it much more easy to interview a homosexual, prostitute, or criminal in Scandinavia than in the United States. When I go to Europe I do not mind filling out the forms required by the police, because I know that the information will not be used against me.

Generally, then, our concerns are to help reduce the systemic total cost of archive network operations by shifting at least parts of certain activities from archives to professional associations or to data suppliers where the local staff can do a job such as cleaning or documentation better and at lesser cost. We desire to improve the utility for secondary analyses of some data collections by developing standards or guidelines about linkage information, basic variables, and coding strategies. It is important that we help improve the links between archives and other information services. We must also undertake research into systems and procedures that (1) speed or otherwise improve the data-collection process *before* the data and documentation are made available to an infromation service or archive and (2) minimize or reduce the problems of retrieval and secondary use of archival data that now plague the user.

Although said before, it must be stressed that our ability to make effective use of information-transfer networks of the future requires more work toward the solution of these problems than has been undertaken so far.

REFERENCES

1. J. C. R. Licklider, *Libraries of the Future*. Cambridge, Mass.: MIT Press, 1965, p. 219.
2. C. F. J. Overhage, and R. Joyce Harman (eds). *Intrex, Report of a Planning Comference on Information Transfer Experiments*. Cambridge, Mass.: MIT Press, 1965.
3. John McCarthy, "Information," *Scientific American*, 215, No. 3 (September 1966), pp. 64–73.
4. National Academy of Sciences, *Communication Systems and Resources in the Behavioral Sciences*, Publication 1575, Washington, D.C., 1967.
5. Bruce Frisbie and S. Sudman, *The Use of Computers in Coding Free Response Answers in Survey Research*. Chicago: National Opinion Research Center, University of Chicago, 1966; P. J. Stone, D. C. Dunphy, M. S. Smith, and D. M. Ogilvie, *The General Inquirer: A Computer Approach to Content Analysis*. Cambridge, Mass.: MIT Press, 1966, p. 651.

6. R. A. Bauer, *Social Indicators*. Cambridge, Mass.: MIT Press, 1967.
7. Sheldon, Eleanor Bernert, and Wilbert E. Moore (eds.), *Indicators of Social Change*, New York: Russell Sage Foundation, 1968.
8. R. L. Bisco, 'Social Science Data Archives: Progress and Prospects," *Social Science Information*, VI, No. 1 (1967), pp. 39–75; W. E. Miller, *Annual Report of the Executive Director of the Inter-University Consortium for Political Research*. Includes current statement of data holdings. Available from the Executive Director of the Consortium. Latest report is for 1969.

Index

Abelson, R. P., 22, 39n, 40n, 209, 274
Acheson, E. D., 250n
Acton, F. S., 201, 206n
ADMINS, 12–13
Afifi, A. A., 203, 206n
Alford, Robert, 53, 60n
Allen, S. I., 157n
Almendinger, V. V., 110n
American Behavioral Scientist, 60n
American Historical Association, 44
Analysis, cohort, 33
  content, 33
  regional, 74
Anderson, T. W., 206n
Angell, Robert C., 36, 41n
Archival facilities, activities of, 5–9
  development of, 3–5
Archival use, problems for users in, 9–11, 279–283
Archive development, problems of, 44–45
Archive organization, alternative for, 11–15
Archives, general-purpose, general service, 13
  general-purpose, local service, 13–14
  relation between individuals and, 47–50
  services of, 8–9
  special-purpose, general service, 13
  special-purpose, local service, 14
Area identification, methods of, 212–216
  problems of, 211–219
Aristotle, 19
Aron, Raymond, 20, 38n
Asch, S. E., 26, 36, 40n
Atkinson, Thomas R., 180n, 197n
Axford, S. J., 250n

Bargman, R. E., 207n
Barnett, G. O., 157n
Bartlett, M. S., 206n
Bauer, R. A., 22, 39n, 285n
Bauman, Richard A., 112, 136n, 197n, 262n, 272n
Bell, Charles G., 52
Berelson, Bernard, 22
Bergson, Abram, 39n
Bernert, Eleanor, 285n
Bhargava, R., 206n
Bisco, Ralph L., 1, 15n, 60n, 80, 250n, 273, 285n
Bobrow, D. B., 60n
Bondi, G., 38n
Boulding, Kenneth, 22
Bowman, Raymond T., 63, 69n
Box, G. E. P., 201, 206n
Braddock, Fred, 158
Brenton, M., 259n
Bruning, Iris, 60n
Buck, S. F., 206n
Bureau of Labor Statistics, 79
Bureau of the Budget, 76
Bureau of the Census, 75–76, 250n
Bwy, D. P., 60n

Calkins, H. W., 237n
Campbell, Angus, 22, 39n, 42
Campbell, D. T., 40n
Canadian Atomic Energy Board, 239
Cantril, Hadley, 21
Careers in Archives, 4, 37
Castleman, Paul A., 139, 156n, 157n
Center for International Studies, Massachusetts Institute of Technology, 12–13
Chamberlin, Edward, 25, 39n
Chammah, A. M., 41n
Chess, J. I., 110n
Clark, Colin, 21, 38n
Clark, W. L., 237n
Cocoran, W. G., 206n
Cohen, A. C., Jr., 204, 205, 206n
Committee for the Collection of Basic Quantitative Data of American Political History, 44
Committee on the Preservation and Use of Economic Data, 44

287

Index

Community profiles, 74–75
Compustat file, 181, 185, 187, 189, 194
Computer programs, 36–37
Computer systems, managing complex data structures, 137–172
Computer technology, influence of, 72–73
Computers, development activities for, 9
Conant, J. B., 39n
Confidentiality, 244–247
  problems of, 134–135
  see also Privacy
Conine, E., 259n
Contingency checks, 98
Cooper, H. C., 251n
Costigan, Gerald, 41n
Council of Social Science Data Archives, 23, 42, 280, 283
Cramer, S. J., 272n
Crawford, R. J., Jr., 237n
Crossley, W. O., 110n

Dahl, Robert, 23, 39n
Data, aggregative, 30, 35
  amount of, by type, 30–34
  "cleaning" of, 6, 98
Data, concerted use of, 6
  content analysis, 30, 34
  control on production of, 121–125
  derived, 36
  documentation, 99
  elite, 29
  historical, 30, 36
  legislative voting, 30
  mass opinion, 30
  missing, *see* Missing data
  multipurpose, 264, 277
  revolutions, 20–38
  secondary use, 52–60
  statistical, social security, 239–243
  survey, 29, 30, 33, 34, 35
  useability of, 10–11
Data and Program Library Service, University of Wisconsin, 12–13
Data base, definition of, 70
Data bases, complex, 28
  impact on the social sciences, 19–41
  priorities in development of, 43–44
Data file, complex, 112–136
Data librarian, 100
Data linkage, confidentiality and, 244–247
  error correction and, 249–250
  statistical, 238–251
Data management system, 140–142
Data management techniques, 142–146
Data not in archives, 45–46
Data processing, 118–119
  problems in, 131–134
Data release, problems of, 134–135
Data users, survey of, 54–55
David, Martin H., 112, 136n, 197n, 262n, 272n
Dear, R. E., 206n
Deutsch, Karl W., 19, 40n
Dexter, L. A., 22, 39n
Dial, R. B., 237n
Drosendahl, R. G., 110n
Dunn, E. S., Jr., 69n, 136n, 251n
Dunphy, D. C., 284n
Durant, Richard O., 125, 136n

Eckstein, Alexander, 39n
Economic Development Administration, 78, 79
Economic Opportunity Council, 77
Edgett, G. L., 207n
Edinger, L. J., 40n
Eklund, G., 207n
Elashoff, Janet D., 174, 198
Elashoff, R. M., 174, 198, 203, 206n
Ennis, Philip H., 53, 56, 59n
Etzioni, Amitai, 40n
Eulau, Heinz, 40n

Fairman, G. W., 110n
Farber, S. J., 136n
Fay, William T., 211, 219n
Federal Information Systems, 70–80
Federal Program expenditure, information systems on, 76
Federal Reserve Board, 259
Federal statistical data center, 64–68, 256
Feige, Edgar L., 253, 261, 262n, 272n
Fellegi, I. P., 250n
Fellner, W. J., 39n
Festinger, Leon, 22, 26, 36, 40n
Fiering, M. B., 207n
File maintenance, 125–127
Findings, compatibility, 23–38
  replicability, 23–38
Fisher, Lawrence, 181

Index 289

Franks, E. W., 110n
Freud, 26
Friedrich, C. J., 40n
Frisbie, Bruce, 284n

Gallagher hearings, 69n
Gallup, George, 21
Geffert, James A., 130, 136n
General Inquirer, 33-34
Geocoding, 221-237
  benefits of, 236-237
Geographic coding, 98-99
Glaser, E., 136n
Glasser, M., 205, 206n, 207n
Goldberger, Arthur S., 261n
Goldmann, Joseph, 39n
Grady, Kathleen M., 110n
Grant-In-Aid programs, 71-72
Greenstein, Ruth, 41n
Grid block, concept of, 223-224
  generalized, 228-229
  referencing mapped imagery, 299-233
  scale considerations, 224-228
Guttman, Louis, 40n

Hackett, W. P., 111n
Hagan, R. L., 219n
Hanson, M. H., 219n
Harman, R. Joyce, 284n
Harmon, H. H., 39n
Hartley, E. L., 40n
Hayashi, Chikio, 32, 40n
Hegel, 21
Heller, W. W., 39n
Herodotus, 19
Higgins, B. H., 39n
Himmler, Heinrich, 256
Hinman, K. A., 110n
Hocking, R., 207n
Horwood, Edgar M., 220, 237n
Human relations area files, 35

Information MARK IV file-management system, 158-171
Information, acquisition, 8
  maintenance, 8
  processing, 8
Information system, definition of, 70-71
Information-transfer networks of the future, description of, 274-278

problems of, 278-284
services of, 276-277
Ingelhardt, Ronald, 32, 40n
Inkeles, Alex, 31, 39n
International Data Library and Reference Service, 54
Inter-University Consortium for Political Research, University of Michigan, 11-14, 49, 50, 54, 283

Jacob, P. E., 40n
Jacobs, R. C., 40n
Jacobsen, 33
Jaeger, W. W., 38n
James, A. P., 250n
Jogdeo, K., 201, 206n

Kant, 21
Kennedy, Norman, 111n
Keynes, John Maynard, 25
Kuznets, Simon, 21, 38n, 39n

Landecker, W. S., 41n
Lane, Robert E., 22, 39n
Lasswell, Harold, 22, 23, 33, 40n
Lazarsfeld, Paul, 22, 31, 39n, 40n, 41n
Leontiev, Wassily, 21, 38n, 39n
Licklider, J. C. R., 275, 284n
Likert, Rensis, 22
Lipset, Seymour Martin, 22
Livant, W. P., 26, 40n
Lockheed Missiles and Space Company, 259n
Long Hearings, 69n
Lord, F. M., 207n
Lorie-Fisher File, 181, 185, 187, 189, 194
Lorie, James, 181
Lowry, Roye L., 70
Luce, R. D., 38n

McCarthy, John, 278, 284n
Maccoby, Eleanor E., 40n
Machiavelli, 20
Macridis, R. C., 40n
MADAM, 110n
Malthus, 24
Mannheim, Karl, 22, 39n
Marshall, Thurgood, 26-27
Marx, Karl, 21, 24
Massachusetts Institute of Technology, 12-13

290 Index

Matthai, A., 207n
Merritt, R. L., 40n
Michael, D. N., 260n
MIDAS, 110n
Miller, Robert J., 83
Miller, Roger F., 112, 136n, 174, 177, 197n, 262n, 272n
Miller, Warren E., 285n
Missing data, 96
   definition of, 172
   handling problems of, 173–207
   probability models for, 199–207
   regression analysis with, 198–207
Montesquieu, 20
Montias, J. M., 39n
Moore, Wilbert E., 285n
Morgenstern, Oskar, 22, 38n
Moses, L. E., 204n, 206n
Moyer, M. Eugene, 129, 136n, 197n

National Academy of Sciences, 284n
National Science Foundation, 43
Neumann, E. P., 22, 40n
Newcomb, T. M., 40n
Newcombe, H. B., 250n
Nicholson, G. E., Jr., 207n
Nolle, Elisabeth, 40n
Numerical Identifiers, social security, 241–243

Office of Business Economics, 76
Office of Economic Opportunity (OEO), 74, 75, 77
Ogilvie, D. M., 284n
Orcutt, G. H., 262n, 272n
Orwell, George, 256
Overhage, C. F. J., 376, 284n

Packard, V. O., 260n
Parsons, Talcott, 23, 30, 40n
Personal income in metropolitan areas, 80
Petty, William, 20
Planning-programming-budgeting system (PPBS), 72–74
Plato, 20
Pool, I. deS., 22, 39n, 40n, 60n, 209, 274
Popkin, S. L., 22, 39n, 40n, 209, 274
Pritzker, Leon, 250
Privacy, 65n, 68–69
   and confidentiality, 64–67
   protection of, 48–49, 253–272, 283–284
   microaggregation and, 261–272
   technical problems and, 258
Public Health Conference on Records and Statistics, 250n

Raiffa, H., 38n
Rao, C. R., 207n
Rapoport, Anatol, 22, 36, 41n
Report of task force on the storage of and access to government statistics, 69n
Ricardo, 24
Riecken, Henry W., 40n
Roberts, Noreen J., 83, 110n, 111n
Robinson, Joan, 25, 39n
Robinson, S. U., III, 157n
Rokkan, Stein, 40n, 60n
Roll, Eric, 38n, 39n
Roper, Elmo, 21
Roper Public Opinion Research Center, 54, 274
Rosenberg, Morris, 39n, 41n
Rosenblatt, D., 136n
Rothman, Stanley, 253
Ruggles Committee, 44
Ruggles, Richard, 51n, 69n
Rummel, R. J., 39n

Sacks, J. R., 40n
Sampford, M. P., 207n
Schacter, Stanley, 40n
Scheuch, E. K., 60n
Shannon, Claude E., 22
Shaw, J. C., 156n
Simon, Herbert, 22, 39n
Simulmatics project, 53
Singer, J. D., 40n
Smith, Adam, 20, 24–25
Smith, D. H., 39n
Smith, M. S., 284n
Smith, W. B., 207n
Social indicators, 77
Social research, financial support of, 45
Social science data archives in U.S., 15n
Social science information center, University of Pittsburgh, 12
Social Science Research Council, 44
Social Security, numerical identifiers, 241–243
   statistical data, 239–243

Sombart, Werner, 20, 38n
SPAN, 102–103
Spencer, Herbert, 21
Standing committee on data archives, 280
Statistics, voting, 30
Steinberg, Joseph, 238, 250n, 251n
Stephenson, Helene L., 111n
Stone, Philip J., 4, 33, 284n
Stolper, W. F., 39n
Sudman, S., 284n
Sunter, A. B., 250n
Survey Research Center, University of Michigan, 43

Teitelbaum, S. G., 157n
Threshold theory, 283–284
Thurstone, L. L., 21, 39n
Tobin, James, 39n
Tocher, K. D., 207n
Toscano, J. V., 40n
Trawinski, I. M., 207n
Truman, D. B., 40n

University of Michigan, 11–14, 32, 43, 49, 50, 54
University of Pittsburgh, 12
University of Wisconsin, 12–13
US Congress Subcommittee on Economic Statistics of the Joint Economic Committee, 69n
US House of Representatives Committee on Government Operations, 51n, 260n
US House of Representatives Subcommittee, of the Committee on Government Operations, 69n
US Senate Committee on the Judiciary-Subcommittee on Administrative Practice and Procedure, 69n
Uytterschaut, L., 53, 56, 59n

Veblen, Thorstein, 39n
Viet, J., 60n
von Neumann, John, 38n
von Thunen, J. H., 21, 38n

Walsh, J. E., 207n
Ward, R. E., 40n
Ware, Willis, 258–259
Washington Post, 251n
Watson, G. S., 201, 206n
Watts, Harold W., 136n, 178, 207n, 253, 261, 262n, 272n
Weber, Max, 22
White, F. T., 110n
Wiener, Norbert, 22
Wigle, James, 111n
Wilcox, A. R., 60n
Wilkinson, G. N., 207n
Wilks, S. S., 207n
Wisconsin assets and incomes studies, 114–115, 121, 132, 178, 180
Witt, E. G., 260n
Wood, M. K., 136n

Yates, F., 207n

Zwick, C. J., 69n